18

Biopolitics, Narrative, [illegible] orality

CONTENTS

Introduction

Rodger Frey and Alexander Ruch

We hope you'll find this issue of *Polygraph* to be a particularly "lively" one. By framing the issue through the prism of three central concepts—biopolitics, narrative, and temporality—we hope to shed some light onto the politics of life, or experience, today. We affirm the argument that politics today assumes as its primary object life itself, a common denominator of the various theories of biopolitics. Rather than focus the issue on one of the various articulations of biopolitical theory, we instead address the common denominator of these theories: the claim that politics today assumes as its primary object life itself. Our intention in taking up "life"—as a concept for critical theory, in its political and philosophical conceits, but also in its real, immediate, and particular existence—in relation to concerns of narrative and temporality is to bring to the abstraction "life" considerations of its concretization and actualization. One of the central conceits of this issue is the belief that the schemata that narratives provide for our understanding of temporality and our figuration of time have political effects: effects on how we imagine change (in both its possibility and its potential forms), agency (be it individual, institutional, or collective), and indeed our own being.[1] As such, narrative has the capacity to modulate our conception of "life"—what it is, as well as what it can be—and, as a consequence, our practice of that life in the everyday.[2] By shifting the focus of biopolitical investigation from the arena of "bare life" to that of the qualified life implied by the everyday, we also hope to open up the biopolitical more directly to questions of discourse and meaning-making.[3] Indeed, the articles contained in this volume demonstrate that, in the construction of "life" as constituted by the biopolitical field, the "real" is never just that, but also imagined; the immediate is already mediated; and the particular is always tempered by the other, the general, and the universal.

It is such a "tempering" with which the *Polygraph* collective lately has addressed questions of the biopolitical, owing to the traditions that those such as Michel Foucault and Gilles Deleuze both took up and instantiated. Recent issues of *Polygraph* examined these traditions and their interlocutors, placing the field of the biopolitical under the microscopic lenses offered by such varied figurations as Deleuze's "line of flight," the ontological planes of immanence and transcendence, and the universalistic mode of thought presented by the philosophy of Alain Badiou. The present consideration continues this refractive examination, at times placing the question of the biopolitical at its focal center, at other times exploring its indeterminable crevices, from its motivating origins in the Greek concept of *bios*, as Sarah Clift examines in our issue's first treatment, to the more recent figures presented by the "inimical life" of the outlaw and the politics of death, or *thanatopolitics*, of the suicide bomber, as Ian Baucom and Stuart J. Murray, respectively, construct them in the final two essays. We would like to imagine that the question of the biopolitical—or of what biopolitics *is*—has been furthered over the time of our recent body of work, and it is time itself that we use to examine the question in this *Polygraph*. Time as life, time as story, time, indeed, as death. Each of these accounts offers hope for the potentiality of time as a constitutive political form—time, that is, as resistance.

Michel Foucault began to tell the story of the biopolitical—some say with great license—through the history of sovereignty and its growing concern with governmentality, or the regulation of the population over which it maintained authority.[4] This focus on the population as a whole relied at once on a subjugation of the human body that arose with the emergence of the disciplinary society in the sixteenth and seventeenth centuries, when, as Foucault describes, "in the army, colleges, workshops, and schools we see the development of a training of the body as a useful body. New procedures of surveillance, control, spatial distribution, and notion, et cetera are perfected. The body is invested by mechanisms of power that seek to render it both docile and useful."[5] Such were the disciplinary "technologies of power" with which sovereign authority concerned itself. However, emerging in the late eighteenth century was a new technology of power, not solely disciplinary and no longer focused specifically on the individual body, but rather a "biopolitics" taking the population or human species as its object, "a global mass that is affected by overall processes characteristic of birth, death, production, illness, and so on."[6] The technologies of power at play in this emerging biopolitics relied less on the disciplining of individual bodies than the techniques it would utilize on the population as a whole, from the study of endemic diseases and illnesses, to the use of statistics, measures, estimates, and forecasts allowing for the popular generalization, the attendancy to mortality and health, and the "rational" mechanisms of insurance, individual and collective savings, safety, and security measures. Foucault refers to these mechanisms as technologies of *biopower*, more specifically, one separate from that of the absolute power of sovereignty: "Sovereignty took life and let live. And now we have the emergence of a power that I would call the power of regularization, and it, in contrast, consists in making live and letting die."[7] This paradigm between sovereignty and governmentality, from "taking life and letting live" to "making live and letting die," presents the early narrative of what would come to constitute the biopolitical as a field of inquiry.

Death, for its part, is excepted from the ubiquitous object of "life" in contemporary politics, and this non-relation produces forms of narrative and concepts of temporality incongruous with those of the previous era. As in Dickens's last novel, *Our Mutual Friend*, which Ian Buchanan examines in this issue, the individual is left to experience death in private, in the body of the malcontent Rogue Riderhood, while his life becomes generalized, the property of those around him to "make live."

Death, indeed, is a common theme throughout this issue, be it in correspondence with the finite tendencies of narrative form or be it as a mode of interpretation. Along with Dickens's final novel, the "last work," the eulogy, and the obituary each become an object of narrative's relation to the constitution of "life." Death is examined here as a contestational praxis against biopolitical power, as well as an anachronistic yet very real deployment of its method of control, as discipline and sovereignty still very much exist as technologies of biopower. Gilles Deleuze locates effects of the two types of power in the figure of Kafka's Josef K., who in *The Trial* finds himself suspended between the *apparent acquittal* of the disciplinary society's techniques of massification and individuation (two poles that operate in tandem to create spaces of confinement) and the *endless postponement* of a society of control, which instead coordinates minute and continuous adjustments in access and behavior through the development of mobile codes or passwords.[8]

Deleuze's use of Kafka's narrative to elaborate his extension of Foucault's biopolitical analysis to the "society of control" indicates his estimation of the political importance of narrative art. Tellingly, he attributes the diagnosis of this regime of control to the literature of William Burroughs, attesting to the creative and productive abilities of fictional narrative to both identify and resist power. "Art is resistance," says Deleuze in another place. "It resists death, slavery, infamy, shame."[9] History tells us the story of a pre-modern William Tell, who, upon shooting an apple from his son's head, proclaimed, "I am free!" and was released from the shackles of sovereign authority. Burroughs, having attempted and failed at a similar feat, renders in *Naked Lunch* the stark reality that, in the control society, freedom is no longer thought to be achievable in a pure form; rather, negotiations, escapes, and resistances must be exacted within, outside, and against the dominant technologies of power.[10] Often such resistance comes in the form of diagnoses (both "clinical" and "critical") of blockages and failures (the extreme example of which is death itself), which fiction raises to the level of resistance through the demand for "the missing people." Or, as Deleuze and Guattari put it in their book on Kafka: "The literary machine thus becomes a relay for a revolutionary machine-to-come, not at all for ideological reasons but because the literary machine alone is determined to fill the conditions of a collective enunciation that is lacking elsewhere in this milieu: *literature is the people's concern.*"[11] Similar figurations and diagnoses of biopolitical "life" arise in the articles presented here, from the ghost-images experienced by the protagonist of Don DeLillo's novella *The Body Artist* to the "diminished" Paul Rayment of J.M. Coetzee's recent novel *Slow Man*. Rachel Smith offers the former as an affective embodiment of "good grief," a mode of biopolitical resistance outside the psychoanalytical discourse of mourning and melancholia, while, for Grant Farred, Coetzee's work articulates a "cosmopolitical life" contesting the controlling manifestations of universalism. The various forms of life engendered here—affective, cosmopolitan, feminist, emergent, prosthetic, and precarious—aim to disrupt biopower's regime of control by negotiating its interstices, borders, and lines of flight.[12]

But these modes of resistance beg yet another question on which we must constantly dwell: in what manner is narrative also a form of control? Narratives provide not only figures that call power into question but also establish normative patterns and preconceptions. This means that narrative can expand our capacity to imagine the world (and ourselves) differently, but it can also limit that capacity through the repetition of normative forms or the management of mediated desire. Particularly in an age in which flexibility, mobility, and choice are so prevalent (at least in those areas which used to be called the "first world"; the periodization of the present appears to us more complex when "underdeveloped" or "developing" nations, peoples, and economies enter the picture), power must operate in the most subtle of ways, offering apparent options while also determining in advance our responses to this apparent freedom. The control that normative narratives (life-narratives, certainly, but also narratives of social development, politics, historicism, etc.) provide takes on a greater role as the forms taken by power become more open and flexible (as opposed to the spaces of confinement of a disciplinary society). If it is indeed the case that politics today takes life as its object, then the analysis of different means by which narrative both figures and regulates temporality, as well as possible modes of subverting or bypassing such regulation, should remain on the agenda.

....

All of the contributors to this issue develop their own connections, explicit or implicit, between biopolitics and modes of meaning-making that impact our experience of time and temporality. Sarah Clift's contribution to this issue develops an historical narrative *of* narrative forms, which provides a framework for thinking about the period specificity of forms of narration as well as the potential political significance of these forms. "Narrative life span, in the wake" does this by revisiting the writings of Hannah Arendt and Walter Benjamin on narrative and history, which chronicle the detachment of narrative forms from that of the finitude of human life. If, as both Benjamin and Arendt claim in different ways, the time of modernity is that of a purely quantitative time, detached from experience, we can also see, along with Paul Ricoeur, narrative as the principal means through which time is (re)made human and meaningful.[13] While not wishing to fall back into a naïve idea of the properly human, neither Benjamin nor Arendt (nor indeed Clift) wishes to abandon the idea of a meaningful time that is neither "empty" nor "homogeneous," but one which remains open to qualitative difference.

The attempt to locate forms of meaningful time (identified here with the function of memory) is one of the consistent threads of this issue, whether it is articulated through Negri's writings on the *kairòs* (which Rachel Smith takes up in her article), Merav Amir's invocation of Elizabeth Grosz's demand for a "reconceptualization of the future," or Matteo Mandarini's utopian vision of a "communist practice of time." Meaningful time is indeed what is at issue, although, as several of the essays included in this volume demonstrate, meaningful time is not necessarily liberatory. Merav Amir, for example, produces an analysis of how a particular mode of temporal meaning-making (producing a form of temporality that she describes as a "linear, goal-oriented, and clock-driven temporal pattern") can function in the service of social control. In "Bio-Temporality and Social Regulation," she takes the relation between human life span and narrative in a different direction than does Clift, employing Gilles Deleuze's thesis about "control societies" to analyze the discourse of the biological clock as a control mechanism for ordering women's life-narratives outside of the enclosed institutional space of the nuclear family. Amir contends that, as the capacity for this institutional space to manage the lives of women has decreased, the discourse of the biological clock has emerged to take its place, replacing a general social demand that women marry, stay at home, and produce offspring with the more flexible option of independence, supplemented with a new medicalized discourse of the "biological clock" (based on but not reducible to a biological reality known for centuries): the command is no longer "marry and reproduce" but "the choice is yours, but never forget that your time to make the (right) choice is running out!" While feminists have traditionally been reluctant to set Deleuze's thought to work,[14] Amir weds Deleuze's thoughts on periodization and the dominant form of contemporary power to a concrete analysis of changing discursive strategies of containment, generating a functional descriptive scheme which should prove suggestive for further feminist research. At the same time, her use of Deleuze to address feminist problems serves as a well-needed reminder (too often forgotten by Deleuze's adherents and detractors alike) that flexibility is not necessarily freedom, or, as Deleuze puts it in the "Postscript on Control Societies," "[a] snake's coils are even more intricate than a mole's burrows."[15] At the conclusion of her analysis, Amir calls, as do many of the contributors to this issue, for us to "conceive alternative temporalities," but her central concern in the article is to document in concrete terms the emergence of a particular normalizing narrative discourse about women's bodies.

Matteo Mandarini provides a more general and abstract approach to temporality and biopolitics. His article continues the reclamation of Gilles Deleuze for political thought by producing an enlightening translation of Marx's analysis of capital into Deleuzian terms, a translation which produces significant effects in Marxist thought (most notably, another approach to recent attempts to historicize and de-center the labor theory of value that has remained, for many, the bedrock of Marxism[16]). As with Benjamin, Mandarini views the homogenization and standardization of time to be constitutive of modernity (although here the term employed is, as Fredric Jameson would have it in *A Singular Modernity*, simply "capitalism," the motor force that throws up "modernity" as its obfuscatory cover).[17] He describes it here in Deleuzo-Guattarian terms as (1) a differentiation of planes followed by (2) an axiomatization of time allowing for correspondences across planes or blocks of qualitatively distinct temporalities. This means that the function of capital is largely that of coordinating transferences and relations between different "practices of time" that are radically heterogeneous. This originary heterogeneity, according to Mandarini, allows for the emergence of crisis as the "possibility of non-conversion," the production of incommensurable times beyond the capacity of capital to coordinate them.

Mandarini remains close to Antonio Negri in his call for "an alternative set of conducts of time" as a constituent form of biopolitical resistance, a call which echoes those of Clift and Amir. Rachel Smith, for her part, attempts to provide one such example of an alternative conduct of time by bringing Don DeLillo's meditation on grief in *The Body Artist* to bear on Hardt and Negri's theorization of biopolitics. In doing so, Smith provides a rejoinder to the focus on the joyful passions in Hardt and Negri's work (at the occasional expense of careful treatment of the sad passions, or Sianne Ngai's "ugly feelings")[18] without resorting to a return to psychoanalytic theories of mourning and melancholia. As do Ian Buchanan and Grant Farred later in the issue, Smith helps literature to perform its own theoretical and philosophical work, producing the corresponding concept to the affects and percepts embodied in DeLillo's novel, as Deleuze and Guattari might have put it. At the same time, Smith's article points to the connectedness between affect and temporality, a connection dating back at least as far as Aristotle's distinction between passion and action, but gaining new relevance as affect reappears on the agenda of political theorists and cultural and literary critics alike: witness thinkers as disparate as Brian Massumi, Eve Sedgwick, Paolo Virno, Lauren Berlant, Philip Fisher, and Sianne Ngai.[19]

Eric Alliez and Jean-Claude Bonne provide a rather different elaboration of non-normative temporality by way of an engagement with Matisse's murals, which they claim create "a becoming that does not produce, that shows nothing but itself, in the events to which it gives body." This process of "giving life" (to use Matisse's term) to space through an un-Formed becoming which opens space to the Outside of a multiplicity of forces brings us in contact with Deleuze's concept of "inorganic life," a concept which problematizes the rapid assimilation of the "bio" in biopolitics to the biological level of "life-processes" through the dehiscence of the term "life" from the idea of an organic entity. Alliez and Bonne thus elaborate a "bio-aesthetic," a concept they develop out of the work of Deleuze and Guattari, that engenders a "becoming-life of art," a "politics of sensation" in which art gives body to thoughts and events.

Ian Buchanan's article "Deleuze's 'Life' Sentences" continues this examination of what a properly Deleuzian notion of biopolitics might entail through a return to Deleuze's encounter with Dickens in "Immanence: A Life..." Although he begins with a critique of Agamben's treatment of Deleuze in "Absolute Immanence," his conclusion that life is, for Deleuze, a presentation of "the possibility of ... judgments being varied" through the encounter/separation of the actual from the virtual brings him quite close to Agamben's claim that "form-of-life" (defined as "a life for which living itself would be at stake in its own living") must not be considered as an ossified form or demographic category, but rather as "thought," a continuous affection by one's own capacity to be affected (and thus to be otherwise).[20] Relevant here is not simply this unlikely proximity between Buchanan and Agamben, but the fact that Buchanan makes explicit the link between "pure thought" as the grasping of the gap between stability and dynamism (and the insufficiency of either of these taken separately) and fiction as a means for making this gap apparent (a claim that resonates with Smith's argument regarding DeLillo's fiction).

In a similar spirit, Grant Farred asks us to reconsider not only what philosophy (what is now more popularly known as that amorphous entity called simply theory) can tell us about narrative, but also what the narrative encoding of experience can contribute to philosophical and political debate, in this case an exposure of the "old secret" of contemporary neo-Pauline universalism. He counters Alain Badiou's influential reading of Paul the apostle with J.M. Coetzee's Paul Rayment, whom Farred offers as an illustration of the titular "politics of prosthesis"—an illustration that unveils particularity as the "remnant" (in the sense Giorgio Agamben gives the term in *The Time That Remains*)[21] of an exclusive universalism. In so doing, Farred locates the recent universalism, in particular that of Alain Badiou and Slavoj Žižek, as a poorly disguised attempt to secure philosophical and political authority for those already holding a majoritarian position, and he uses Paul's suppression of contending versions of possible Christianity (particularly those represented by the Gnostic Gospels) as an allegory of the present intellectual situation.

Our final two articles both deal with one of the major critiques of biopolitical theory: the concept of *necropolitics* (the "subjugation of life to the power of death")[22] proposed by Achille Mbembe as a demand that the attention to a politics of life not elide the difficult fact that the administration of death remains a significant function of contemporary political power. Mbembe is less interested in arguing against biopolitics as a concept than in avoiding a too-rapid assumption that biopolitics as the management of life has simply replaced an older form of sovereignty based on the right to put to death. Thus, he writes (regarding Palestine) that "late-modern colonial occupation is a concatenation of multiple powers: disciplinary, biopolitical, and necropolitical."[23] For the purposes of this issue, we consider the thesis of a necropolitics to be internal to the discourse surrounding biopolitics, not only because it was occasioned by Foucault's discussions of biopower and biopolitics but also because, if our wish is to develop more descriptive and efficacious terms to describe contemporary politics, we would do well to consider the "multiple powers" described by Mbembe in their complexity rather than simply avoiding questions of death in favor of a myopic view toward life. As the contents of this issue demonstrate, the terms of life and death are mutually co-implicated, as are the terms of any traditional dualism, and any attempt to isolate one from the other is fated to collapse in its own aporias.

Ian Baucom expands Mbembe's questioning regarding the limits of the theories of biopolitics by seeking a necropolitical figure that would serve a parallel function to that played by "bare life" in Agamben's version of biopolitics. The narrative he charts of the work of Francisco Goya leads him to designate such a figure as "inimical life," an enemy that does not fulfill the traditional requirements of enmity and that, for this reason, emerges as an enemy "not so much of any *particular* state but of the very concept, possibility, or institutions of *the state-form itself*." This form of life (a term we invoke here to signal Baucom's differentiation of inimical from bare life), epitomized by the figure of "the traitor, the robber, or the brigand," appears to the state as one of Kant's "unjust enemies," whom the state is authorized to dispose of in any way it deems fit. Inimical life then marks, for Baucom, the site at which the rights of the state become unlimited, as bare life does for Agamben.

Both biopolitical and necropolitical thought have been forced by recent geo-political events to address the nature of contemporary war, and it is instructive to juxtapose the illuminations these two theories shed on the question of war. Hardt and Negri begin *Multitude* with an attempt to provide a biopolitical theory of war dealing with many of the same figures as does Baucom, but with a slight difference. The enemy, for example, does not so much *become* "unjust" as his or her existence allows for a "just" *war*, and in this way provides for the sovereign, as Baucom argues, "the constitutive function of legitimacy." However, the difference becomes pronounced when we approach the functions that these figures serve for sovereignty. For the biopolitical theory of Hardt and Negri, the power of the sovereign to "rule directly over death" is a form of biopower rather than necropower because it produces a type of direct control over life in the form of torture.[24] Further, Hardt and Negri contend that this power is legitimated by the production of an enemy so "unknown and unseen" (and therefore indestructible—think of "terrorism" as an enemy) that its monstrous abstraction allows the imperial power to enact the most rigid forms of control over daily life under the guise of security.[25] For Baucom, the "unjust enemy" becomes not abstract but all-too-concrete in the "terrifying realism" of Goya's engravings, as well as in the photos of abused and tortured detainees from the Abu Ghraib prison, both of which mutely speak the truth of sovereignty. It seems to us virtually undecidable whether one is correct and the other false, as they describe different aspects of contemporary geo-power. More productive is the attempt to produce a mapping capable of demonstrating the lines of force, which might accord the necropolitical a greater role in the legitimation of sovereign power as such, while the biopolitical approach allows for a greater grasp of the mechanisms of control that this legitimation allows the state (or post-state agencies or assemblages) to develop and refine.

Stuart J. Murray's article also develops from Mbembe's work, proposing a concept of *thanatopolitics* that cannot help but recall Mbembe's theses regarding necropolitics. Murray, however, concedes more to Foucault's diagnosis of contemporary politics as primarily directed toward the control of populations than does Mbembe. While Mbembe locates necropolitics primarily on the side of power and the state (a move which Baucom furthers), Murray uses the term thanatopolitics to refer to an oppositional politics that uses death as a means of resistance to the biopolitical as such. To discuss what this might mean, Murray focuses on the rhetorical significance of the suicide bomber (whom Hardt and Negri declare to be "the ontological limit of biopower in its most tragic and revolting form"),[26] asking what *productive* rather than simply *destructive* effects emerge from the suicide bomber's symbolic assault (which accompanies but is not reducible to his or her physical assault) on the contemporary political discourse of life. This is perhaps a limit case of Gilles Deleuze's articulation of ethics in *The Logic of Sense*: "Either ethics makes no sense at all, or this is what it means and has nothing else to say: not to be unworthy of what happens to us," to "will death" *as an* (indeed *the*) *event* (and as such not the occurrence of death but the "purely expressed" within what occurs).[27] Murray insists (as does Mbembe) that this refocusing of the debate on contemporary politics must call into question the dualism of life and death, rather than simply insisting on the recognition of the importance of the "marked" pole (death as somehow "more important" than life, or vice versa). For Murray, this involves the difficult task of imagining a society and a selfhood in which death is interlaced with life, occasioning a deliberately improper relation to self and to rational sovereignty. It is in this sense that Murray believes that we can learn from the discomfort and confusion that the suicide bomber, as someone who has rejected our own self-serving rational calculation and valuation of life as such, occasions.

Beyond the threshold of the body marked for death, whether in the very real figure of the suicide bomber or in the more literary accounts addressed in these pages, the increasingly nuanced inscriptions deployed by narrative structures—and the temporalities for which they account—enact a complex politics of life that is experienced in both subtle and transparent forms every day, in habit and in thought. The existence and nature of biopolitics is currently an object of debate across such fields as philosophy, political science, cultural studies, and anthropology; as such, we do not expect that a single journal issue will decide the fate of the concept, nor even provide a definite answer as to the best theorization of what biopolitics might be or mean. Our aim is more modest: that the encounter of biopolitical theory with considerations of narrative and temporality might bring the role of the imagination and of cultural mediation into these debates, in the hopes that the sparks thrown off by such a forced collision might prove instructive across the borders of different fields. It is not our role to determine how successful this experiment has been. An introduction is only another narrative, providing a frame for, in this case, a series of articles that cross this frame transversally rather than resting stably within it. Nor would we wish for it to be otherwise. A thoroughly planned encounter occasions no friction, which is what animates the sparks. ▪

....

1 The most significant thinker in recent years to make the link between narrative and temporal schemata is Paul Ricoeur, to whom this formulation owes a significant debt. See Paul Ricoeur, *Time and Narrative*, vol. 1, trans. Kathleen McLaughlin and David Pellauer (Chicago: University of Chicago Press, 1984).

2 This formulation is meant to recall Michel de Certeau's work on everyday life. While we use the term everyday here relatively uncritically, we also wish to point out that the everyday, as it has variously been described by thinkers such as Heidegger, Lefebvre, and de Certeau, is itself a (historically specific) temporal category, based on a notion of a particular form of repetition. This is obvious in the writings of Heidegger and Lefebvre, but even de Certeau's formulation of a "practice" as a "way of operating" assumes a repetitive temporal framework, although this repetition is certainly evaluated differently by de Certeau than it is by Heidegger or Lefebvre. As such, the delimitation of a sphere that we can call the everyday (as well as evaluations of that sphere based on differing normative models for what constitutes meaningful activity) is itself a product of narrative-influenced expectations of different types of temporal being. See Michel de Certeau, *The Practice of Everyday Life*, trans. Steven Rendall (Berkeley: University of California Press, 1988);

Martin Heidegger, *Being and Time*, trans. Joan Stambaugh (Albany: State University of New York Press, 1996), 307-340; and Henri Lefebvre, *Critique of Everyday Life*, vol. 1, trans. John Moore (New York: Verso, 1991).

3 For any who have somehow missed the elaborate discussions revolving around "bare life" in the last few years, see Giorgio Agamben, *Homo Sacer: Sovereign Power and Bare Life*, trans. Daniel Heller-Roazen (Stanford: Stanford University Press, 1998).

4 Foucault takes up the discussion of sovereignty and governmentality in his lectures at the *College de France*, particularly those lectures running from 1974-1976, translated in English and published as Michel Foucault, *Abnormal: Lectures at the College de France, 1974-1975*, eds. Valerio Marchetti and Antonella Salomoni, trans. Graham Burchell (New York: Picador, 2003) and Michel Foucault, *"Society Must Be Defended": Lectures at the College de France, 1975-76*, eds. Mauro Bertani and Alessandro Fontana, trans. David Macey (New York: Picador, 2003).

5 Foucault, *Abnormal*, 193.

6 Foucault, *"Society Must Be Defended,"* 242-3.

7 Ibid., 244-7.

8 Gilles Deleuze, "Postscript on Control Societies," *Negotiations*, trans. Martin Joughin (New York: Columbia University Press, 1990), 179.

9 Gilles Deleuze, "Control and Becoming," *Negotiations*, trans. Martin Joughin (New York: Columbia University Press, 1990), 174.

10 William S. Burroughs, *Naked Lunch* (New York: Grove Press, 1990). See Timothy S. Murphy, *Wising Up the Marks: The Amodern William Burroughs* (Berkeley: University of California Press, 1997), 74-102, for a reading of *Naked Lunch* indebted to Deleuze and Guattari (as well as Horkheimer and Adorno).

11 Gilles Deleuze and Félix Guattari, *Kafka: Toward a Minor Literature*, trans. Dana Polan (Minneapolis: University of Minnesota Press, 1986), 17-18. The term "the missing people" appears in the second volume of Deleuze's *Cinema* books, where he articulates most clearly the capacity of the aesthetic (in this case, film) to call for the creation of an absent people. See Gilles Deleuze, *Cinema 2: The Time-Image*, trans. Hugh Tomlinson and Robert Galeta (Minneapolis: University of Minnesota Press, 1989), 215-224.

12 "Forms of life" is meant here in the technical terms that Giorgio Agamben proposes in the essay "Form-of-Life." Giorgio Agamben, "Form-of-Life," *Means Without End: Notes on Politics*, trans. Vincenzo Binetti and Cesare Casarino (Minneapolis: University of Minnesota Press, 2000), 8-12. See our discussion of Ian Buchanan's contribution to this issue below for a brief treatment of this concept.

13 Ricoeur, *Time and Narrative*.

14 The possibility of a place for Deleuze's thought within feminism is an issue too complicated for us to address in this introduction. Those interested in this question may wish to consult Claire Colebrook's "Introduction" to the volume *Deleuze and Feminist Theory*, ed. Ian Buchanan and Claire Colebrook (Edinburgh: Edinburgh University Press, 2000), 1-17. Many of the articles contained in that collection also dwell on this question.

15 Deleuze, "Postscript on Control Societies," 182.

16 See, for example, Antonio Negri, "Value and Affect," trans. Michael Hardt, *Boundary 2* 26, no. 2 (1999): 77-88; and Moishe Postone, *Time, Labor, and Social Domination* (New York: Cambridge University Press, 1993), 362-366.

17 Fredric Jameson, *A Singular Modernity: Essay on the Ontology of the Present* (New York: Verso, 2002).

18 See Sianne Ngai, *Ugly Feelings* (Cambridge, MA: Harvard University Press, 2005).

19 Brian Massumi, *Parables for the Virtual: Movement, Affect, Sensation* (Durham: Duke University Press, 2002); Eve Kosofsky Sedgwick and Adam Frank, *Touching Feeling: Affect, Pedagogy, Performativity* (Durham: Duke University Press, 2003); Paolo Virno, *A Grammar of the Multitude*, trans. Isabella Bertoletti, James Cascaito, and Andrea Casson (New York: Semiotext(e), 2004), 73-93; Lauren Berlant, *The Queen of America Goes to Washington City: Essays on Sex and Citizenship* (Durham: Duke University Press, 1997); Philip Fisher, *The Vehement Passions* (Princeton: Princeton University Press, 2001); and Ngai, *Ugly Feelings*.

20 Agamben, "Form-of-Life," 8-12.

21 Giorgio Agamben, *The Time That Remains: A Commentary on the Letter to the Romans*, trans. Patricia Dailey (Stanford: Stanford University Press, 2005).

22 Achille Mbembe, "Necropolitics," *Public Culture* 15(1), 39.

23 Ibid., 29.

24 Michael Hardt and Antonio Negri, *Multitude: War and Democracy in the Age of Empire* (New York: Penguin, 2004), 19. Once again, it is a literary example that fuels the discussion of mechanisms of control: in this case, Orwell's *1984*.

25 Ibid., 18-19, 30.

26 Ibid., 54. The suicide bomber is also a figure with which Mbembe briefly deals in "Necropolitics" under the rubric of a "logic of martyrdom." Mbembe, "Necropolitics," 36-39.

27 Gilles Deleuze, *The Logic of Sense*, trans. Mark Lester with Charles Stivale (New York: Columbia University Press, 1990), 149.

Narrative life span, in the wake

Sarah Clift

> *The divine art is the story. In the beginning was the story. At the end we shall be privileged to view, and review, it—and that is what is named the day of judgement.*
>
> —*Isak Dinesen*[1]

Derrida's lecture "Mnemosyne," written shortly after the death of Paul de Man and devoted both to his work and to the friendship they shared, opens with a statement that is as complex as it is succinct. Its tone is sorrowful, compounding the loss to which it testifies by indicating from the outset what the lecture will *lack*: "I," he writes, "have never known how to tell a story."[2]

His disquiet, Derrida goes on to explain in the lines that follow, is grounded in what is said to link storytelling to memory: "And since I love nothing better than remembering and Memory itself—Mnemosyne—I have always felt this inability as a sad infirmity. Why am I denied narration?" Recalling Socrates' influential formulation of that relationship in the *Theaetetus*, that it is Mnemosyne or "Memory itself," "*tes tôn Mousôn metros*, the mother of all muses," who bestows the gift of narrative,[3] what Derrida has set in motion is, in fact, a renewed thinking of the complexity of both memory and narrative as well as of their relation to each other.

An apostrophe to an absent other, a lover scorned, withheld gifts, and memory sickness—it is not by ruse that Derrida's remarks are inflected with such erotic and melancholy accents. Indeed, far from obscuring the rigor of what is being claimed in those remarks, the precision of the formulation consists in its rehearsing the union that produced narration as its offspring. A self-professed "lover of Mnemosyne"—note the double genitive—Derrida begins by invoking echoes of a tryst, one re-staged between Mnemosyne and the "I" of his own text. Though, unlike the ancient coupling that has—just barely—been invoked, its reflection, its echo and repetition in Derrida's text is an encounter that yields no gifts and bears no offspring.

Derrida's remarks attest to a blocked encounter: one that leaves no narration in its wake and so presumably admits of no generation or transmission. Precisely the contrary, then, of how the West will so often have thought of memory and its origin, its offspring, and its destiny. On the margins of this disjunction between memory and narration, however, one still senses occasion for thought:

> Why didn't I receive this gift from Mnemosyne? From this complaint, and probably to protect myself from it, a suspicion continually steals into my thinking: who can really tell a story? Is narrative possible? Who can claim to know what a narrative entails? Or, before that, the memory it lays claim to? What is memory?[4]

In drawing attention to the long-established links between narration and memory and in underscoring the canonical figures according to which those linkages are normally understood—the figures of generation and procreation, of the lover-mother and her offspring—Derrida restages the inaugural moment of a tradition in which narrative, born of the goddess of memory Mnemosyne, is given the task of preserving the past. But he restages that birth, not in order to set a generative logic into motion but rather to expose the relation between memory and narration to thought, including even the most basic assurance that narrative memory guarantees continuity between generations. And this, too, is an act of re-staging: it was Socrates who, on the verge of (his own) death, is reported to have confessed, "I was not good at inventing stories."[5]

At the risk of doing violence to Derrida's gesture, it might be possible to situate it in relation to work done by Walter Benjamin and Hannah Arendt on narrative and memory. By asking the question of what is at stake when the relation between memory and narration is not simply given or assured, Derrida effectively inherits memory as a *dilemma*, a dilemma that had started to become especially pressing in Benjamin and Arendt's time. Both Benjamin's essay "The Storyteller" (1936) and Arendt's "The Concept of History" (published first in 1958 and then again in *Between Past and Future: Eight Exercises in Political Thought* in 1961) recall the figure of Mnemosyne and, also like Derrida, displace the operation of its traditional meaning as a force of unity between past and present. The motif functions as a kind of touchstone for their work, through which they are able to gauge the ruptures in memory itself—ruptures for which, according to Benjamin, Mnemosyne has become practically synonymous. The very name, he says, "takes the observer back to a parting of the ways in world history."[6]

With Benjamin writing as Nazism was on the steady rise and Arendt writing in its "long shadow," the violent shock of historical events intensified and accelerated what was already a precarious connection between past and present. Neither Arendt nor Benjamin seem to have had any doubts that historical discourse, determined in some measure by the legacy of nineteenth-century historicism, would prevail over all other forms of transmitting the past. Both were convinced, in this respect, of the need to submit historicism to a thorough-going critique, in particular by emphasizing the ways in which its own structures were complicit in the discontinuity between the past and the needs of the present. Critiques of its abstract notion of "humanity," of its own specific forms of selective memory and the violence of its ideas of progress and perfectibility, thus had to form the basis for a rethinking of historiography. And while Arendt's and Benjamin's essays both adopt the thematic of memory as the ground upon which to motivate certain aspects of this critique, it is not in order to set up a strict opposition between memory and history; rather it is to discern what remains legible of memory within modern historical discourse itself and, specifically, within its conception of time.

Arendt examines the potentially endless linear sequence of what Benjamin calls historicism's "homogeneous, empty time,"[7] seeking to establish the temporal conditions under which historicism as such could become possible. Historicism, she argues, is the apotheosis of a generalized temporal structure of modern historical discourse, one that became formalized in the chronological reforms of the eighteenth century. These reforms, wherein "the history of mankind reaches back into an infinite past … and stretches ahead into an infinite future," created the conditions within which mankind could achieve a "potential earthly immortality."[8] One of the most serious consequences of the formalization of this endless temporal sequence as "historical time"—and one of the potentially most violent—was how it inaugurated an alarming "lifelessness" at the heart of modernity's historical time, the endlessness of which bears no traces of human finitude.

Benjamin's well-known description of the Angel of History in the "Theses on the Philosophy of History" (1940) also addresses this continuous narrative of inexorable progress, transforming it into a nightmare of destruction and indecipherability:

> Where we see a chain of events, he sees one catastrophe which keeps piling wreckage upon wreckage and hurls it in front of his feet. The angel would like to stay, awaken the dead, and make whole what has been smashed. But a storm is blowing from Paradise. … This storm irresistibly propels him into the future to which his back is turned, while the pile of debris before him grows skyward. This storm is what we call progress.[9]

The dangers of historicism are, for Benjamin, at their most legible in its notion of progress, the goal of which, while being assured as an ideal, is especially pernicious in that it is indefinitely, indeed infinitely, postponed. One of the strengths of the passage consists in how it links "seeing" (a continuous succession of events) to language or, more specifically, to the only word explicitly registered as such: the word, simply, "progress." By thus drawing attention to the role played by language in determining what counts and becomes visible as history, his disastrous counter-image powerfully undermines the conception of language according to which words signify the "real"; this kind of language is turned into the very force of blindness itself. Moreover, it is also through this act of denaturalizing the word "progress" that Benjamin is also able to register the need for another thinking of the language of history, one that can challenge historicism's notion of infinite progress and, perhaps, restore to history the potential of its own finitude.

Recent theoretical work in historiography has also responded to critiques of progress in ways that are relevant to Benjamin's and Arendt's critical interventions. Jacques Le Goff's *History and Memory* (1977), for instance, begins by soundly rejecting the notion of "a linear, continuous, irreversible progress" implicit to the dominant historiography of the nineteenth and early twentieth centuries: according to Le Goff, such a conception of history is "practically dead."[10] Along with many historians of his generation, Le Goff is concerned to undermine any residual power this notion of history may have, in part by problematizing the "category of the real"[11] contained in the postulate that historical discourse represents the past "as it really happened." To that end, he attends to the complex textual operations involved in the historian's construction of a "real" historical event and in particular, to the irreducible groundedness of historical discourse in language.

If what is traditionally at issue for historiography is the epistemological status of "real" events and their transmission in historical discourse, the task of contemporary historiography is to develop criteria of truth that move beyond the naïve understanding that historical language represents a "real" past. As Le Goff asserts, "It is vain to believe in a past independent of the one constituted by the historian."[12] Drawing out the implications for historical work of the contention that the historian does not have access to a "real" event but rather draws on the textual and social traces of memory in order to construct it, Le Goff approvingly cites Barthes's notion of a "reality effect" that "in 'objective' history, the 'real' is never more than an unexpressed signified, sheltered behind the apparent omnipotence of the referent. This situation defines what could be called 'the reality effect.' … [H]istorical discourse does not follow the real, it only signifies it, ceaselessly repeating *it happened*; but that assertion can never be anything but the signified obverse of any historical narrative."[13]

The contention that the "real" event is an effect of discourse has, of course, a myriad of repercussions for the discipline of history, but one of them in particular has bearing on our readings of Arendt and Benjamin: the notion that the "real" is a discursive effect allows Le Goff to bracket the claim of language's strict referentiality and to focus instead on how historical narratives—and, indeed, all narratives—have internal structures and logics, ones for which close analysis provides a means of understanding how the time of historical narrative does not simply represent or mirror "real time" but is, in fact, a product of the text's narrative structure.[14] As such, the call Le Goff makes for a precise study of the temporal modalities operative both in the documents used by historians and in historical narrative itself[15] can be understood as a means both to counteract the sense of an over-arching and endless temporal process and to open up the notion of "historical time" to new understandings. Of course, in this regard one cannot fail to mention Paul Ricoeur, who has also analysed the temporal parameters of both literary and historical narratives and has drawn important links between narrative and human finitude on the basis of their shared temporality. He writes in *Time and Narrative* that "time becomes human time to the extent that it is organized after the manner of a narrative; narrative, in turn, is meaningful to the extent that it portrays the features of temporal experience."[16]

The ways in which Arendt and Benjamin advance the notion of narrative memory as orientation for a theorization of history has relevance for the turn being made within contemporary historiography to the question of narrative time, especially for the possibility that narrative time be configured as a site or expression of finitude. Insofar as both thinkers articulate the structure of memory in terms of the affinities it shares with the structure of human life span, they also conceive of memory to be an expression, first and foremost, of the *time* of human finitude. As such, theorizing narrative memory in terms of life span will have implications both for an understanding of memory as well as for its temporal modality, beyond the strictly linear time of modern historical discourse.

Memories of Life Span

Were one to raise objections to the way in which memory is being conceived here, namely, as a form of anteriority in tension with the modern historical time of chronological succession (past-present-future), one might do so on the grounds that, in fact, the historical record belongs among the most magisterial of memory's expressions. After all, doesn't history show itself to be a kind of memory when it rescues things from time and secures for them, as well as for the time of their unfolding, a more lasting resting-place in its own discourse?

This objection is a good one and so deserves serious consideration. In "The Concept of History," Hannah Arendt argues to the effect that, at its inception in Ancient Greece, historical narrative was unthinkable outside of the general rubric of memory, for which the task of immortalizing human action involved narrating historical events in accordance with the structure and the temporality specific to the life span of the individual human, or *bios*. By tracing the development of the concept of history from the Greeks up to that of the moderns, Arendt shows how, as historical narrative continued to be understood as the means for securing human immortality under the radically changed conditions of modernity, its chronicle of the events of human political life became gradually less and less tethered to the kind of temporality specific to human life.

The historical account provided of this gradual unmooring of historical discourse from the time of human lives serves as a basis upon which Arendt can gauge the relevance of modern history for human memory and for the finitude to which memory was originally called upon to attest. As well, her formulation of the rift between human experience and modern history, both in the development of the essay's arguments as well as in its less clearly articulated aspects, will provide us with clues to an as-yet unassimilated aspect of modernity's time.

....

For the Greeks, history consisted of preserving great political action, action deserving of remembrance. Invoking Herodotus, Arendt writes that history's aim was "to preserve that which owes its existence to men, lest it be obliterated by time, and to bestow upon the glorious, wondrous deeds of Greeks and barbarians sufficient praise to assure their remembrance by posterity and thus make their glory shine through the centuries."[17] By virtue of its capacity to safeguard that which is at risk of perishing, the writing of history for the Greeks was a form of memorial preservation: "the human capacity to achieve this was remembrance, Mnemosyne, who therefore was regarded as the mother of all the muses."[18]

Arendt argues that the key to understanding the importance of memory for the Greeks lies in their notion of human mortality: "Since the things of nature are ever-present," she writes, "they are not likely to be overlooked or forgotten; and since they are forever, they do not need human remembrance for their further existence."[19] Unlike this "ever-recurring life" of nature but also unlike "the deathless and ageless lives" of the gods, humans require memory because they are the "only mortal things there are,"[20] that is to say, beyond being members of a species, they also exist as individuals. According to the Greek conception, it is only as individuals that humans can, strictly speaking, be said to be born, to live, and to die.

Against the backdrop of temporal passing by virtue of which all human action was continuously subject to the threat of oblivion, memory was conceived of as a means by which the transient nature of actions and deeds could be mitigated. As such, the Greek notion of memory was what enabled men to overcome their perishable nature and to foster truly divine aspirations:

> By their capacity for the immortal deed, by their ability to leave non-perishable traces behind, men, their individual mortality notwithstanding, attain an immortality of their own and prove themselves to be of a "divine" nature.[21]

The distinction between the mortality of men and the immortality of nature and the gods was the tacit assumption of these memorial practices. The passage of an action or deed from the transient, mortal world of men to the realm of immortality depended upon what Arendt describes as a kind of "translating" into the written word: a recasting of human action and deed—which, on their own, "would never outlast the moment of their realization"—into a medium that could grant them longer life: this was the task uniting poet and historian.[22]

The line of inquiry that Arendt pursues in these discussions of mortality and immortality serves to emphasize what was generally at stake in Ancient Greek memorial practices and what the underlying assumptions of those practices were. Memory, expressed as history or poetry, served as a bridge between the transient, temporal realm of humans and the realm, both divine and natural, of "everlastingness."[23] The seeming irreconcilability of these two realms notwithstanding, to what do the actions of men owe their "translatability," or, in other words, what characterizes mortality such that it can be translated into a kind of immortality? Probing this question, Arendt writes:

> The mortality of man lies in the fact that individual life, a *bios* with a *recognizable life-story from birth to death*, rises out of biological life, *zoē*. This

> individual life is distinguished from all other things by the *rectilinear course of its movement*, which, so to speak, cuts through the circular movements of biological life. This is mortality: to move along a *rectilinear line* in a universe where everything, if it moves at all, moves in a cyclical order.[24]

According to this description, the formal structure of *bios* corresponds to that of narrative; mortal life is not only life that is born, lives, and then passes away but is also one whose very life span provides the key to narrative immortalization. The strong affinities that the "form of life" or *bios* bears to a life-story or plot show how difficult it is, at a certain level, to discern life-story from life: at some level, the *bios* of individual life is always already *biography*.[25]

The most readily discernible temporal parameter of this linear movement is what Arendt, in the book's preface, refers to as "historical or biographical time" and describes in terms of the "unidirectional flow of time. … [T]he traditional image according to which we think of time as moving in a straight line [is] a rectilinear temporal movement."[26] The linear chronology implied by an unfolding or sequence is, though, secondary in importance to what she calls in *The Human Condition*, "birth and death, natality and mortality."[27] This "general condition of human existence," she argues, provides the structure according to which a successive series of events or episodes can be circumscribed and turned into something meaningful. In other words, the work of memory is said to immortalize the actions and deeds of humans as it gives expression both to the time of their unfolding as well as to the time of their emergence and their completion—actions, in other words, are inscribed within a structure bound to and by the events of human birth and death.

Arendt's description of the structure of finitude bears strong resemblances to the theory of narrative structure advanced by Aristotle in *The Poetics*, in particular to the requirement that a narrative is complete only "if it has a beginning, a middle and an end."[28] Notably, Ricoeur has taken up this requirement in *Time and Narrative* as "the pivot" of Aristotle's formulation, one which warrants consideration in terms of the temporality implicit to plot-structure. While Aristotle himself did not articulate poetic structure in terms of its temporality—for Aristotle, poetry could only teach the universal on the condition that it maintain an "achronicity"[29]—Ricoeur draws on the Aristotelian notion of "wholeness" to argue that:

> The act of emplotment combines in variable proportions two temporal dimensions, one chronological and the other not. The former constitutes the episodic dimension of narrative. It characterizes the story insofar as it is made up of events. The second is the configurational dimension properly speaking, thanks to which the plot transforms the events into a story. This configurational act consists of "grasping together" the detailed actions. … It draws from this manifold of events the unity of one temporal whole.[30]

Ricoeur conceives of the temporality of plot-structure as a unified "double-time": on the one hand, the linear succession of events which is, for Aristotle, the domain of the plot's "middle"[31] and, on the other hand, the logical limits of the beginning and the end in accordance with which the contingent episodes become meaningful as part of a temporal whole. According to Ricoeur, the unexpected, the surprising, and the perplexing are what "the plot tends to make necessary and probable. And in so doing, it purifies them, or, better, purges them."[32]

While no mention of Arendt is made in the context of Ricoeur's discussion,[33] her innovation is to have placed this narrative logic in relation to human finitude and to have discerned the paradoxical source of narrative's immortalizing power in the structure of *bios*. Moreover, the connection that she articulates between the structure of narrative and the finite structure of individual life is the basis upon which she is able to draw out the importance of singularity in Greek history, for which historical events "are not seen as parts of either an encompassing whole or a process; on the contrary, the stress is always on single instances and single gestures."[34]

It might be useful, at this point, to clarify a possible misconception: for Arendt, the Greeks did not commit human action to the memorial structure of individual life span in order to "humanize" political action, and her intention is certainly not to focus on how "great men" become immortal on the basis of an individualistic conception of personal biography. Rather, the task of her argument is to show how Greek political action retains its singularity in historical discourse by virtue of being narrated *like* an individual human life. As she argues in *The Human Condition*, in distinct contrast to an individualistic conception of politics, the basis of action—and all action was political, took place in the polis—was the human condition of plurality: "that men, not Man, live on the earth and inhabit the world."[35] Moreover, for the Greeks, it simply would have been inconceivable that anyone outside of the polis—or, what amounts to the same thing, anyone not in possession of the potential to act that the "being-with" and the plurality of the polis enabled—could be conceived as a human.[36] So, far from heralding the individual as the agent of political action, her discussion of the relation between the structure of the individual human life and that of immortalizing narrative demonstrates that the emphasis on singular instances in Greek historical discourse is due to its narrative structure, conceived in terms of natality and mortality.[37]

On that basis, Arendt insists on the following points: first, that history and poetry were given the task of inscribing politics into memory; second, that it is through the "acting in concert" of politics that humans were able to obviate their own individual mortality; and, third, that insofar as political action and human life were thought to be inseparable, the memorial inscription of politics came to be emblematic of humanness as such.[38] This means that, for the Greeks, memory rids human life of its propensity simply to pass away by taking up its most memorable political actions and, within the structure of historical or poetic discourse, granting to those actions their singular and unique importance by narrating them in accordance with a specifically human form of temporality.

....

Arendt gives a preliminary idea of just how unfamiliar and foreign these notions of history and poetry would become by noting the radical changes introduced by the

Socratic school of philosophy into the conception of human immortality. In this respect, Arendt describes Plato's philosophy as a "culmination."[39] In addition to various other attacks launched against man's attempts to immortalize himself, the philosopher in *The Symposium* responds to man's desire to achieve human immortality by having Diotima suggest that the impulse be satisfied by encouraging the masses to procreate.[40] Otherwise, it is a vain and imprudent undertaking.

The emergent authority of metaphysics is grounded in a more or less explicit rejection of the framework of mortal life in accordance with which the memorial forms of poetry and history had been structured. Nowhere is this metaphysical transformation exemplified with greater clarity than in Plato's dialogue *Phaedo*, wherein testimony is given of Socrates's final conversation with his disciples and a perspective on immortality and human finitude is developed that differs in almost every respect from the notion that immortalizing memory is moored to human life span.

In order to give his listeners a sense of the serenity he feels as he faces imminent death, the *Phaedo* has Socrates put forward the famous argument that what is worthy of remembrance and recollection exceeds the boundaries of human life. Death, the separation of body and soul, is welcomed by the philosopher, given that all things proper to the mortal body—what in *The Symposium* is described in graphic and disparaging fashion as "a perpetual process of loss and reparation: hair, flesh, bones, blood, and the whole body are always changing"[41]—must be abandoned as worthless or dangerously seductive if the soul is to perceive the eternal and unchanging world of the ideas.

Philosophical recollection is, thus, death-rehearsal. In the *Phaedo*, Socrates approves the popular understanding that philosophers are half-dead: "anyone who thinks nothing of physical pleasures has one foot in the grave."[42] The philosopher gains access to the eternal realm only by denying the fugacity of mortal life; he has always allied himself to what does not pass away, change, or grow old. Thus the philosopher need not fear his own death since he has been preparing himself for it all along.

What is especially significant for our purposes is the enormity of the changes in perspective on human life and memory being proposed here. Whereas poetry and history found the form of immortalizing memory in human life, philosophy will overturn this valorization and conceive of human life as deeply corruptive for all that is truly immortal.[43] Memory, no longer cast as a narrative repetition of the temporal structure of a human life, is a struggle away from the temporality of all things mortal. Socrates evokes this struggle as he discusses what happens to the soul when it is forced to seek shelter in the body:

> it is dragged away by the body into the realm of the variable, and loses its way and becomes confused and dizzy, as though it were fuddled. … But when it investigates by itself, it passes into the realm of the pure and everlasting and immortal and changeless, and being of a kindred nature … strays no longer, but remains in that realm of the absolute, constant and invariable, through contact with beings of a similar nature.[44]

According to this perspective, for as long as the immortal soul is embodied, it is condemned to an existence that is "human, mortal, multiform, unintelligible, dissoluble, and never self-consistent."[45] The embodied soul is errant, its state one of temporary confusion. Leaving aside for a moment the question of whether or not the temporariness of this confused state—and so, the fact of its temporality—compromises the radically unchangeable nature of the soul, the official meaning of these statements is clear: since truth does not change, it is neither subject to processes of aging or decay, nor could it ever be manifest in the processes of human finitude. It is not, like mortals are, enslaved by time. Wholly immersed in their bodily finitude, men are incapable of truth.

It would be difficult to overstate the influence that these formulations have had on Western thinking, particularly how they oppose the activity of thinking to the human world and how they authorize a disdain for the human body that has scarcely abated since.[46] Less obvious, perhaps, but no less decisive are the consequences that this estimation of human life has for memory. When, for instance, Plato has his Socrates denounce "wars and revolutions and battles" by virtue of their belonging to the realm of "the body and its desires," it is to disqualify politics *tout court* as the site of memory.[47] Since political events happen in time as a dimension of human finitude, they only serve to distract the philosopher, whose recollection is directed toward what is timeless. Philosophical memory, out-of-step with the time of politics, is also patently non-political; attempting to rid itself of the traces of human temporality, it is a form of resistance to politics and to finitude as such.

These conceptions of life, death, and memory are a reversal of all the themes and formal structures that had been established within Greek history and poetry: death for philosophy, as the radical separation or separability of the soul from the constraints of finitude, is the condition upon which philosophy stakes its claim to memory's ultimate timelessness. According to this schema, human death is not what it was for the pre-Socratic narrative arts: not an end or a loss to which narrative responds by ensuring an ongoing relation to that loss (in the memorial form of its own temporality). Philosophy conceives of human death in a more radically upbeat sense, according to which whatever loss it entails is registered as pure gain.[48] And in direct proportion to how philosophy tends to value death as a force of unqualified redemptive potential, it also subjects human birth to a radical depreciation, seeing it as the soul's catastrophic fall into the mortal world of humans. It is a kind of amnesia-inducing trauma, *avant la lettre*.[49]

....

This detour has, I hope, served to lend a measure of clarity to the two dominant notions of memory and to the lines along which their opposition can be understood. On the one hand, the immortalizing claims of narrative resided in the chronicle it produced of human political events and which it expressed in accordance with the course of a human life. On the other hand, disdain for the mortal life of humans was central to developing a radically different notion of memory: one that, by virtue of having as little as possible to do with human life, could be defined as a form of pure and a-temporal contemplation. The aim of this contemplation—knowledge of the ideas—lay at the end of a long metaphysical journey that resembled death and that had to be taken largely alone.

In other words, philosophy did not just take memory in a direction that turned out to be incompatible with the political realm or with the social world of humans; rather, it actively directed memory *against* human life. Arendt emphasizes how philosophy turned memory away from the world of humans when she draws attention to the silence of its ultimate undertaking:

> Thus the proper attitude of mortals, once they had reached the neighbourhood of the immortal, was actionless and even speechless contemplation: the Aristotelian νοῦς, the highest and most human capacity of pure vision, cannot translate into words what it beholds, and the ultimate truth which the vision of ideas disclosed to Plato is likewise an ἄρρητον, something which cannot be caught in words.[50]

When memory enters the domain of solitary or philosophical-sectarian contemplation, it is severed from the world of human affairs. By highlighting the ineffability of philosophical memory, Arendt is laying particular stress on the centrality of language for human action and its immortalizing memory.[51]

In many ways the gap dividing Greek memory into the immortalizing chronicle of political events on the one side and the transcendent and eternal realm of the ineffable on the other, is one legacy which Christianity would inherit and attempt to resolve. For, how else are we to specify the uniqueness of Christianity if not in its having given its god a life span? Hegel's description of Christianity proceeds along these lines: "The fact that Christ is a child," he writes in the *Aesthetics*, "does in one way definitely express the meaning he has in our religion: he is God who becomes man and therefore goes through the stages of human life."[52] If the specificity of Christianity does indeed lie in having granted to its God a human life span—submitting him to a birth and, even more scandalously, to suffering and death—then the process by which he is immortalized must, if he is not to be subject to an internal division (and so consequently not absolute at all), also be articulated in terms of this life span. The Christian God is thus made immortal by virtue of the immortalization of his human life span, a process that Catherine Malabou has described in terms of the "absolutizing of finitude."[53]

Christianity attempted to resolve the dual nature of the claim to immortality through its deification of life span. In so many ways a parallel to Plato's parable of the cave, just as the philosopher must first leave the cave that is man's earthly prison, so too is Christ's departure from his earthly tomb the condition upon which his place in eternity is assured. Though, as Christianity immortalizes human life span and so resolves the contradiction between two competing notions of memory, it produces another tension, one between politics and memory.

Arendt argues that by immortalizing the life span of the single human individual, Christianity effectively reversed the Greek order according to which men could aspire to everlastingness. She makes the point as follows: "[I]n Christianity neither the world nor the ever-recurring cycle of life is immortal, only the single living individual. It is the world that will pass away; men will live forever."[54] In order for Christianity to immortalize human life span (noting that its immortalization is predicated upon departure from *this* world), life span itself will have had to forfeit any attachment to a changing and changeable world.[55] Beyond the assurance Christianity gives of membership in a community of the faithful, Christianity's resolution of Greece's two competing claims to immortality means that life span and finitude have had to take leave of their specifically political and "worldly" character.[56]

The effects of the Christianization of life span are not limited to its transformation of the notion of immortality vis-à-vis human life; it also brought about radical transformations to how the unpredictable and changeable world of politics was to be narrated. To the extent that Christianity draws a distinction between human life span and the world of politics and raises individual life above political concerns, it also provides Arendt with a backdrop against which to examine what little has remained of human finitude within the discourse of modern history. Very much in contrast to the more life-affirming aspects of the Greek narrative arts, the story she offers of modern history is that of its radical depopulation.

....

The characterization Arendt gives of modern history underscores how decisively it differs from the Greek conception of history. Modern history, she argues, is incompatible with its notion of history as narrative life span insofar as

> [s]ince the seventeenth century the chief preoccupation of all scientific inquiry, natural as well as historical, has been with processes. ... In the modern age history emerged as something it never had been before. It was no longer composed of the deeds and sufferings of men; it became a man-made process, the only all-comprehending process which owed its existence exclusively to the human race.[57]

Thus, just as she had linked the Greek conception of history to its conception of nature on the basis of history's being that which allowed humans to escape their transience and partake of immortality, so too does she link modern history to nature, but for different reasons. For Arendt, the similarity of their claim to immortality lies in the quintessentially modern concept of "process: both [history and nature] imply that we think and consider everything in terms of processes and are not concerned with single entities or individual occurrences and their special separate causes."[58]

As Arendt directs her attention to the consequences of this process-oriented thinking for human life, her discussion becomes increasingly critical of its dehumanizing aspects. Regarding the decline of the humanities and the rise of the social sciences as the logical heir of modern history, she writes:

> If their vocabulary is repulsive and ... our deplored impotence to "manage" human affairs through an engineering science of human relations sounds frightening, it is only because they have decided to treat man as an entirely

> natural being whose life process can be handled the same way as all other processes.[59]

When meaning is generated solely on the basis of an overarching process, the implications are potentially catastrophic, beginning with how the plurality of individual entities are reduced to a function within a process that itself cannot be made the subject of human understanding. "Invisible processes," she writes, "have engulfed every tangible thing, every individual entity that is visible to us, degrading them into functions of an over-all process."[60]

When Arendt raises the issue of the chronological reforms introduced in the eighteenth century, it is to show what impact the modern conception of historical process has on notions of temporality once the former are freed from the formal constraints of life span. Arguing that modernity bestows "upon mere time-sequence an importance and dignity it never had before," she goes on to suggest that what is truly decisive about those reforms is that the birth of Christ becomes "a turning point from which to count time both backward and forward"[61] and that, for the very first time,

> the history of mankind reaches back into an infinite past to which we can add at will and into which we can inquire further as it stretches ahead into an infinite future. This two-fold infinity of past and future eliminates all notions of beginning and end, establishing mankind in a potential earthly immortality … as far as secular history is concerned, we live in a process which knows no beginning and no end.[62]

According to this understanding, what is distinctive about the temporality of modern history is how it continues to be dependent upon the rectilinear, consecutive time of *bios*, but only after the latter has been stripped of birth and death. Thus, the temporal standard adopted from the life span of the human individual has given way to a rather more alarming constellation: one in which the history of modernity's mankind, because it is neither born nor dies, is told in a kind of infinite and un-dead narrative time.

Set in relief against her description of Greek historiography, the discourse of modern history emerges in Arendt's thinking as the site of a two-fold dehumanization: first, since historical events only become meaningful when seen as part of an ever-expanding historical process that neither begins nor ends, history in the modern period ceases to derive its narrative form from the temporal structure of human life span, the result of which being that birth and death no longer figure in the formal structure of the modern historical account. For modern history, Arendt argues, nothing ever begins or ends. Secondly, in its unmooring from the conditions of finite existence, historical discourse is deeply complicit with the broader modern phenomenon of the gradual disappearance of representations of finitude from the public sphere, a disappearance which, according to one prominent historian of death, is now practically complete.[63]

Arendt's account shows how decisively the structure of modern historiography differs from that of Greek historiography. Grounding her distinction in the uncanny sense that the structure and temporality of human life span has "gone missing" from modern historiography, her account invites us to consider modernity as an epoch whose historical discourse generates no narrative memory proper to human finitude. And, although not explicitly stated in these terms, in a sense she is also asking us to consider modernity as an epoch to which no one can truly bear witness.

Less despairingly perhaps, another challenge raised by Arendt's theory of narrative memory involves asking the question of what remains of finitude *within* modern history's open-ended linear succession, especially since this claim of open-endedness is made as a function of historical time. For if the time of modern history is an endless succession of distinct moments, couldn't it also be argued that *bios* is *everywhere* at work within this temporality, governing the operation whereby each moment is constituted by virtue of the break it makes from the one preceding it?

Michel de Certeau has also taken up the logic of this temporality, grounding his description in the relation it bears to death. Like Arendt, he too suggests that modern history is conceived in terms of how it presumes to have evacuated death from its own temporality. But de Certeau's account also differs from Arendt's; he sees in this temporality, one supposedly purified of all death, the strangely ubiquitous presence of death itself. The source of this ubiquity, he argues, lies precisely in the modern notion of time as a constant *rupture*, that is, as a process of constant differentiation by means of which the production of the new "provides the place for a discourse considering whatever preceded it to be 'dead.' … Breakage is therefore the postulate of interpretation (which is constructed as of the present time)."[64] De Certeau's account draws out the implications of history's relation to the past when its "heterology" consists of a weighty deadness:

> On its own account, historiography takes for granted the fact that it has become impossible to believe in this presence of the dead that has organized (or organizes) the experience of entire civilizations; and the fact too that it is nonetheless impossible "to get over it," to accept the loss of a living solidarity with what is gone, or to confirm an irreducible limit. What is *perishable* is its data; *progress* is its motto. … It is an odd procedure that posits death … and that yet denies loss by appropriating to the present the privilege of recapitulating the past as a form of knowledge. A labor of death and a labor against death.[65]

What de Certeau's formulation suggests is not so much that modern history has evacuated finitude from its discourse as that its own temporal structure has inadvertently multiplied or intensified it. From this perspective, the chronological time of modern historical discourse appears to have formalized *bios* as its own temporal principle; the claim of every moment, epoch, or period is asserted by virtue of the "death" of the one preceding it. Consequently, we might say that every moment of a historical succession has itself become finite: it possesses "a life of its own" as well as a death, one that historiography can no more readily mourn than abandon.

Insofar as Arendt limits her discussion of memory in modernity to the perils of modern historical discourse, she leaves open the question of the relation between memory and human finitude in art. Indeed, while both Greek history and poetry are clearly tethered to the exigencies of memory in Arendt's thought, her silence on the question of modern poetry and, more generally, on the issue of modern literary language *as such*, leaves open the possibility that perhaps its own sustained relation to finitude can help draw out the implications for history of a *bios* that has not simply disappeared, but that occurs at every single moment.

Mourning Stories

> *The past carries with it a temporal index by which it is referred to redemption. There is a secret agreement between past generations and the present one.*
> —*Walter Benjamin*[66]

Some twenty years before Arendt, Walter Benjamin had directed his attention to the question of narrative and cultural transmission, inflecting what he saw as the widening disjunction between them with a kind of historical specificity. In "The Storyteller," Benjamin offers clues to suggest not only that consideration of the relation between modern culture and storytelling must take into account the demise of storytelling as a means of cultural transmission but also—and more oddly—that it is *only* with the demise of storytelling that such a relation can be accurately characterized at all.[67] Beyond the at-times awkwardly nostalgic feel to the essay (which perhaps accounts for why it is not read as rigorously or as systematically as many of his other writings), Benjamin wishes to situate the end of narrative in light of a broader, markedly non-nostalgic question: what it might mean, namely, for a culture to be no longer transmissible by narrative. As well as attempting to clarify what might be implied by storytelling's loss of authority as a "medium" for cultural transmission, the essay thus also asks what it might mean for a culture to take stock of that loss, in a mode that resists simply capitalizing on it, as part of its own continued survival.

Given these aims, it seems fitting that the essay begins by developing an image of the storyteller using a dense interplay of remoteness and proximity, of the immediacy of "living presence" and more complex modes of encounter. For, it is only from a perspective of this sort—near and far, visible and yet barely discernible, accessible only in its inaccessibility, and so on—that, Benjamin suggests, we will be able to "see" what is at stake in the end of storytelling. Then he goes on to suggest that

> the art of storytelling is coming to an end. Less and less frequently do we encounter people with the ability to tell a tale properly. More and more often there is embarrassment all around when the wish to hear a story is expressed. It is as if something that seemed inalienable to us, the securest among our possessions [*Vermögen*], were taken from us: the ability to exchange experiences [*nämlich, das Vermögen, Erfahrungen auszutauschen*].[68]

What Benjamin claims is assured property, and what is at stake when stories are no longer told is not really a possession at all, at least not in the strict sense of the word. To the contrary, what is called "possession" here actually seems more like the relinquishment of one; the act of transmission itself is what Benjamin suggests may be at stake in the loss of storytelling. And, if storytelling is no longer able to act as a means by which people can share their experiences with one another—if, as Benjamin contends, people experience embarrassment at the mere mention of the word—then, presumably, changes undergone at the level of experience must have had a hand in this demise, changes that have made experience incompatible with the narrative mode of language.

In fact, while the essay's title "*The* Storyteller" ("*Der Erzähler*" and not, say, "A Storyteller") evokes the work of Russian storyteller Nikolai Leskov (whose writings had already been largely consigned to literary oblivion in Benjamin's own time) as a figure of utter singularity, the essay's most powerful and provocative moments are provided by a double sense of Leskov's exemplarity—that is, both his singularity *and* his example—of which the "pastness" of his literary achievement is a not insignificant trait. In fact, Leskov's exemplarity seems most productive for Benjamin at the level of the general insights it affords regarding this loss of narrative as an articulation of experience. For Benjamin openly contends that the loss of a literary means to express experience cannot be isolated from other, graver ruptures in experience, the historical weight of which is brought to bear on the text as a whole. As he describes it in the first paragraphs of the essay, every aspect of experience has been brought face-to-face with what has the power to overwhelm it. Beginning with the limit-experience of men returning from the battlefields of World War I, "grown silent—not richer, but poorer in communicable experience," Benjamin writes:

> And there was nothing remarkable about that. For never has experience been contradicted more thoroughly than strategic experience by tactical warfare, economic experience by inflation, bodily experience by mechanical warfare, moral experience by those in power. A generation that had gone to school on a horse-drawn streetcar now stood under the open sky in a countryside in which nothing remained unchanged but the clouds, and beneath these clouds, in a field of force of destructive torrents and explosions, was the tiny, fragile human body.[69]

Describing a world in which the only constants are clouds—which, in most people's estimation, do nothing if not change—the essay's very first impulses are to insist on the disjointedness of experience and time as a way of explaining why narrative practices have become impossible to sustain, either as a literary genre or as a discursive mode of everyday life. The return home of soldiers burdened with extreme and un-narratable experience is itself marked as a historical threshold, one by virtue of which modernity's generalized crisis of experience has become legible.[70] Benjamin articulates this crisis as a confrontation with an unrecognizable world, one which has made an anathema of human life: it offers no orientation or scale with which the measure of human lives could be taken. Assurances of this kind belong to the past, of which even the most recent moments seem so remote that they can only be conjured through the nostalgic, almost quaint image of going to school "on a horse-drawn streetcar."

This invocation of a bygone era has a melancholy ring to it—longing, perhaps, for a *temps perdu*—but on a formal level the contrast that it affects captures a sense of the gap separating past from present.[71] Reducing even the very recent past to the status of a faded cliché accentuates the toll that the destructive violence of the world has taken on time and memory. For a world wherein the only continuity is provided by the strange permanence of clouds in the sky, the past can no longer be appropriated or understood by the present, much less can it offer meaningful and narratable orientation for the future; it can only be invoked mechanically, as drearily unassimilated and un-assimilable as a stale metaphor.

It is in the context of this rift between the past and the present that the critical force of Benjamin's reflections on the possible end of narrative as well as its implications for experience are to be situated. For, both here and elsewhere, Benjamin is resistant to the notion that experience constitutes the "raw material" for memory, narrative or otherwise; rather, Benjaminian experience is already implicated in memory and is, as we shall see momentarily, already irreducibly literary. In his essay on Baudelaire, published just a few years later, Benjamin writes approvingly of Bergson's contention in *Mémoire et Matière* that "the structure of memory [i]s decisive for the philosophical pattern of experience [*Erfahrung*]."[72] It is partially on the basis of memory's primacy that Benjamin affects the contrast between *Erfahrung* and *Erlebnis*; whereas *Erfahrung* is the name given to impressions which already have been lifted out of the time of their occurrence by memory, *Erlebnis* elicits the sense of impressions which have remained "at a certain hour in one's life" and so have proven resistant to narration.[73]

While certainly this stance had become more explicit in the later essay, one can sense the urgency with which it was beginning to emerge in the descriptions of "The Storyteller." The excessive and violent stimuli of the modern world threaten narrative memory, making the structures of memory unstable and, even more radically, calling into question the very possibility of experience itself. Over and against a past which yields only silence or neutralized clichés when confronted with an overwhelming present, Benjamin seems to postulate hidden conjunctions between what has past—storytelling—and the needs of the present. This he does by locating affinities between the temporal register of the life and death of narrative and that of the "tiny, fragile human body." Thus, he lingers at the end of storytelling, draws it out and lets it take its time in order to make a point, precisely, about time.

Among the various factors which contribute to the demise of storytelling—the novel and its solitary individual, the rise of the middle class, the invention of the printing press, capitalism, etc.—Benjamin singles out one factor in light of the seriousness of the threat it poses. After having discussed the emergence and transformation of epic narrative forms in terms that hyperbolize the tectonic slowness of their tempo (in rhythms, he emphasizes, which are "comparable to those of the change that has come over the earth's surface in the course of thousands of centuries"), he writes:

> we recognize that with the full control of the middle class, which has the

> press as one of its most important instruments in fully developed capitalism, there emerges a form of communication which, no matter how far back its origin may lie, never before influenced the epic form in a decisive way. But now it does exert such an influence. And it turns out that it confronts storytelling as no less of a stranger than did the novel, but in a more menacing way, and that it also brings about a crisis in the novel. This new form of communication is information.[74]

As information is brought into sharper focus, greater and greater emphasis is placed on the character of its temporality. And, pointedly, Benjamin accentuates how it is that as information becomes more and more pervasive, its rationalization and acceleration of time stand to annul questions of time altogether.

One aspect of information targeted by Benjamin involves its sense of immediacy, beginning with the prerequisites that it "appear understandable in itself" and that it be subject to "prompt verifiability" by means of other sources.[75] This "prime requirement" suggests that information has direct and immediate access to the real, that it is somehow able to circumvent language's potential complications, including questions of authority, translation, the use of rhetoric and trope, and those involving referentiality itself.[76]

Benjamin draws attention to the temporal implications of this kind of language by noting how value is accorded to information on the basis of how *little* time it takes. By definition, he notes disparagingly, information is transitory and short-lived: so tightly wedded to the present, it is almost always rushed. Evoking a kind of confrontation with the law, Benjamin writes that information "does not survive the moment [*dem Augenblick*] in which it was new. It lives only at that moment; it has to surrender to it completely and explain itself to it without losing any time" and, quoting Valéry, that "the time is past in which time did not matter [*Die Zeit ist vorbei, in der es auf Zeit nicht ankam.*]. Modern man no longer works at what cannot be abbreviated."[77]

Story-telling, on the other hand, takes time. In what on a certain level seems an implausible comparison, Benjamin contrasts information's *Augenblick* with what is so "exemplary" about a story by Herodotus, its potential for practically infinite generation—a trope for earthly immortality if ever there was one. Benjamin renders the story with a clear focus on the scene of unforeseeable mourning staged within it:

> When the Egyptian king Psammenitus had been beaten and captured by the Persian king Cambyses, Cambyes was bent on humbling his prisoner. He gave orders to place Psammenitus on the road along which the Persian triumphal procession was to pass. And he further arranged that the prisoner should see his daughter pass by as a maid going to the well with her pitcher. While all the Egyptians were lamenting and bewailing this spectacle, Psammenitus stood alone, mute and motionless, his eyes fixed on the ground; and when presently he saw his son, who was being taken along in the procession to be executed, he likewise remained unmoved. But when afterwards he recognized one of his servants, an old, impoverished man, in the ranks of the prisoners, he beat his fists against his head and gave all the signs of deepest mourning.[78]

Benjamin likens the story to "seeds of grain which have lain for millennia [*jahrtausandelange*] in the chambers of the pyramids ... and have retained their germinative power up to this day [*bis auf den heutigen Tag*]."[79] Despite the hyperbole of Benjamin's description here—one verging on the Biblical—the simile is no mere flight of fancy on Benjamin's part. In fact, this is no ordinary simile at all, but rather the citation of one. We cannot fail to read the subtext of Benjamin's description as a reference to the pyramid that had figured so prominently in Hegel's theory of the sign in the *Encyclopedia of the Philosophical Sciences*, among other places. Set in contrast to the highly critical appraisal of information's language of immediacy preceding it, one is also reminded of how the pyramid's formal structure had provided Hegel with the means to explain the disjunction of the sign: how its inside and its outside are irresolvably disjoined. The visibility of its exterior can, for Hegel, never be subjected to processes of reconciliation with the invisibility and the indeterminacy of what, if anything at all, resides on its interior.[80]

There is, thus, an important sense in which Benjamin's pyramid demands a twofold reading: on the one hand, by virtue of its force as citation, it acts as an implicit critique of the assumption that language directly refers to what is outside it and, on the other hand, it operates metaphorically to draw attention to the story's incredible longevity by accentuating the role that a *different* kind of language plays in that longevity.

Indeed, the language of the story being privileged here has little in common with the kind used in the transmission of information. The story endures, Benjamin seems to suggest, precisely because of how its language fails to guarantee any kind of direct relation to the real; it is likened to a pyramid, after all, and so to the irresolvable indeterminacy of its content. In other words, language does not simply register what, beyond language, is of enduring value by granting form to the formlessness of "timeless truths" or the like. Rather, Benjamin's notion of language is grounded in another kind of endurance, one less reliant on metaphysical notions of representation and one which attunes him to how inexhaustibility is posited by and within language. In short, for Benjamin, it is precisely *because* language does not signify in any direct or natural way that it is able to generate any history at all.

Beyond the manner in which the story's own history gets generated, there is also the decidedly enigmatic instance of mourning which takes place within the story and in which Benjamin clearly locates the source of the story's lasting power. Mourning, like memory, is most often understood in terms of the clear temporal parameters according to which the present turns toward the past or toward what has assuredly passed. There is a majestic stability to this temporality and to this stance; so rarely shaken, they seem to have come from the work of mourning itself. Nothing, in fact, would seem more detrimental to mourning than doubt or confusion. Here though, the story's scene of mourning is just such an arresting instance of unpredictability, one which takes its readers—of the past, the present, and the future, says Benjamin—by surprise. Benjamin clearly locates the exemplary force of this mourning, as well as its momentum toward the future, in how it thwarts all expectation and defies understanding. As if this weren't surprising enough—given the general conviction that understanding forms the basis of historical or cultural longevity—what kind of mourning is it that disturbs the "expected" so quickly and unpredictably as to seem practically to come *from* the future?

Let us defer the question of the futurity of mourning for a few moments and pursue another one related to it. Returning to the suggestion Benjamin makes at the beginning of the essay regarding the relation between storytelling and experience: to what aspect of narrative language could experience have ever possibly owed its transmissibility, especially when the story is praised for a kind of language which does not in the first instance transmit content? Although Benjamin is clear on the point that unmediated language is incompatible with the narrative transmission of experience, he is less clear on what it is about narrative that allows it to generate insights about experience. In that light, it makes sense to turn to a more complicated form of affinity between language and experience, one not reducible to a relation of representation. The essay's almost-constant preoccupation with time suggests that affinities between the literary structure of narrative and the structure of experience are to be found in the kinds of temporality that they share.

Benjamin will specify these affinities by inquiring into how the two prose genres of the story and the novel manage to negotiate the question of their own endings. In some respects similar to how Arendt praised Greek narrative for the relation it sustains to human finitude and life span, Benjamin had nonetheless already gone further than Arendt by taking the notion of life span beyond its objective representation in language—that is, beyond the notion of life span as it is seen from the perspective of its completion. I will argue that, by exposing the limits of such an objective representation, he had also already exposed the conventional understanding of the relation between experience and narrative memory to what, in the Baudelaire essay, he would call the "shock experience" of modern life.

....

In the final analysis, the range of life must be determined by history.
—Walter Benjamin, "The Task of the Translator"[81]

In part to explain how the notion of eternity and, along with it, memory's immortalizing claim both get eclipsed by an increasingly rationalized temporal structure, Benjamin begins by pointing out a paradox: how eternity is related to death. "The idea of eternity," he writes, "has ever had its strongest source in death."[82] Relating death's disappearance to the decline of this idea, he suggests that the epoch in which information—along with its reduction of time to *mere* moments—has flourished is also the epoch in which "people [can] avoid the sight of the dying":

> In the course of modern times dying has been pushed further and further out of the perceptual world of the living. … Today people live in rooms that have never been touched by death, dry dwellers of eternity, and when their end approaches they are stowed away in sanatoria or hospitals by their heirs.[83]

Thus, modernity is an epoch which, "by means of hygienic and social, private and public institutions,"[84] has almost entirely succeeded in evacuating death and dying from its midst.

Unsurprisingly, Benjamin's rendering of the phenomenon emphasizes its literary dimension, by tying Ariès's "denial of death" to the demise of narrative. What Benjamin asserts will later resonate in Arendt's claim that the authority of narrative is furnished by the relationship it sustains to human finitude, a relation that modernity threatens to make superfluous or to negate altogether. Thus Benjamin can state that "[d]eath is the sanction of everything that the storyteller can tell" and that "it is … characteristic that not only a man's knowledge or wisdom, but above all his real life—and this is the stuff that stories are made of—first assumes transmissible form [*tradierbare Form am ersten*] at the moment of his death."[85]

No sooner does Benjamin make the claim that death plays a singular and authoritative role in literature than he complicates it by multiplying the essay's perspectives on death. In the passage just cited, for instance, Benjamin situates death's authority in terms of the kind of "closure" it affords. Similar to the force exerted by death in Arendt's account of narrative life span, Benjamin's account places decidedly greater emphasis on how narrative gives meaning and form to life *for the very first time* in order to radicalize the sense of what is at stake in the loss of narrative. Benjamin is proposing that only in literary narrative does human life have any chance of becoming meaningful at all.

Although this stance might seem to indicate a rather uncomfortable slide toward an aestheticization of human existence, Benjamin's conviction of the all-encompassing scope of language demands it to be read otherwise than as a denigration or trivialization. The possibility that literature might offer insights into experience that experience itself can not offer—especially in light of the breakdown of experience sealed by modernity—is brought to bear on his discussion of the novel, for example, which derives part of its explanation of the genre's appeal on the basis of what can be gleaned from the lives of the characters through their deaths. Beyond that, though, Benjamin also seems to suggest that the death of a character can reveal something about a future death to which the reader will never have access: his or her own.

> This stranger's fate by virtue of the flame which consumes it yields us the warmth which we never draw from our own fate. What draws the reader to the novel is the hope of warming his shivering life with a death he reads about.[86]

What might it mean, in accordance with this formulation, that death—a death that, paradoxically, has the power to warm—has gone missing? On the one hand, if death is the condition upon which a life in its totality first becomes meaningful, then death's absence is clearly going to have massive repercussions, both within literary discourse and outside of it, for issues of cultural transmission, what Benjamin calls "the chain of tradition which passes a happening on from generation to generation."[87] Arendt too alludes to this crisis of transmission, seeing it exemplified by the post-war experience of the French Resistance after a return to normalcy had made the "essential years" of the Resistance fundamentally incommunicable. For Arendt, this experience is best encapsulated by René Char's aphoristic "Notre héritage n'est précèdé d'aucun testament" ("Our inheritance was left to us by no testament"), a claim that she explains in the preface to *Between Past and Future* in the following terms:

> The point of the matter is that the "completion," which indeed every enacted event must have in the minds of those who then are to tell the story and to convey its meaning, eluded them, and without this thinking completion after the act, without the articulation accomplished by remembrance, there simply was no story left that could be told.[88]

As was suggested at the outset of the paper, both Arendt and Benjamin were only too aware, and not just in theory, that a world in which death's finality only ever takes place off-stage distorts the task of remembrance and threatens to turn it into an endless "triumphal procession"[89] in which human death has only instrumental value. As such, a central aspect of Benjamin's critique of history was to situate the violence of this "deathless" history in relation to its temporality: "The concept of the historical progress of mankind," he writes toward the end of the "Theses,"

> cannot be sundered from the concept of its progression through a homogeneous, empty time. A critique of such a progression must be the basis of any criticism of the concept of progress itself.[90]

Given the contention that a critique of progress must begin with a critique of the temporal parameters of progression, what insight does Benjamin's analysis of temporality in literature bring to bear on this critique of progress?

Let us pick up the thread of the argument regarding literature and time. We saw how Benjamin had begun outlining the temporality of the novel by situating it in relation to the finality that comes with death, be it a figurative death (the end of the novel) or a literal one (the death of a character). We saw, too, how important this sense of closure was for the kind of memory inhabiting the novel. But what of its time? Subscribing to Georg Lukács's dictum that "the novel is the only art form which includes time among its constitutive principles,"[91] Benjamin's formulation bears quoting at some length, beginning with the claim it makes of the novel's inherent suspense:

> The suspense which permeates the novel is very much like the draft which stimulates the flame in the fireplace and enlivens its play. … It is a dry material on which the burning interest of the reader feeds. "A man who dies at the age of thirty-five," said Moritz Heimann once, "is at every point of his life a man who dies at the age of thirty-five." Nothing is more dubious than this sentence—but for the sole reason that the tense (*Tempus*) is wrong. A man—so says the truth that was meant here—who died at thirty-five will appear to *remembrance* at every point in his life as a man who dies at the age of thirty-five. In other words, the statement that makes no sense for real

> life becomes indisputable for remembered life. The nature of the character in a novel cannot be presented any better than is done in this statement, which says that the "meaning" (*der "Sinn"*) of his life is revealed only in his death.[92]

According to this description, the form of remembrance best exemplified by the novel is one in which each of its moments is infused with its end. According to Benjamin, this means that the moments of a remembered life cannot be read in isolation from other moments (which is another way of saying that they are never, or never quite, *momentary*), nor are they to be read as simply part of a continuous sequence. Rather, remembered moments are shot through with a deep and irrevocable sense of the end to which they are directed. Not to be confused with how conventional wisdom usually associates "knowing how it ends" with the deadening boredom of predictability, Benjamin attributes what is so suspenseful about a novel—a quality which gives it its life, its breath—to a structure within which remembrance is literally inseparable from anticipation.

The novel inaugurates a particularly *suspenseful* experience of reading in part because of how it is able to *suspend* or complicate its own narrative and temporal sequence of a past-present-future unfolding. While linearity doubtless plays a role in the novel, it is supplemented—and its temporal hegemony ultimately compromised—by the force of the novel's end, which is given by remembrance and which should, theoretically at least, make itself felt at every moment. The end of the novel is able to exert this kind of force, not because the novel makes no claim to truth but because of the irreducible textuality of its structure—its inscriptive quality not being subordinated to language's representative function. Each moment of a novel is, then, divided within and against itself, to be read both in terms of the unfolding temporal sequence according to which it is literally impossible to see what is coming and in terms of how each moment is filled with a sense of its own fulfilment and completion, its own memory. Thus, no moment of the novel—nor any minimally discursive moment at all, for that matter, save those saturated with information—can be read in a pure way, isolated from other moments or from its own internal doubling; rather, each moment is inextricably linked to the end.

Whereas Benjamin locates the force of the novel's temporality in the finality of its end by virtue of which each of its moments is suffused with the immanence of that end, a remark made in an unaccountably off-hand way suggests that something else is at stake at the end of a story. The contrast of the story with the novel is affected by how their temporal and narrative parameters are differently oriented toward to their respective endings:

> Actually there is no story for which the question as to how it continued [*Wie ging es weiter?*] would not be legitimate. The novelist, on the other hand, cannot hope to take the smallest step beyond that limit at which he invites the reader to a divinatory realization of the meaning of life [*den Lebenssinn ahnend sich zu vergegenwärtigen*] by writing "Finis."[93]

What we read here as the novel's requirement of completion contrasts with the story's withheld ending, with its literal "open-endedness." That the end of the story is conceived as "to be continued…" does not mean that the story is itself meaningless, just that it offers no promises or guarantees of meaning. Nor does it mean that the story's time is one of an endless linearity. All along, Benjamin has been clear on this last point: like the novel, the story's authority is also given by the relation it sustains with death. The challenge of the remark lies, I think, in understanding what the authority of death might mean in the context of its being *withheld*.

The challenge might be taken up in the context of insights Benjamin has just generated around the question of the novel's temporality. The temporality of the story is marked by a future that is much more uncertain and open than that of the novel; nonetheless, its temporality is still structured around futurity—around the *Wie ging es weiter?*—and needs to be considered as such. Whereas the novel's future is given in each and every one of its moments as a kind of Marquezian "death foretold," the story's futurity permeates every one of its moments with a kind of restlessness, a power that could arrest time or explode its continuity. Filled with an unforeseeable future, every moment of the story harbors the possibility of a surprise yet to come.[94]

……………

In order to see how Benjamin's analysis of literature's temporality might bear on his critique of historicism's time, let us turn briefly to one of the most celebrated statements of the "Theses": "To historians who wish to relive an era," Benjamin writes, "Fustel de Coulanges recommends that they blot out everything they know about the later course of history. There is no better way of characterizing the method with which historical materialism has broken."[95] Here, Benjamin describes the violence of a historicist approach to the past in terms of how its "process of empathy"[96] sacrifices the present to a past untouched by futurity. In its drive to identify with the past, historicism effaces any sense of the foreignness that accrues by virtue of lapsed time. It is to this lapse of time—precisely, to what we have seen emerge in the analysis of literary time as the past's imminent and perhaps surprising futurity—that Benjamin is alluding when he describes the necessary *afterwardness* of history as "posthumous":

> Historicism contents itself with establishing a causal connection between various moments in history. But no fact that is a cause is for that very reason historical. It became historical posthumously, as it were, through events that may be separated from it by thousands of years. A historian who takes this as his point of departure stops telling the sequence of events like the beads of a rosary. Instead, he grasps the constellation which his own era has formed with a definite earlier one. Thus he establishes a conception of the present as the "time of the now" which is shot through with chips of Messianic time.[97]

Despite the haste with which these thoughts were likely formulated—they were among his very last—it is nonetheless not simply a shortage of time that had led Benjamin to move quickly from a discussion of the history of historicism to a kind of history that is not even identified or named as such. Rather, "a conception of the present as the 'time of the now'" registers what no historicism ever could, that a historical moment is never simply at one with itself and that the time for its futurity is, literally, "now."

How seriously should we take the proposal that literature serve as a model for historical discourse? It would have the definite advantage of denaturalizing history and of making its discourse a matter for reading and writing—a far cry from the modes of transparency and idealist reflection of much nineteenth-century historiography. Far from simply turning history into an eclectic literary genre, though, if an approach to history is conceivable along lines similar to those that Benjamin ascribes to the reading of a story—and in particular, the indeterminacy of its *to be continued*...—the implications of modernity's own withheld ending can be drawn to a conclusion quite different from one leading to a despairing sense of the future's emptiness: namely, that none of the moments of modernity's past are ever really or simply passed and that each one of them is powerfully infused with the possibility and the potential of a deeply surprising future.

On the one hand, this means that the future is literally inseparable from the ways the past is read, from the way its forms and figures are put back into play, and from the way that it is mobilized to open up new perspectives. On the other hand, the notion that history be conceived as "reading the past," especially in relation to the unfinished story of modernity, means also that the experience of reading the past will itself be exposed to more than one time at once. If, as Benjamin suggests, every moment of a narrative is doubled within itself, split between its position in a chronological sequence and the eruptive power of the (withheld) end inhabiting it, this also means that reading the past would entail being exposed to both of these temporalities, marked by the impossibility of being in both of them at once. An approach to reading modern history in this way—and certainly not just its texts—could perhaps resist the tendency to flatten out the complexity of historical time, by exposing its own practices of reading to the irreducible and irreconcilable double-time of history's moments—a finite time, then, that is only unified and thus rendered timeless at the price of considerable violence to the past, as well as to its future.

On another level, it seems highly significant that the re-emergence of literary time in Benjamin's notion of historical discourse is so utterly in keeping with the itinerary that Benjamin follows as he traces the passing of literary modes of experience. The passing of the literary narration of experience turns out to be the very condition for it to yield a temporal modality that is directed toward an as-yet unarticulated future. As such, the unforeseeable emergence of that temporal mode in a history "to come" is as much a performance of the theory as it is its suspenseful affirmation. ▪

....

1 Cited in Hannah Arendt, *Denktagebuch*, ed. Ursula Ludz and Ingeborg Nordmann, vol.2 (Munich: Piper Verlag, 2002), 639.

2 Jacques Derrida, *Mémoires for Paul de Man*, trans. Cecile Lindsay, Jonathan Culler, Eduardo Cadava, and Peggy Kamuf (New York: Columbia University Press, 1989), 3.

3 Plato, *Theaetetus*, in *The Collected Dialogues of Plato*, ed. Edith Hamilton and Huntington Cairns, trans. Hugh Tredennick (New York: Pantheon Books, 1961), 191d.

4 Ibid., 10.

5 Plato, *Phaedo*, in *The Collected Dialogues of Plato* (see note 3), 61b.

6 Walter Benjamin, "The Storyteller," in *Illuminations*, ed. Hannah Arendt, trans. Harry Zohn (New York: Schocken Books, 1968), 97.

7 Walter Benjamin, "Theses on the Philosophy of History," in *Illuminations* (see note 6), 261; 262; 264. The newer translation of this work (in German,"Über den Begriff der Geschichte") as "Theses on the Concept of History" brings out the title's resonance with Arendt's "The Concept of History." See *Walter Benjamin: Selected Writings, Volume 4, 1938-1940*, ed. Howard Eiland and Michael W. Jennings (Cambridge: Harvard University Press, 2003).

8 Hannah Arendt, "The Concept of History," *Between Past and Future: Eight Exercises in Political Thought* (New York: Penguin, 1968), 67-68.

9 Walter Benjamin, "Theses on the Philosophy of History," 257.

10 Jacques Le Goff, *History and Memory*, trans. Steven Rendall and Elizabeth Claman (New York: Columbia University Press, 1992), xii. Although it is certainly true that our own historical moment can hardly be said to be under the exclusive sway of historicist notions of progress and perfectibility, Dipesh Chakrabarty has recently warned against overly hasty pronouncements of the end of historicism. Chakrabarty points out that, in fact, a great deal of contemporary historical writing remains deeply historicist and that even when historicism as such is rejected as an outdated mode of historiography, its notion of linear historical time continues to dominate historical writing, often to the point of foreclosing consideration of other temporal configurations. See Dipesh Chakrabarty, *Provincializing Europe: Postcolonial Thought and Historical Difference* (New Jersey: Princeton University Press, 2000), 22-23, 73.

11 Le Goff, *History and Memory*, 102.

12 Ibid., 107.

13 Roland Barthes, "Le discours de l'histoire," cited in Le Goff, *History and Memory*, 119. For the English translation of Barthes's essay, see Roland Barthes, "The Discourse of History," trans. Stephen Bann, *Comparative Criticism* 3 (1981): 7-20. In *The Writing of History*, Michel de Certeau makes a similar point regarding the referential function of language, namely that it has the ability to "introduce into the text an effect of reality." Michel de Certeau, *The Writing of History*, trans. Tom Conley (New York: Columbia University Press, 1988), 94.

14 For instance, when Le Goff addresses the account given by linguistics of the culturally determined modalities of past-present-future, he draws attention to how "language [expresses] temporal relations." This leads him to consider the insights of linguists who "insist on the construction of time in language, which goes far beyond the verb [tense] and concerns vocabulary, the sentence, and style. This leads some to refer to a 'chronogenesis.'" Le Goff, *History and Memory*, 4-5.

15 Ibid., 108, 135n.

16 Paul Ricoeur, *Time and Narrative*, vol. 1, trans. Kathleen McLaughlin and David Pellauer (Chicago: University of Chicago Press, 1984), 3.

17 Arendt, "The Concept of History," 41.

18 Ibid., 43.

19 Ibid., 42.

20 Ibid.

21 Ibid., 19.

22 Ibid., 45. See also Hannah Arendt, *The Human Condition* (New York: Doubleday Anchor, 1958), 44ff.

23 For a penetrating reflection on death as "border," see Derrida, *Aporias*, trans. Thomas Dutoit (Stanford: Stanford University Press, 1993), especially the first section "*Finis*," 1-42.

24 Arendt, "The Concept of History," 42. (Emphasis added.)

25 This point is also made by Julia Kristeva. See Julia Kristeva, *Hannah Arendt: Life is a Narrative*, trans. Frank Collins (Toronto: University of Toronto Press, 2001), especially chapters 1 and 2.

26 Arendt, "The Concept of History," 11-13.

27 Arendt, *The Human Condition*, 10.

28 Aristotle, *Poetics*, ed. Frank L. Lucas (Oxford: Oxford University Press, 1968), 50b26.

29 Ricoeur, *Time and Narrative*, vol. 1, 170.

30 Ibid., 66.

31 Aristotle, *Poetics*, 50b31.

32 Ricoeur, *Time and Narrative*, vol. 1, 44.

33 Although the explicit focus of *Time and Narrative* is not the theme of memory (as Ricoeur says later in *La Mémoire, l'histoire, l'oubli*), it is nonetheless surprising that Ricoeur does not mention Arendt's work in the course of his treatment of historical discourse and narrative time, especially considering that he wrote a preface to the re-issue of the French translation of *The Human Condition* in 1983 (the same year in which *Time and Narrative* first appeared). See Paul Ricoeur, *La Mémoire, l'histoire, l'oubli* (Paris: Editions du Seuil, 2000).

34 Arendt, "The Concept of History," 43.

35 Arendt, *The Human Condition*, 9.

36 Ibid., 23n.

37 To be sure, there is much more at stake for Arendt's political theory than a formal or structural analogy between politics, its remembrance, and the condition of finitude. In both *The Human Condition* and *On Revolution*, she insists on birth and natality as the central categories of political thought, on the basis that political action would be unnecessary if humans were not born but were simply carbon-copies of the same model. Biological natality then, what she calls "the constant influx of newcomers" (a term she also fondly used in reference to her students), constitutes the very literal condition for the possibility of new beginnings, one implicit to all political action: "[T]he new beginning in birth can make itself felt in the world only because the newcomer possesses the capacity of beginning something anew, that is, of acting" Arendt, *The Human Condition*, 11. See also *On Revolution* (London: Penguin Books, 1965), 42, 210-211.

38 Arendt, "The Concept of History." In these sections, Arendt is more interested in the similarities between classical historiography and poetry than in their differences. In this respect, her analysis differs from Aristotle's—and is perhaps a kind of implicit quarrel with him over the claim that poetry has nothing to do with time—who differentiated between the two on the basis that poetry teaches the universal and history is concerned with particulars. In drawing out the affinities between Ancient Greek poetry and history, though, Arendt is making good on what is seldom recognized in readings of Aristotle's appraisal, namely, that history and poetry contend with each other precisely because they both claim the transmission of the past as their own task.

39 Ibid., 46.

40 Plato, *Symposium* in *The Collected Dialogues of Plato* (see note 3), 209b-c.

41 Ibid.

42 Plato, *Phaedo*, 65a.

43 Le Goff has commented on this "removal of Memory from the temporal realm" in terms of the radical separation it inaugurates between memory and history: "When [memory] is put in the service of eschatology, it also nourishes itself on a veritable hatred for history." Le Goff, *History and Memory*, 65.

44 Plato, *Phaedo*. 79d-e.

45 Ibid., 80b.

46 Julia Kristeva has recently shown the degree to which Arendt's conception of human corporeality participates in this dualist legacy. Insofar as Arendt's thought locates what is properly human in *bios*, its "form of life," it is opposed to the undifferentiated *zoē* which humans share with animal and vegetative life and which concerns labor, biology, and the mute survival of the species. In her privileging of *bios* over *zoē*, Arendt expresses her denigration of the latter by bringing it into association with incommunicability, suffering, isolation, and the dumb repetitive labor of survival. As Kristeva argues, "the body presents itself as a major target of that tearing away from the *zoē*, if not as sworn enemy—the principal paradigm of alienation." Kristeva, *Hannah Arendt*, 63. For an examination of how various artists of the post-communist period challenge the Arendtian sense of unredeemable labor, see Charity Scribner, *Requiem for Communism* (Cambridge: MIT Press, 2003). Coming to Arendt's (partial) defense, though, could one not argue that her analysis offers some of the most compelling—if disputed—terms within which to articulate the political crises of modernity and that, as such, her work opens up ways to situate some of the memorial dilemmas implicit to the crises to which modernity has given rise? Arendt's conceptions of memory and human life, beyond any particular bias on her part, are meticulous in how they clarify the problems associated with mourning communism, both in light of the cynical brutality with which labor was instrumentalized in the twentieth century and in light of the way in which the repetitive and monotonous structures that it puts into place make it peculiarly resistant to memorial expression. A forceful examination of modernity's processes of dehumanization that takes Arendt's work as one of its points of departure is Giorgio Agamben, *Homo Sacer: Sovereign Power and Bare Life*, trans. Daniel Heller-Roazen (Stanford: Stanford University Press, 1998).

47 Plato, *Phaedo*. 66c. Doubtless it is statements like these that made Arendt resistant to the idea that her work be categorized as political philosophy. In the 1964 Gaus-Arendt interview, for instance, she takes issue with Gaus's characterization of her as a philosopher on the grounds that philosophy has never been concerned with politics as such. Hannah Arendt, *The Portable Hannah Arendt*, ed. Peter Baehr, trans. Joan Stambaugh (London: Penguin Books, 2004). For a theoretical development of this position, see her posthumously published *Lectures on Kant's Political Philosophy*, ed. Ronald Beiner (Chicago: Chicago University Press, 1982), in particular the "Fourth Session," 22ff.

48 This substitution of loss for pure gain is consistent with the means of Socrates' death: by poison (in the Greek, *pharmakon*). Given that the hemlock is presented to Socrates throughout the *Phaedo* as a *pharmakon*, the undecidability of its meaning (both "poison" and "remedy") to which Derrida has drawn attention has important implications for the argument as a whole. Derrida writes that the poison "is transformed, through the effects of the Socratic *logos* and of the philosophical demonstration in the *Phaedo*, into a means of deliverance, a way toward salvation, a cathartic power. The hemlock has an *ontological* effect: it initiates one into the contemplation of the *eidos* and the immortality of the soul. *That is how Socrates takes it*." Jacques Derrida, "Plato's Pharmacy," *Dissemination*, trans. Barbara Johnson (Chicago: University of Chicago Press, 1981) 126-27.

49 Plato, *Phaedo*. 75c-76b.

50 Arendt, "The Concept of History," 47.

51 In *The Human Condition*, Arendt affects the contrast between these two competing forms of memory in her historical account of the relation between the *vita activa* and the *vita contemplativa*. For the Greeks, the *vita activa* was, first and foremost, political life, the life of action that owes its existence solely to the human condition of plurality. "Action, in so far as it engages in founding and preserving political bodies, creates the condition for remembrance, that is, for history," Arendt argues, a condition that allows men to obviate their own individual mortality. According to the hierarchy subsequently established by what Arendt calls the "philosophical *apolitia*" of late antiquity, the *vita contemplativa* began to be valued over all forms of human activity as the only truly free way of life, free not only from labor and work but also from political life (the Greek word for which—*skholē*—bears close ties to *askholia* or "unquiet"). The primacy of contemplation over activity rests on the conviction that no human activity, however lasting, can equal the unchanging eternity of the *kosmos*, itself unspeakable and unapproachable through human activity: "[I]t is decisive," Arendt concludes, "that the experience of the eternal has no correspondence with and cannot be transformed into any activity whatsoever." Arendt, *The Human Condition*, 20.

52 This description occurs in the context of Hegel's analysis of painting, in particular the argument regarding the suitability of painting for the portrayal of the Christian God. G.W.F. Hegel, *Hegel's Aesthetics: Lectures on Fine Art, vol. II*, trans. T.M. Knox (Oxford: Oxford University Press, 1972), 822.

53 Catherine Malabou, *The Future of Hegel: Plasticity, Temporality and Dialectic*, trans. Lisabeth During (London: Routledge, 2005), 108.

54 Arendt, "The Concept of History," 52.

55 In a journal entry from May 1954, Arendt had started articulating the difference between the Greek and Christian world-views in terms of man and world: "Im Altertum ist der Mensch vergänglich; im Christentum ist die Welt, aber nicht der Mensch, vergänglich. Jeder christliche Tod ist eine Art Weltuntergang; jeder klassische Tod ist eine Art Gemordetwerden." *Denktagebuch*, vol.1, 482.

56 Werner Hamacher has recently addressed this issue of Christianity's withdrawal from politics and has pointed out that Christianity's claim to universality was the end-result of the gradually widening distinction between the political community and the community of faith. He argues that Christianity's doctrinal *dis*interest in politics was the condition upon which its claim to universality could be made, a claim which would eventually lead to its expression in politics—its submission to what Hamacher calls "a particular kind of politicity"—as democracy's universal equality of individuals. See Werner Hamacher, "The Right to Have Rights (Four-and-a-Half Remarks)," ed. Ian Balfour and Eduardo Cadava, *The South Atlantic Quarterly* 103, no. 2/3 (Spring/Summer 2004): 343-356. The insight that modern democracy is the structural heir to Christianity's universal equality of individuals has important implications for how we understand memory with respect to politics. In particular, it can help to clarify the often confusing assertion that an inherent affinity exists between them. From a certain perspective, of course, there is a degree of truth to the claim if, by politics, we are referring to democracy's politicized version of the Christian claim to immortalization on the basis of the universal equality of individuals. While it is no doubt the case that democracy's claim to universal equality forms the basic condition of receptivity upon which memorial claims can be submitted to contestation and open scrutiny, the result is often that those claims to memory are read through the

cipher of individualistic notions of identity which can sometimes work to de-politicize the intervention (especially since memory is so often structured by figures of collectivity that, by virtue of their irreducible attention to particularities, are often marginalized within a democracy, like those of particular ethnicities, of gender and sexuality, of class, of linguistic belonging, etc.). That is not to say that memory is simply a-political; rather, by accounting for the remnants of an a-political Christian tenor in the ways that memory is made audible in a democracy, I am attempting to clarify misconceptions regarding where memory's political potential actually resides. In fact, recent developments of studies in collective memory—those taking place under the rubric of trauma theory, theories of witnessing, law and memory, etc—are in the process of submitting the notion that memory is an expression of identity to rigorous questioning, precisely in order to gauge other ways of thinking about its political and ethical potential. See, among others, Cathy Caruth, ed. *Trauma: Explorations in Memory* (Baltimore: Johns Hopkins University Press, 1995); Caruth, *Unclaimed Experience: Trauma, Narrative, and History* (Baltimore: Johns Hopkins University Press, 1996); Lisa Yoneyama. *Hiroshima Traces: Time, Space and the Dialectics of Memory* (Berkeley: University of California Press, 1999); Dominick LaCapra, *Representing the Holocaust: History, Theory, Trauma* (Ithaca: Cornell University Press, 1996), *History and Memory after Auschiwtz* (Ithaca: Cornell University Press, 1998), *Writing History, Writing Trauma* (Baltimore: Johns Hopkins University Press, 2000); Kai Erikson, *A New Species of Trouble: The Human Experience of Modern Disasters* (New York: Norton, 1995).

57 Arendt, "The Concept of History," 57-58.

58 Ibid., 61.

59 Ibid., 59.

60 Ibid., 63.

61 Ibid., 65, 67.

62 Ibid., 67-68.

63 Philippe Ariès devotes the final section of *The Hour of Our Death* to "Death Denied," a phenomenon that he sees as unique in the history of death and specific to industrialized, urbanized, and politically secular areas of the West. Ariès articulates the central hypothesis of the section—that, baldly, "society has banished death"—in terms of its temporal implications: "there is no way of knowing that something has happened: the … hearse has become indistinguishable from the flow of traffic. Society no longer observes a pause; the disappearance of an individual no longer affects its continuity." Philippe Ariès, *The Hour of Our Death*, trans. Helen Weaver (New York: Oxford University Press, 1991), 560. Despite the difficulties of Ariès's text in terms of its historicization and delimitation of the phenomenon of death—just how delineable can death be, asks Derrida, when it is delineation itself?—its suggestion that the temporality of mourning disrupts sequential, continuous time is an interesting one. For a powerful reading and a thorough-going critique of Ariès's text, see Jacques Derrida, *Aporias*, trans. Thomas Dutoit (Stanford: Stanford University Press, 1993), 43n.

64 Michel de Certeau. *The Writing of History*, 4.

65 Ibid., 5.

66 Benjamin, "Theses on the Philosophy of History," 254.

67 Walter Benjamin, "The Storyteller": 83-110. "The Storyteller" first appeared in German in 1936 and was translated into English in 1968 for *Illuminations*, the first collection of Benjamin's work to appear in English, which Arendt both edited and introduced. Although Arendt worked on the *Illuminations* volume some years after she wrote *Between Past and*

Future and *The Human Condition*, she was undoubtedly familiar with the essay when developing her own formulations on memory, time, and narrative. Benjamin and Arendt were acquainted in Berlin and became friends during their exile years in Paris; Arendt was certainly in attendance when Benjamin lectured there. It is puzzling, to say the least, that Benjamin's essay is never explicitly mentioned by Arendt, either in her introductory essay to *Illuminations* or, to my knowledge, in any of her other works (including "The Concept of History," where its relevance is most evident). The most one can say, then, is that whatever influence it did have on her own thinking about narrative and memory was indirect or of a deeply complex nature. For an account of their friendship, as well as of the publishing endeavors Arendt undertook in the U.S. to honor it, see Elizabeth Young-Bruehl, *Hannah Arendt: For Love of the World*, 2nd ed. (New Haven: Yale University Press, 2004), especially 157-168. See also Shoshana Felman, *The Juridical Unconscious: Trials and Traumas in the Twentieth Century* (Cambridge: Harvard University Press, 2002), 131-166 for an examination of Arendt's *Eichmann in Jerusalem* (London: Penguin Books, 1994), both in terms of how it defends legal testimony as a narrative means by which to contain historical trauma as well as how its stylistic aspects are governed by insistent and complex references to "The Storyteller": ones which constitute a subtext of unmourned loss—a story, in short, that Arendt cannot tell.

68 Benjamin, "The Storyteller," 83.

69 Ibid., 84.

70 To be sure, the threshold or rupture is historical (Benjamin does implicitly "date" it at 1918), but not in the sense that would situate this moment along a temporal continuum and thereby neutralize its effects. In fact, the essay's first indication of a more complex perspective on history is its clear resistance to the conventional understanding of dating as part of the process by which history becomes recuperated in narrative. Cf. Shoshana Felman's reading of this passage and its strategy of dating in *The Juridical Unconscious*, 26ff. See too Agamben's brief description of this passage in terms of how it marks out the difficult, because constantly shifting, historical threshold of modernity in *Infancy and History: An Essay on the Destruction of Experience*, trans. Liz Heron (London: Verso Books, 1993), 13.

71 On the nostalgic strains of Benjamin's thought and, in particular, on how nostalgia functions in his work as an important force of political motivation, see Fredric Jameson's early essay "Benjamin; or, Nostalgia." Contrary to the ways in which fascisms deploy nostalgia—that is, to efface the present so as to long for a vanished past of plenitude and unity—Jameson argues that Benjamin sought to recover a nostalgic mode as a principle means by which to register the present in terms of the remorseless dissatisfaction that it provokes. As such, Jameson sees the appeal made to "a simpler cultural past" in "The Storyteller" as Benjamin's way of working out a Marxist aesthetics: to draw out "a vanished form of social and historical existence" and to establish correlations between "the activity of storytelling and the concrete form of a certain historically determinate mode of production." Fredric Jameson, "Benjamin: or, Nostalgia," in *Marxism and Form: Twentieth-Century Dialectical Theories of Literature* (Princeton: Princeton University Press, 1971), 80.

72 Walter Benjamin, "On Some Motifs in Baudelaire," in *Illuminations* (see note 6), 157.

73 Ibid., 163. Not only does *Erlebnis* resist narration; it also resists translation. Zohn prudently avoids translating both *Erlebnis* and *Erfahrung* as "experience" (or translating *Erlebnis* as "lived experience," which simply obscures the difference between them) by emphasizing how, with *Erlebnis*, impressions remain fixed to the moment in which they were lived.

74 Benjamin, "The Storyteller," 88.
75 Ibid., 89.
76 Benjamin's early essay on language, "On Language as Such and the Language of Man," denounces as "bourgeois" the notion that language is primarily communication. As Ian Balfour notes, however, the category of bourgeois is not at all circumscribed within the historical, social, or political conditions of modernity; in fact Benjamin locates the provenance of this conception of language in the Garden of Eden, where the seducing serpent promises Adam and Eve the knowledge of good and evil. Walter Benjamin, "On Language as Such and the Language of Man," in *Reflections*, ed. Peter Demetz, trans. Edmund Jephcott (New York: Schocken Books, 1978), 314-332, and Ian Balfour, *The Rhetoric of Romantic Prophecy* (Stanford: Stanford University Press, 2003), 6-12.
77 Benjamin, "The Storyteller," 90, 93. Benjamin's use of *Augenblick* in this particular context is far from Heidegger's understanding of the term. Here, the term is being used to generate a sense of how the hegemony of information's mode of language stands to normalize temporal fracture; when information dominates, time is constituted as a conglomeration of unrelated, random, and disconnected moments, the time in which the event or occurrence (*Ereignis*) happens in "real time," instantly passing into oblivion. Not only does the time of information preclude the possibility of narrated experience (*Erfahrung*), the normalization of its temporal fracture also stands to neutralize the disruptive force of any singular instant. This latter brings us closer to Heidegger's interpretation of *Augenblick* which possesses an epiphantic quality: it is the force of a singular moment which suspends linear time. See Martin Heidegger, *Being and Time*, trans. Joan Stambaugh (Albany: State University of New York Press, 1996), especially section VI.
78 Benjamin, "The Storyteller," 90.
79 Ibid. (Translation slightly modified.)
80 G.W.F. Hegel, *Enzyklopädie der philosophischen Wissenschaften* III (Frankfurt: Suhrkamp Verlag, 1999) § 458. For Derrida's reading of Hegel's semiology, see Jacques Derrida, "The Pit and the Pyramid," in *Margins of Philosophy*, trans. Alan Bass (Chicago: University of Chicago, 1982): 69-108.
81 Benjamin, "The Task of the Translator" in *Illuminations* (see note 6), 71
82 Benjamin, "The Storyteller," 93.
83 Ibid., 93-94.
84 Ibid., 93.
85 Ibid., 94.
86 Ibid., 101.
87 Ibid., 93.
88 Arendt, "The Concept of History," 6.
89 Benjamin, "Theses on the Philosophy of History," 256.
90 Ibid. 261.
91 This claim is one made by Benjamin to sum up Lukács's position, rather than a direct citation from Lukács. Benjamin, "The Storyteller," 99. Cf. Georg Lukács, *The Theory of the Novel*, trans. Anna Bostock (Cambridge, MA: MIT Press, 1971), especially 70-83.
92 Benjamin, "The Storyteller," 100-101.
93 Ibid., 100.
94 On the relation between the "to come" (*à venir*) and futurity (*avenir*), see the *Passages* interview with Derrida. Jacques Derrida, "The Deconstruction of Actuality," in *Negotiatons: Interventions and Interviews, 1971-2001*, ed. and trans. Elizabeth Rottenberg (Stanford: Stanford University Press, 2002), 85-117.

95 Benjamin, "Theses on the Philosophy of History," 256.
96 Ibid.
97 Ibid., 263.

Bio-Temporality and Social Regulation: The Emergence of the Biological Clock

Merav Amir

"Reproduction" has long been a central feature in regulating sexualities and gender identities. During the last quarter of the twentieth century, fundamental political, techno-scientific, social, and cultural shifts occurred, which changed the manner in which "reproduction" operates.[1] This paper examines these transformations as they occurred in the United States, claiming new forms of biopolitical patterns have appeared, altering the dynamics of the construction of gender difference and regulating heteronormativity.[2] More particularly, it maintains that the biological clock of the female reproductive system is one such construction, a form of imprinting gender difference onto the body. The biological clock first appeared as a concept in the popular discourses in the United States during the last two decades of the century and has since functioned as a new regulatory mechanism for producing the gendered body.[3]

Portraying the emergence of the biological clock enables us to depict the manner in which normative constructs of temporality materialize the gendered body as a locus of social- and self-regulation. This analysis also elucidates the emergence of a biopolitics, in the Foucauldian sense of the term, which inscribes the heteronormative order into the bodies of women, by intertwining contingent and culturally specific social arrangements with what are perceived to be objective biological facts. In the name of the temporal "logic" of the female body, new forms of intervention and management of life foreclose future possibilities and life narratives in order to suit ideological formulations of the family.[4] Analyzing the discourses from which the biological clock derives its cultural significance illustrates how they are genealogically linked to the eugenic discourses that dominated concerns about reproduction and population control at the turn of the twentieth century in the United States. By employing selective pronatal discursive strategies, this new form of biopolitics implicitly demarcates socially advantaged women using biological criteria.

The gendered aspects of prevalent concepts of time, the different temporality regimes which govern gendered subjects, and the gendered differentials in the ways men and women experience time have been well researched by feminist scholars. Feminist analysis suggests that there are feminine and masculine patterns of experiencing time due to the gendered division of labor, different ways men and women experience time because of their socialization and relative social positions and the gendered conceptualization of time in capitalist societies.[5] Following the emergence of the biological clock and the ways it operates provides an additional perspective to these discussions as it enables the portrayal of how patterns of temporality are constructed onto and then articulated as derivative of the gendered body. Analyzing and identifying the construction of the differential temporal regimes as located in the biological functioning of the body undermines essentialist presuppositions about the nature of sexual and gender difference, which are sometimes left unquestioned in feminist discussions. Moreover, the linear, goal-oriented, and clock-driven temporal pattern of the biological clock which exclusively marks the female body differs from prevalent accounts of gendered classifications of time. As prior feminist research has shown, linear time is perceived as primarily applying to masculine subjects or to male social positions. The entailments of this particular temporal regime of the biological clock are therefore in need of further examination.

The manner in which the age-related decrease in female fecundity poses constraints on the life-course decisions of young women, constraints which put them at a relative disadvantage in comparison to their male counterparts, has not eluded feminist criticism. While these studies tend to resort to economic models of analysis, some accounts deal with sociological and psychological aspects as well.[6] Other discussions by feminist scholars consider the manners in which new reproductive technologies may offer women an escape path from these constraints, adding a cautiously optimistic viewpoint to the on-going debates within feminism on the pros and cons of these innovations for women.[7] While these accounts raise crucial issues concerning the function of the biological clock in determining women's current and expected experiences, they share common assumptions, leaving gender definitions and the materialization of the body as sexed unquestioned. Yet, except for a single study by Nicole Keating, which clearly demonstrates how the regulatory aspects are intertwined into the metaphor of the clock and how it conceptualizes reproductive decisions for women in terms of constraints,[8] the manner in which the concept of the biological clock operates as a regulatory mechanism has received little attention in prior research. The aim of this paper is to understand some of the current discursive practices which construct and regulate the "biological reality" of the body, for the purpose of establishing gender difference by analyzing the biological clock. As a relatively novel phenomenon, the biological clock provides a rare opportunity to examine these processes as they materialize, in a sense, right before our eyes. Even more so, since the biological clock is a concept which directly relates to the functioning of the sexed body in the realm of reproduction, it is, seemingly, the last uncontested biological fact which enables the drawing of the line of sex and therefore also of gender distinctions.

Judith Butler provides a conceptual framework for considering the construction of the sexed body by claiming that it is erroneous to consider sex as an attribute of the body, a consideration which implies the body precedes its sexual assignment, since the sexual assignment is a condition of possibility for the material signification of the body as such. If sex is a precondition for the materialization of the body and not a derivative of its biological nature, then sex is a product of discursive practices. There is, therefore, an ever-present need to reinscribe the sexual demarcation of the body through what Butler calls gender performativity.[9] The concept of gender performativity implies particular temporal relations: while the past provides a fictitious link with an origin from which the normalized identity draws the authenticity of its appearance in the present, the future holds the promise of a repetition with an intentional or unintentional difference, in which unexpected change may occur. Thus, the articulation of gender performativity, according to Butler, implies progressive temporal relations. This progressive temporal formulation holds the future as an open horizon of potential radical political changes.[10] Yet, Butler's insistence that the persistence of the body is not a property of its biological nature but a demand of language[11] means that not only the past but also the future plays a role in preserving normalized identities, since this consistency is projected onto the future of the individual body. Nevertheless, this is a primarily static conceptualization of the future. Drawing on Butler's account, the aim of this paper is to provide an analysis for how dynamic patterns of the future mark gender difference in our understanding of the body and how they are configured as normative imperatives for individuals.

Transition from Disciplinary to Control Societies

In *Discipline and Punish* Michel Foucault makes his famous assertion that the human subject as we know it is a product of modern society. The modern subject is produced through the operation of disciplinary institutions, for which prisons serve as the model. The same disciplinary techniques, also found in schools, factories, families and hospitals, which differ only in scale and in the severity of their rituals, create the modern soul as the regulatory principle of the subject.[12] In his "Postscript on Control Societies" Gilles Deleuze writes that, according to Foucault's description, disciplinary societies operate through well-defined spatial enclaves which yield to coherent rules. He claims that the Foucauldian description shows that while these enclaves are analogical and exercise the same mechanisms, they are discrete. Years after Foucault's death, Deleuze continues their interrupted dialogue by claiming that in the latter half of the twentieth century, disciplinary societies, which were so accurately described by Foucault, have dissolved into what can now be called control societies.[13]

According to Deleuze, the spatial enclaves, so crucial for the disciplinary institutions, are now, in control societies, breached and can no longer operate as a means of social regulation. In control societies, space has turned into an endless continuum, characterized by differential potentialities, and the distinction between interiority and exteriority can no longer be sustained. Thus the factory, which was the basic manufacturing unit, has been replaced by the business, which is everywhere and anywhere and which places all individuals in constant competition. Similarly, the educational process, which took place in the school, has yielded its place to an ongoing training procedure in which continuous assessment replaces the function of the examination. Deleuze claims that while disciplinary societies were built on the irresolvable tension between the individual and the masses, in control societies "individuals become '*dividuals*,' and masses become samples, data, markets, or '*banks*.'"[14]

In an introduction to Deleuze's text, Ariella Azoulay writes that one fundamental contribution of Foucault is the notion that, in the institutions of disciplinary societies, life is constantly managed; however, she continues, the constant management of life does not come to a halt in control societies. The locus of management shifts in control societies from the enclosed environment to the body of the singular: "The body of the singular is invaded by the different 'superpowers' which cross through him turning him into a satellite unit, a control post." While in disciplinary societies one would enter and exit the enclosed environments, which were run by the "superpowers," in control societies "where the simulation of being outside no longer exists and the singular is completely woven into the channels in which he is managed … the superpower has completely collapsed into the self and the self has turned into the object of resistance." Thus, according to Azullay, since social regulation no longer takes place in the disciplinary institutions, in control societies the body has become the locus of constant social management.[15]

Deleuze claims that the manner in which temporality operates has also changed in the transition from disciplinary to control societies: "Control is short-term and rapidly shifting, but at the same time continuous and unbounded, whereas discipline was long-term, infinite, and discontinuous."[16] Time, in the disciplinary regime, was sharply divided into distinct periods by the spatial enclaves: the lesson at school, the shift at work and the time of incarceration. However, since in control societies these enclaves can no longer maintain their distinctness, they can also no longer bestow meaning on time; no longer is the nature of time determined by spatial definitions; it is time which constructs space. Working hours, for instance, are no longer defined as the duration one spends in the work environment. It is instead the time devoted to work which turns the immediate space—be it the home, the airport terminal, or the car—into productive space. Losing its differential segmentation, time has also turned into a continuum. Hence, in an ongoing postponement of any conclusion, in control societies each person is the spatial unit which is subjected to a continuous management of life over time.

Deleuze states, "We're in the midst of a general breakdown of all sites of confinement—prisons, hospitals, factories, schools, the family. The family is an 'interior' that's breaking down like all other interiors—educational, professional, and so on. … Family, school, army, and factory are no longer so many analogous but different sites converging in an owner, whether the state or some private power, but transmutable or transformable *coded configurations*."[17] Deleuze does not argue that under a radically different regime the old order simply disappears without a trace, or that in control societies the former configurations of social regulation become redundant, but that their *modus operandi* undergoes a fundamental transformation. In his analysis, Deleuze focuses on the consequences of the emergence of the business from the ruins of the factory, hinting that the reorganization of the economic logic of late capitalism may provide the explanatory power for the changes he describes. However, his description also allows us to draw conclusions about the implications of these changes for the family.

Since the concrete institution of the family can no longer sustain its interiority, our spatial relations to the family in control societies is, therefore, one of proximity. Thus, now that it does not operate as a disciplinary institution and the family has turned into a "coded configuration," its main function has shifted to its role as a regulatory principle, an organizing ideal. It is not that the family did not traditionally operate as an organizing ideal nor that families ceased to exist in control societies, but while families still constitute a central social arrangement, they can no longer fulfill their traditional disciplinary role. Hence, families as sites of social regulation are displaced by "The Family," the latter functioning as a dense ideological construct which can then operate in particular social situations as a moralistic and normalizing yard-stick loaded with social values. For the purpose of determining one's proximity to "The Family," one can then be subjected to enquiries and assessments which are the basis for interventions and regulation.

While in disciplinary societies all environments of enclosure were central in constructing modern subjectivity, the spatial configuration created by the family in the disciplinary regime had an additional role to play. By enabling the distinction between the public and the private, the family was a central site for interweaving the gender difference into the framework of society. Since in disciplinary societies the categories of the private and the public served as a means for establishing the difference between man and woman, the family, as a social institution which allowed the creation of spatial differentiations between the private and the public, was therefore instrumental in conceptualizing gender difference and maintaining it.[18] What, then, has become of the mechanisms of the construction of the gender difference in control societies, in which the family can no longer secure this fundamental spatial dichotomy? As I will later show, many shifts occurred in the manner in which gender operates in the latter half of the twentieth century, but gender difference has yet to disappear altogether, and the family has not ceased to operate as a central means for securing it. Alternative mechanisms for securing gender difference have appeared, which, while drawing on particular aspects of traditional methods, are better suited to the logic of control societies. The biological clock of the female reproductive system is one such mechanism.

The fact that the reproductive abilities of women end at a certain age is in no way new;[19] yet, as I will attempt to show, the biological clock is not a modern and scientifically proven version of this knowledge but a new form of constructing gendered bodies. The biological clock is produced as a means for regulating forms of living according to heteronormative perceptions which ensure the persistence of gender difference. My claim is that this form of social regulation, which operates according to dominant political and economic agendas, first appeared in the last quarter of the twentieth century as a product of developments in techno-science and of cultural and social changes. The term "biological clock" first appeared in the mainstream press in the United States in the context of the female reproductive system in a 1978 *Washington Post* article. Then, in 1979, a book entitled *Up Against the Clock: Career Women Speak on the New Choice of Motherhood* was published. Only in the early 1980s did the term make its debut appearance in other publications.[20] The shift which I wish to portray here, from gender regulation through the institution of the family as a disciplinary enclave to the temporal mechanism of gender management through the biological clock, may help illustrate the changes in the forms of social organization which occurred in the transition from disciplinary societies to control societies. Understanding how the biological clock operates may illustrate how aspects of gender difference and heteronormative order, which can no longer be regulated through the institution of the family, are made to construct the sexed body. The biological clock of the female reproductive system gives meaning to time by managing life-courses while examining the gender performance of the individual and reinscribing gender difference. While primarily operating in the temporal domain, the biological clock inherits its divisions from the spatial configuration of gender difference; once again the female is located inside and the male outside: the biological clock constructs a crude gender differentiation between the female bodies, to which it applies, and the male bodies, which are beyond its reach.

Yet the gender regulation which the biological clock allows is not merely constituted by its differential range of validity. The breakdown of institutions which Deleuze describes has led to an epistemological crisis in relation to gender difference since neither the distinction between the private and the public, specifically, nor the family as a disciplinary institution, in more general terms, could effectively regulate it any longer. However, since gender difference was in no way extinct, regulatory anxiety emerged, questioning how gender difference might be secured as traditional forms of gender management withered away.[21] In this light, we must consider the emergence of the biological clock as a substitute mechanism: the biological clock contains the relics of the crisis which begot it, and its conceptual framework is constituted by a compensation for a loss. The biological clock, therefore, includes the wish to turn back the clock and remedy a disrupted order. For instance, as I will later show, the biological clock is often referred to as a problem which emerged as a result of the disruption of the normal, natural, or otherwise desirable way of life. Since this disruption might presumably bring about confusion in gender roles, the gender performativity of the individual, be it a concrete "case" or a hypothetical one, is the primary target of investigation and can then be deemed inadequate and in need of intervention.

Understanding the operation of the biological clock from this perspective allows us to articulate the ways in which the regulation of gender performance functions through ideological narration of time. The biological clock functions primarily in the name of the family, but it is not an actual familial institution; it is in the name of the family as an *a priori* ideological construct, and it allows the measuring of one's proximity to it over time. As a temporal regulatory mechanism, the biological clock constructs time as a continuum of successive checkpoints, permitting constant management of the gender performativity of individuals while framing life-courses according to a pseudo-biological determinism which forecloses future possibilities in order to suit a narrow definition of familial narratives.

The Role of Medical Experts and Medical Knowledge in a Historical Perspective

While Deleuze's depiction of the shift from disciplinary to control forms of social management provides the framework for understanding the modes in which governmentality operates, these changes occurred in and were enabled by concrete social conditions. Following the emergence of the biological clock may help elucidate how these changes have transformed the way in which sexuality, gender, and reproduction are mutually configured.

Barbara Ehrenreich and Deirdre English echo the claim Foucault made about the medicalization of the female body[22] from an ideological and economic perspective. Focusing on the American context, they claim that the early stages of the industrial revolution opened up the possibility for women to make their living outside the home, as it did for men. Yet, at that stage, the market increasingly relied on the nuclear family as the basic unit of consumption, and women's work in the family was needed to maintain it. However, since the logic of the market and the dominant capitalistic liberal ideology could not rationalize and ensure this division of labor and the traditional sources of authority could no longer play this role, a new social player appeared and provided for this need: the scientific expert. Ehrenreich and English claim that the business of the new scientific authority "was not to seek out what is true, but to pronounce on what is appropriate." Professional physicians, psychologists, domestic scientists, and parent educators could explain how woman's "nature" differed from that of man, why the home environment better suited the female character and needs, and how to remedy cases of discontent and deviation.[23]

Written in 1979, the book describes an escalating process of pathologization of women's bodies and minds, which reached its climax in the 1950s. Then, the authors claim, fundamental social changes occurred, which brought about the sexual revolution and the second wave of women's liberation movements and freed women from the authority of the medical experts.[24] Without committing to Ehrenreich and English's narrative of liberation, one can still see that for a wide range of reasons, the medical establishment and its medical discourse significantly lost their cultural centrality and their incomparable ability to impact the construction of gender and sexuality during the 1960s and 70s, as competing social forces and configurations of power/knowledge emerged.[25]

The social transformations which occurred in the United States during those two decades included a general trend of a steadily rising age of marriage and of first becoming parents, a decrease in the number of children per adult, an increase in sexual activity outside of marriage, especially for young people, and an increase in women's absolute and relative level of education and their participation in the work force. These changes were accompanied by fundamental cultural shifts, which reflected the fact that, relatively speaking, life-courses of men and women became more similar, with fewer sexually segregated social arenas and more socially sanctioned options for women than there had been previously.[26] As gender definitions lost some of their definitive association to particular and well-defined social roles, the need for the medical expert to guard the difference which assured these definitions also diminished.[27]

Different perspectives may yield different combinations of economic, demographic, or cultural and social reasons for explaining the changes occurring during the 1960s and 70s;[28] paradoxically, the social transformations which undermined the centrality of the medical establishment were also enabled by an innovation in the field of medical intervention in reproduction: the development and the commercial distribution of new types of birth-control methods. While almost all societies have been known to exercise some kind of birth-control techniques, the birth-control pill, which was first distributed commercially in 1960, and, later, the intrauterine devices (IUDS) were the first widely available birth-control methods that allowed prevention of pregnancy without any temporal relation to actual sexual intercourse. By enabling large segments of the population to maintain forms of living which were shaped by the ability to exercise long-term reproduction control, the new birth-control methods were instrumental in bringing about the social changes which have occurred since the 1960s. The most significant implications of this development was for the generation of the baby-boomers, who were just coming of age and were given the means for prolonging their child-free years while remaining sexually active.[29]

In the first volume of *The History of Sexuality,* Foucault claims that "in the socialization of procreative behavior, 'sex' was described as being caught between a law of reality … and the economy of pleasure."[30] Thus, in addition to facilitating these life-course changes for young adults, conceptually speaking, the birth-control pill specifically transformed the cultural signification of sexuality by undermining the "law of reality" which linked it to reproduction. Even more so, it rendered traditional forms of socialization of procreative behavior inadequate, destabilizing one of the fundamental axes of biopolitics and creating a void. During the 1960s and 70s, several discourses and forms of knowledge production, some scientific, such as the field of demographics, and some which grew from oppositional politics, such as the growing movement of feminism, cooperated and competed to fill this void by resignifying reproduction.[31]

Thus, it may be stated that approaching the end of the 1970s the conjunction of social, political, economic, cultural, and technological conditions transformed the signification and mutual configuration of gender, sexuality, and reproduction. Social structures which, for a long time, defined the relations between these factors were irreversibly reconfigured, and new narratives formed and competed for their re-articulation. However, in the early 1980s a neo-conservative sentiment swept the United States. "Something strange has happened to citizenship," states Lauren Berlant in an analysis of the social and political circumstances of this period, "[d]uring the rise of the Reaganite right, a familial politics of the national future came to define the urgencies of the present."[32] Berlant claims that although rhetorically it draws its legitimacy from the past, neo-conservative politics is in fact a new and distinct national political discourse. This discourse equates the violence and injury experienced by stereotyped individuals, women, gays, people of color, with the complaints of citizens who feel enraged at losing their dignified and unmarked social standing, mainly white heterosexual men. To mend the harm, a nostalgic image of the nation is evoked, which is fantasized as conflict-free and in which people are imagined to have lived "normal" intimate lives. In the effort to sustain this image, the political public sphere was transformed into what Berlant calls the *intimate public sphere*, in which, in the name of the future of a presumably fragile nation, a preoccupation has developed with the behavior of citizens in the intimate aspects of their lives:

> [T]he intimate public sphere of the U.S. present tense renders citizenship as a condition of social membership produced by personal acts and values, especially acts originating in or directed toward the family sphere. No longer valuing personhood as something directed toward public life, contemporary nationalist ideology recognizes a public good only in a particularly constricted nation of simultaneously lived private worlds.[33]

In the intimate public sphere of the 1980s, medical experts returned once again to center stage, and the knowledge produced by them, which was given the cultural centrality it had lacked during the previous two decades, could return to its traditional role and provide the conceptual framework in which reproduction was culturally articulated and socially managed. The fluctuations in the social standing of the medical establishment and, as a result, that of medical discourse, can be seen not only by analyzing changes in the cultural construction of gender and sexuality, but also in the changes which occurred in social attitudes towards services and treatments offered by doctors. In the pronatalist, technologically and scientifically optimistic atmosphere of the 1950s, couples who encountered infertility problems rushed to infertility clinics. However, the doctors in those clinics had very little to offer them in terms of new treatments. While infertility specialists in the mid 1950s had newly acquired knowledge concerning the human reproduction process, due to the discovery of hormones and their roles in reproduction, they did not have at their disposal any procedures of medical intervention which were not already in use in 1940.[34] Nevertheless, during the 1970s, when both progressive and conservative skepticism towards medical and technological innovations was most prevalent and the authority of medical experts reached an all-time low, some of the most significant developments in reproductive technology were made.[35]

During the 1970s, hormonal drugs, such as Clomid and Pergonal for treating ovulation irregularities, were authorized for use, new techniques for inserting semen into the womb to facilitate the process of insemination were developed, and the discovery of the procedure for freezing sperm led to the establishment of sperm banks and made the use of donor semen much more accessible for couples in which the man suffered from fertility deficiency.[36] However, these innovations did not raise interest in the possibilities they allowed: in 1968 there were 600,000 visits to doctors concerning infertility problems; this number did not change significantly until 1980. As of 1981, there was a sharp increase in the number of visits of couples searching for infertility treatments, and by 1983 this number exceeded two million annually.[37] These figures show that the issue of infertility was rediscovered at the beginning of the 1980s and became the focus of interest for the general public during this period. Although research shows that the frequency of infertility problems in the United States did not change during the twentieth century, the renewed interest in this issue was perceived, as one infertility specialist described it, as a growing public health problem of epidemic proportions.[38]

Contrary to what we might expect, neither scientific developments nor changes in the prevalence of infertility can account for the shift in general attitudes toward the medical establishment. We can assume that the neo-conservative and reactionary political atmosphere beginning in the early 1980s, accompanied by new waves of pronatalist sentiment, can explain it.[39] The familial politics of the neo-conservative period required, once again, the authority of the medical experts and the knowledge they developed in their medical discourses for rearticulating the significance of gender identities and behaviors, since in the intimate public sphere of the period they were inseparably linked to the biological functioning of the individual body.

In-Vitro Fertilization and the Emergence of the Industry of Assisted Reproductive Technology

The implications of menopause on the reproductive abilities of women were already recognized in ancient times; however, the effect of the age of pre-menopausal women on their reproductive abilities first became a subject of medical research only in the early 1980s. Until then, physicians believed that the fecundity of women reached its peak at the age of 25 and remained at that level until 35, yet this knowledge was based on commonplace observations and was not regarded as requiring scientific examination.[40] In 1982, a team of French doctors published a research paper in the *New England Journal of Medicine*, which analyzed data accumulated at infertility clinics regarding couples in which only the man was diagnosed as suffering from fertility deficiencies and who were therefore undergoing artificial insemination procedures using donor semen. The research, which was the first to scientifically examine this issue, concluded that the fecundity of women starts to drop around the age of 30.[41] In the introduction to their research, the authors of the paper stated that assisted reproductive technologies provided conditions for isolating the factor of age in women from other interfering variables: "Artificial insemination with donor semen (AID) seems to present an opportunity to control certain variables in the study of female fecundity over time."[42] They claimed that since age might also have an effect on the reproductive abilities of the male partner and since older women tend to have older partners and older couples tend to decrease their intercourse frequency, which might also significantly influence pregnancy success rates, it is difficult to isolate the influence of age in women on success rates of couples who are trying to have children without medical intervention.[43]

However, assisted reproductive technology did not only provide the conditions for performing a long-awaited analysis of the impact of women's age on their reproductive potentiality; *it is the assisted reproductive technology which turned women's age into an issue in need of scientific examination.*[44] One might argue that the rising age of first marriage and women postponing their first child into their thirties have brought about the need to explore this issue, but as Stephanie Coontz shows in her 1992 book *The Way We Never Were: American Families and the Nostalgia Trap*, "the age of marriage today is no higher than it was in the 1870s, and the proportion of never-married people is *lower* than it was at the turn of the century."[45] My claim is that reproductive technologies provided the conceptual framework in which the age-related reproductive potentiality of women was attributed with new-found value and, therefore, gained significance.

In 1978, what would prove to be the most significant development in the field of the new reproductive technologies was accomplished, as Louise Brown, the first baby to be born as the result of an in-vitro fertilization (IVF) procedure, was born.[46] Asexual reproduction, epitomized in the IVF procedure, gained new public interest not only due to the renewed pronatalist atmosphere, which sent infertile couples to the specialists, but also because of the heated debates which the new technologies stirred. The "Pro-Life" conservative organizations which were organized during the 1970s had gained significant political visibility and influence by the end of that decade. The main focus of these organizations was the abortion debates, but they perceived the new reproductive technologies as unholy interventions of god-playing doctors in natural processes, which would bring about the ruin of the institution of the family while condemning numerous fetuses to death.[47]

The loud objections conservative organizations raised had a profound influence on the field of assisted reproductive technologies. Turning it into a delicate political issue, these organizations deterred the federal government from addressing such controversies and caused it to refrain from funding research clinics which were developing IVF-related treatments.[48] Yet, while the opponents of these technologies assumed that the lack of government funding would halt all progress in the field, the withdrawal of these funds had a paradoxical effect. IVF technology was still funded privately by infertile couples, who were willing to pay significant sums for the chance of having a biological baby of their own. IVF and the public interest it drew attracted the attention of investors to the field of assisted reproductive technologies and turned it into a rapidly growing market.[49] By the end of the century, the market of assisted reproductive technologies was estimated to exceed several billion dollars annually.[50] Relying on private funds, researchers and doctors in this field did not have to adhere to regulations and restrictions which are imposed on publicly funded research.[51] However, the shift from public to private funds did not mean that the researchers and doctors were freed from all regulation; it simply meant that the field was now subject to a different type of regulation—that of the market. As governmental regulation not only sets the boundaries of research but also channels it in certain directions, the dynamic of supply and demand has a profound influence on the knowledge produced by fields of research which operate as an industry.[52]

The greatest novelty of IVF with regard to infertility treatments does not stem from the fact that the conception process takes place in a Petri dish instead of in a woman's body; the novelty lies in the fact that, unlike other methods for inducing pregnancy at the time, IVF is not a method of treatment for the problem which caused the infertility in the first place. IVF is a method for bypassing any deficiency which hinders conception, even if the reason for the deficiency is unknown; it may therefore be regarded as a type of medical *service*, rather than a method of medical *treatment*. In order to perform the IVF procedure, all that is needed is the "raw material"—the eggs and sperm—no matter how they are obtained and whether they are extracted from the body of the patient or from other sources.[53] The development of the IVF method disassociated the field of assisted reproductive technologies and the services it offered from infertility as a medical condition with a particular history and with demographic characteristics.[54] The services IVF offered were at least potentially applicable to the population at large, and now that it was subjugated to the economic regulation of the market, the only question which remained open was who its potential customers would be and how they might be reached.[55] Hence, while infertility is much more prevalent among members of disadvantaged groups and minority populations, the assisted-reproductive-technologies industry targeted upwardly mobile educated professional couples and single women, who could afford the high costs of infertility treatments, as its primary client base.[56] In this context, the age-related decrease in the fecundity of women was attributed a financial value, since it was one of the primary causes of impregnation difficulties in its potential clients,[57] and as such, it demanded research and frequent re-evaluations. However, the industry was quick to discover that it was not the actual biological findings which had such significant value; it was the widespread perception of the social and cultural meanings derived from this fact, framed in everyday language as the "biological clock," that drew patients to the clinics.[58]

The Cultural Signification of the Biological Clock

The fundamental social changes which occurred during the 1960s and 70s persisted and even grew during the 1980s.[59] The mass life-long participation of women in the work force was not only a well-established fact by the early 1980s, it was also an economic necessity, since women's work was needed to support the growth of the service portion of the market, which was dependent on increasing numbers of white- and pink-collar professionals.[60] Therefore, now that social domains were not sufficiently segregated, traditional configurations of signifying and regulating reproduction, the heteronormative order, and gender difference could no longer operate effectively since they relied, among other things, on gendered spatial configurations and on the distinction between the private as the realm of the feminine and the public as that of the masculine. Additionally, in spite of being under reactionary attack, the social movements and scholarly efforts of oppositional politics, such as feminism and the gay liberation movement, managed to reconceptualize gender roles and sexuality in many ways and redefined the conditions in which these issues were now addressed. Thus, while historical differentiations of social roles and divisions of labor allowed the marking of particular social functions as essentially feminine or masculine, the profound disruption of traditional assumptions concerning the essence of the genders during the 1960s and 70s rendered these definitions inadequate for securing these concepts.

However, despite all these changes, men, women, and gender difference did not cease to exist as central social and cultural categories. The neo-conservative familial atmosphere of the 1980s called for reinforcement of the heteronormative order and, by extension, the gender difference which makes it possible;[61] new forms of signification and regulation were therefore explicitly called for.[62] In this atmosphere, the renewed public trust in the medical experts and their knowledge allowed for the articulation of these social and cultural categories once again in the conceptual framework of biological determinism. As a result of the oppositional political movements of previous decades, by the early 1980s assumptions about how women's "nature" differed from that of men, which used to provide the basis for rationalizing the gender order, were politicized and could no longer be unwaveringly accepted. Hence, the new knowledge produced by medical experts concerning the deterioration of women's fecundity with age could, at last, provide a seemingly objective and impartial scientific fact about gender difference.

The influence of age on female fecundity as a scientific fact has become a form of temporal regulatory force which is coined in the term "biological clock," by enveloping it in an extensive framework of normative presuppositions.[63] On the level of the individual, the biological clock narrates notions of life-course for women as governed by a succession of essential checkpoints drawing their logic from a familial determinism which is portrayed as derivative of their bodies. As Foucault claims, the norm is "a mixture of legality and nature, prescription and constitution."[64] The construct of the biological clock, binding the natural and the social, allows one to condemn inevitable deviations from the desirable narrative it constructs as a breach of constituent principles. Foucault continues: "The judges of normality are present everywhere ... it is on them that the universal reign of the normative is based; and each individual, wherever he may find himself, subjects to it his body, his gestures, his behaviour, his aptitudes, his achievements."[65] Indeed, as a norm, the biological clock turns the family into a temporal regulatory principle, allowing a continuous assessment of the relative proximity of women in relation to the complete and successful fulfillment of a particular familial configuration. This exclusive familial configuration, comprised of a discrete family unit constituted by a man and a woman who are married to each other and parent their biological offspring, is constructed both as an imperative and as an ideal, and the continuous measurement and analysis of deviations from it set a path for increased management of life by self and others.

For instance, for single childless women in their twenties and thirties, the biological clock dictates notions of the future according to the following logic: if women's chances of getting pregnant sharply decrease in their mid-thirties, they should reach that age after meeting their future partners, spending a few years getting to know him and deciding that he is the one, and a few more enjoying a child-free relationship.[66] Provided that they plan to have more than one child, the time span between each pregnancy and the period of time it might take to conceive also have to be considered.[67] This formula shows that according to the "nature" of their bodies, approaching the age of thirty, women who do not completely forfeit the possibility of having children should already be in a committed relationship with the future father of their unborn children. On more general terms, it implies that in their late twenties and early thirties, years which are most crucial for developing one's career, women should invest their energies building a home, lest they be left without one.[68] It is most evident that this articulation of the implications of the biological clock on the life-course decisions of women is loaded with socially specific assumptions about how and under which conditions one should become a parent, yet it is constructed as the inevitable conclusion of a "natural law."

While imprinting familial and heteronormalizing notions of the individual future onto the body, it frames life-courses according to normalized narratives, which foreclose future possibilities. It might seem strange to claim that the concept of the so-called traditional family forecloses future possibilities for women in a society in which most adults live outside this familial arrangement.[69] However prevalent these diverse forms of living are, when examining the available narrations of the future for single childless women in their twenties and early thirties, these possibilities exist first-and-foremost in relation to that family formulation and as degraded variations thereof. Moreover, such regulatory mechanisms eradicate unforeseen forms of kinship, not only as personal aspirations but also as lived experiences.

....

The following are two prevalent strategies for exemplifying the normative regulation which the biological clock allows; the first focuses on regulating gender performance using essentialist claims, and the second promotes the fulfillment of perceived demands of heterosexuality. The former claims that although in current-day society women are not bound to the home and may strive to fulfill themselves professionally, the biological clock "reveals" the fact that the "natural laws" of women's bodies do not coincide with the values and lifestyles they are so eager to adopt, which are, according to this logic, masculine. For example, an article in *Time Magazine* quotes Ann Hewlett saying that "women embraced a 'male model' of single-minded career focus, and the result is 'an epidemic of childlessness' among professional women."[70] The underlying assumption here is that it is not merely an erroneous management of time which leads to these grave results, but an inappropriate mind-set, a masculine one, which manifests in the nullification of their reproductive abilities.

These arguments, which once again evoke the well-worn dichotomies placing man and culture on the one side and woman and nature on the other, may account for the paradigmatic theme of these texts: the need to make women aware of the "ticking" or the "ringing" of their biological clocks.[71] Thus, while on the one hand, heteronormative desire and appropriate gender performance are constructed as constitutive of the female body and as originating from its "nature," on the other, they are portrayed as in constant need of regulation, due to a discrepancy between women's masculine mind-sets and the temporal law governing their bodies. This discrepancy is historically narrated as resulting from novel social conditions, implying that in the past women naturally assumed their appropriate roles.[72]

The second strategy, which may be found in abundance in "how to" books and advice columns for single women, is aimed at correcting the gender performance of women without resorting to essentialist presuppositions, instead relying on speculative notions of "male desire." These texts claim that as the adolescence stage extends and both men and women tend to postpone the age at which they want to "settle down," the biological clock, which applies only to women, creates an inter-gender imbalance, putting women at a disadvantage. Thus, according to this viewpoint, which draws from economic models of supply and demand, around the age of thirty women become more eager to enter committed relationships and are, therefore, forced to comply with the demands of choosy male candidates.[73] The male desire constructed in these texts is not as progressive as the society at large; apparently, men are searching for "old-fashioned women" who express "true femininity" (i.e. women who are not too independent, successful, smart, assertive, or have short hair).[74] This form of intervention and regulation is notably illusive since its proclaimed aim is not to correct deviations but to aid and to better the lives of its addressees by gently persuading, correcting, and improving their chances of succeeding in the singles market.

....

Examining statements made by medical experts in the popular press about the biological clock shows that there are two different narratives portraying the relations between the newly developed medical technologies and the reproductive female body. The first tells a story of technological progress and medical optimism; the second repudiates the first, urging women and couples not to be led to false expectations and unjustifiable beliefs as to the abilities of these same technological means. With the first signs of positive results in a new procedure of reproductive technologies, feeble as these signs might be, the popular media is swept up with headlines announcing that science has finally found a way to stop, delay, or completely turn back the biological clock.[75] These reports are soon followed by others, giving voice to experts who occupy the position of the friendly realists, warning women not to be caught in these over-optimistic portrayals of the abilities of the new reproductive technologies.[76] While these two narratives seemingly contradict each other, a closer look reveals that, in fact, they serve the same interests and completely coincide, forming a single coherent narrative.

Considering the historical fluctuations in the standing of medical authority in popular discourses, as above-mentioned, it is important not to overestimate the importance of the apparently contradictory narratives drawn by disagreeing medical experts, since such disagreements only call for the proliferation of these discussions. The prolonging of any decisive conclusion in these debates ensures their persistence while it emphasizes the need to turn to the medical specialist for knowledge about the nature of the female body and the truth about sexual and gender differences. Moreover, the commercial interests of this industry do not lag far behind, for they are advanced by the underlying message conveyed by both voices: while the optimistic speaker bluntly promotes reliance on what this industry has to offer, the cautious warns potential clients not to be caught in complacency and postpone resorting to medical interventions until it is too late. Adding a grain of paranoia to this analysis, it is also possible to see how the split between these two narratives completely coincides since, in fact, their addressees are two different groups. While the former, speaking of forthcoming developments which are not available just yet, is aimed at younger women and couples, assuring them that they should not worry about postponing their childbearing years since technology will be there to aid them conceive when the time comes, the latter turns to older potential clients, reminding them that there are also limits to what technology may have to offer them if they do not rush to the nearest infertility clinic immediately. It is important to re-emphasize the fact that since the IVF procedure is designed to produce a pregnancy without having to address the causes of infertility, it may be exercised on couples who would have succeeded in conceiving without medical intervention, provided they had continued trying to do so in the traditional way.[77] Hence, we once again see the crucial role of the continuous reminder given by the fertility expert of the biological clock for this industry.

From this perspective, one of the idiosyncratic features of the biological clock as a temporal pattern can be understood. Analyzing the most common gender differentiations of temporality, an obvious pattern appears: masculinity is articulated in terms of linear time and femininity in non-linear temporal patterns. This is not to say that women are not governed in particular ways by linear constructions of time, but the gender split is articulated in the manner in which women's experiences and the temporal logic of the work which is assigned to women in the gendered division of labor exceed linear time. A prevalent example shows how the time demands posed on wage-workers, both male and female, yields to linear logic, while the labor which relates to the sustenance of life cannot operate under the same temporal pattern. Thus, the labor of raising children, feeding and caring for family members, and doing house work, which is performed largely by women and more generally associated with female social positions and feminine attributes, is governed by temporal patterns which do not coincide with a linear perception of time. Feminist discussions of this issue emphasize the manner in which these types of labor are expelled from the logic of the market in capitalist societies; deemed to reside outside of the economy, they cannot be considered work which can be assigned a value in the economic sense of the term.[78] Similarly, as Emily Martin shows, the male and the female reproductive bodies are regarded as governed by two types of logic which imply two different patterns of time. She shows how descriptions of both human reproductive systems are caught in their own metaphors as they illustrate reproduction in terms of industrial factories:

> In reproductive biology, bodies are organized around principles of centralized control and factory-based production. Men continuously produce wonderfully astonishing quantities of highly valued sperm, women produce eggs and babies (though neither efficiently) and, when they are not doing this, either produce scrap (menstruation) or undergo a complete breakdown of central control (menopause).[79]

Although, seemingly, both reproductive systems adhere to the same temporal framework, while the male epitomizes the highly efficient well-managed production line, the female is illustrated as a degraded version of this model, in which much time and effort are wasted. Thus, according to Martin's analysis, the temporal logic of the female reproductive body differs from that of male by its inability to coincide with the demands of efficiency posed by linear time.[80]

The biological clock diverges from these gendered temporal constructions since it is articulated as linear time in the strictest sense of the term: according to most medical experts the biological clock is defined as the time period between a woman's first period and the onset of her menopause.[81] Thus, as a linear construction, the biological clock deviates from the prevalent temporal form of demarcating gender difference, a deviation which can only be understood as resulting from the commercial interests which brought it into being, as portrayed above. Once the age-related decrease of female fertility was assigned with financial value in the assisted-reproductive-technologies industry, it was also subjected to the linear temporal logic of the capitalist market.[82]

....

Determined by commercial considerations, the biological clock is not only constructed according to economic formulations of time but its range of applicability is also restricted accordingly. As mentioned above, in the process of establishing itself as an industry, research in the field of assisted reproductive technologies turned its gaze from the infertile body as such to that of the potential client, and the knowledge it produced reflects this diversion. The biological clock, as a brainchild of this new knowledge, is emblematic of this process, and the strong class bias at its core is evident. When speaking of the applicability of the biological clock, it is important to distinguish between the act of ascribing the biological clock to a particular body and reference made to it as an abstract phenomenon in the media by medical experts and others. Being a regulatory mechanism, it easily yields itself to ascription and may, therefore, refer to almost all subject positions in its application to particular instances;[83] however, in the latter instance, abstract of any concrete body, its fundamental range of validity becomes apparent. Thus, media references to the biological clock consistently associate it with university graduates, professional women who are single and childless, from the middle- to upper-classes, and in their twenties and thirties. This categorization also entails other classifications, which are not explicitly mentioned. For instance, it is obvious that it strictly refers to heterosexual, able-bodied women who are living in urban areas. Additionally, since in the United States the divisions between class and race tend to show relatively high degrees of correlation, it is also a racial category and, to a certain degree, an ethnic one as well.[84]

Texts dealing with the biological clock as a general social phenomenon repeatedly state that single motherhood is one of the unfortunate consequences of women's erroneous management of their lives, as they do not take into account their temporal constraints. However, as Robin Silbergleid suggests, analysis of statements made in conservative texts which relate to single mothers shows that they explicitly refer to those who are single mothers by choice, mainly white financially secure professional older women who decide to have children on their own, while, in fact, they are concerned with young black single mothers who earn low incomes or are welfare-dependent.[85] Thus, positioning a class- and culturally specific notion of the family within the framework of the biological clock serves as a means to implicitly regulate other forms of kinship relations which do not coincide with it. The normative concept of the family at the root of the biological clock is constructed first-and-foremost in contrast to other familial configurations against which it positions itself, which in addition to single mothers include homosexual couples and families, black kinship networks,[86] and the Latino and immigrant families which supposedly have more children than they can support.

The biological clock therefore encapsulates the notion euphemistically called "demographic concern" which, in fact, claims that while the "right" segments of the population are not procreating enough, the "wrong"' ones are breeding out of control. Hence, it is apparent that the discourses which bring into being the biological clock can be genealogically traced back to the eugenic discourses of the turn of the century, such as that of the concept of "race suicide," which was introduced by Theodore Roosevelt in 1903.[87] The fact that the construct of the biological clock reflects eugenic considerations should come as no surprise since, as suggested above, it is a product of the knowledge produced by the field of assisted-reproductive-technology discourses. As prior research has suggested, eugenic impulses are in no way foreign to present-day practices of assisted reproductive technologies.[88] This new form of eugenics differs from the old not simply by the technologies at its disposal but by the fact that it "naturally" operates through commercial interests and consumer desire instead of being centrally controlled by the sovereign power.

Conclusions

The biological clock of the female reproductive system first appeared in the neo-conservative political climate of the early 1980s as a result of the newly acquired interests on the part of the assisted-reproductive-technologies industry and was quickly adopted into everyday language as the temporal signifier of inter-gender difference. After two tumultuous decades, where traditional forms of social regulations were irreversibly disrupted, the biological clock enabled the reconfiguration of lost forms of marking gender difference in new cultural circumstance. As a configuration of regulatory mechanisms, the biological clock imprints an abstract, ideal notion of the family as the marker of the female body, especially that of educated professional middle- to upper-class single women. Constructed as resulting from a disrupted social order which is nostalgically attributed as agreeing to the natural constitution of women's bodies, this regulatory mechanism reconstructs traditional forms of spatial definitions into the temporal domain.

Thus, it may be asserted that the biological clock draws the heteronormative order from the bodies of women by intertwining contingent and culturally specific social arrangements with what are perceived to be objective biological facts. In addition, operating as a means for normative regulation, the biological clock forecloses the horizon of future possibilities by defining narratives which coincide with ideological formulations of the family as determined by the temporal nature of women's bodies. Privileging these narratives undermines the viability of alternative life-courses, whether they are lived experiences or imagined possibilities, while it naturalizes an ideologically loaded and narrow definition of desirable familial arrangements. Additionally, it provides a seemingly scientific and value-free point of departure for stigmatizing stereotyped social groups.

Since this paper focuses on the productive aspects of a particular configuration of power, it does not discuss potential positions of resistance produced by its operation. The question of how we might articulate such forms of resistance is therefore in need of further discussion. We should assume that since the normalizing impulse is at its core, it is possible to imagine identities, modes of identification, and forms of living which are anti-normative in ways that undermine the operation of the regulatory mechanism of the biological clock. It is important to note that I am not referring to mere declarative objections to it or to life-narratives which seemingly do not conform to its demands since they might still operate according to its logic, for every rule also sustains its exemplary deviations, which do not undermine its existence. Forms of resistance are enabled by attempts to give meaning to ways of living which do not comply with the normative imperatives the biological clock dictates, while striving to sustain their intelligibility. Such forms of living may produce opportunities to imagine narratives which do not comply with the linear logic of life-courses of birth-marriage-reproduction-death and rearticulate prevalent binaries such as that of youth-versus-adulthood. As normative articulations portray a life-course narrative that links the transition from a dependent childhood and a rebellious adolescence to responsible maturity as enabled by marriage and reproduction, oppositional manners of living may give way to new forms of adulthood which are not determined by family and reproduction. My aim here is not to promote alternative temporal templates, such as seeing life as cyclic or living in an everlasting present, to replace the linear temporality the normative perspectives provide, but to suggest that complex and unpredictable patterns of relating to one past and future may be configured.[89]

Elizabeth Grosz suggests a radical departure from dominant concepts of time through her reading of scholars such as Bergson, Deleuze, and Irigaray. Claiming that our phallocentric framework of thought does not enable us to conceive of differences which are not in reciprocal relation to each other, our concept of time is highly restricted. Thus, prevalent notions of time foreclose the ability to draw from the past in order to open uncalculated and unexpected possibilities in the future and enable radical change to occur—a change in kind and not only a change in degree. For Grosz, since the female and sexual difference are emblematic of all that was left out of the phallocentric rationale, it is through the aberration from this rationality, which femininity may offer us, that we may imagine such possibilities:

> One of the most challenging issues facing any future feminism is precisely

> how to articulate a future in which futurity itself has a feminine form, in which the female subject can see itself projected beyond its present position as other to the one.[90]

Thus, Grosz's suggestion that the re-conceptualization of the future may be achieved by feminist endeavors may aid us in departing from the prevalent concepts of time and guide us in our efforts to conceive alternative temporalities.

The analysis of the biological clock as a temporal regulatory mechanism and its broad cultural implications underscores the need to re-think time in order to enable new interpersonal relations to appear. The centrality of temporality in contemporary modes of biopolitics indicates the radicality of the possibilities these "new futures" may hold for us. ▪

....

1 Helen Malson and Catherine Swann, "Re-producing 'Woman's' Body: Reflections on the (Dis)place(ments) of 'Reproduction' for (Post)modern Women," *Journal of Gender Studies* 12, no. 3 (2003): 191; Margaret Marsh and Wanda Ronner, *The Empty Cradle: Infertility in America from Colonial Times to the Present* (London: John Hopkins University Press, 1996); Stephanie Coontz, *The Way We Never Were: American Families and the Nostalgia Trap* (New York: Basic Books, 1992); John A. Robertson, "Assisted Reproductive Technology and the Family," *Hastings Law Journal* 47 (1996); Rosalind Gill and Keith Grint, ed., *The Gender Technology Relations: Contemporary Theory and Research* (London: Taylor & Francis, 1995); and Sarah Franklin, "Postmodern Procreation: Cultural Accounts of Assisted Reproduction" in *Conceiving the New World Order: The Global Politics of Reproduction,* ed. Faye D. Ginsburg and Rayna Rapp (Berkeley: University of California Press, 1995).

2 I use the term "heteronormativity" to describe the manner in which social institutions and cultural mechanisms support clusters of presuppositions about the natural sexual order. These presuppositions include the beliefs that individuals naturally fall into two distinct and complementary categories, male and female; that the social institution of marriage is rightfully privileged; that only heterosexual sexual relations are normal; that marriage should unite only a man and a woman; and that each gender has certain natural roles in life. Thus, according to these presuppositions, the alignment of biological sex, gender identity, and gender roles may be assumed in any given person according to male or female norms, and heterosexuality is considered to be the only normal sexual orientation. See Lauren Berlant and Michael Warner, "Sex in Public," *Critical Inquiry* 24, no. 2 (1998): footnote no. 2 and Chrys Ingraham, "The Heterosexual Imaginary: Feminist Sociology and Theories of Gender," *Sociological Theory* 12, no. 2 (1994): 204.

3 The term "biological clock" is also used to describe the operation of other bodily functions, such as sleeping patterns and circadian rhythms. Yet, in this paper I am only referring to its use in relation to the reproductive system.

4 In accordance with a long tradition of associating infertility deficiency with women, the biological clock links the decreased ability of older couples to conceive with the age of the female partner, despite the fact that reproductive specialists have known for years that age also significantly decreases the reproductive ability of men. See, for instance, March and Ronner, *The Empty Cradle.* In 2002, research was published claiming that in comparison to women "[f]ertility for men is less affected by age, but shows significant decline by the

late 30s." David B. Dunson, Bernardo Colombo and Donna D. Baird, "Changes With Age in the Level and Duration of Fertility in the Menstrual Cycle," *Human Reproduction* 17, no. 5. (2002): 1399-1403. Since then, mentions of the male biological clock have appeared in the popular press. See "Male biological clock is ticking," *BBC News* (2002), http://news.bbc.co.uk/1/hi/health/2328909.stm. However, the modes of operation of the male biological clock significantly differ from that of women. This issue requires an extensive discussion which cannot be developed here.

5 For a discussion of the gendered division of labor, see Karen Davies, "The Tensions Between Process Time and Clock Time in Care-Work: The Example of Day Nurseries," *Time & Society* 3, no. 3 (1994): 277-303, Carmen Leccardi, "Rethinking Social Time: Feminist Perspectives," *Time & Society* 5, no. 2 (1996): 169-186; and Barbara Adam, "Within and Beyond the Time Economy of Employment Relations: Conceptual Issues Pertinent to Research on Time and Work," *Social Science Information* 32 (1993): 163-184. For differences in socialization and social positions, see Pamela Odih, "Gendered Time in the Age of Deconstruction," *Time & Society* 8, no. 1 (1999): 9-38; and Victor J. Seidler, *Rediscovering Masculinity: Reason, Language and Sexuality* (London: Routledge, 1989). For an analysis of the gendered conception of time and capitalism, see Mary Mellor, "Women, Nature and the Social Construction of 'Economic Man,'" *Ecological Economics* 20 (1997): 129-140.

6 See Aloysious Siow, "Differential Fecundity, Markets, and Gender Roles," *Journal of Political Economy* 106, no. 2 (1998): 334-54; Claudia Goldin, "The Long Road to the Fast Track: Career and Family" (NBER Working Paper No. 10331, 2004); and Sylvain Dessy and Habiba Djebbari, "Career Choice, Marriage-Timing, and the Attraction of Unequals" (Institute for the Study of Labor (IZA), Discussion Paper No. 1561, 2005). For an non-economic account, see Valerie Oppenheimer, "A Theory of Marriage Timing," *American Journal of Sociology* 94, no. 3 (1988): 563-91.

7 Elaine Hoffman Baruch and Amadeo F. D'Adamo, Jr. "Resetting the Biological Clock: Women and the new Reproductive Technologies," *Dissent* 32, no. 3 (1985): 273-6.

8 Nicole Keating, "And Sarah Laughed: The Biological Clock Metaphor and its Entailments," International Communication Association (University of Pennsylvania, 1999).

9 Judith Butler, "Introduction," *Bodies that Matter: On the Discursive Limits of Sex* (Routledge: New York, 1993): 1-23.

10 Elizabeth Freeman, "Packing History, Count(er)ing Generations," *New Literary History* 31, no. 4 (2000): 727-44. Freeman also finds in other writings of Butler other formulations of the past which articulate its radical potentiality.

11 Butler, *Bodies that Matter*, 67.

12 Michel Foucault, *Discipline and Punish: The Birth of the Prison* (New York: Vintage Books, 1977): 30.

13 Gilles Deleuze, "Postscript on Control Societies," *Negotiations* (New York: Columbia University Press, 1995): 178.

14 Ibid., 180.

15 Ariella Azoulay, "P.S.—An Introduction to Post-Scriptum on Control Societies," *Theory and Criticism* 24 (2004): 233.

16 Deleuze, "Postscript," 181.

17 Ibid., 178, 181 (emphasis added).

18 See, for instance, Amanda Vickerey, "Propriety," in *The Gentleman's Daughter: Women's Lives in Georgian England*, (New Haven: Yale University Press, 1998): 225-84 and Karin Hausen, "Family and Role-Division: The Polarization of Sexual Stereotypes in the Nineteenth Century; An Aspect of Dissociation of Work and Family Life," in *The German*

Family: Essays on the Social History of the Family in Nineteenth and Twentieth Centuries Germany, ed. Richard. J. Evans & W. R. Lee (London: Barnes and Noble, 1981): 51-83.

19 D. W. Amundsen and C. J. Diers, "The Age of Menopause in Classical Greece and Rome," *Human Biology* 42 (1970): 79-86.

20 In the *New York Times*, for instance, it first appeared in 1981, and the first time it was mentioned in *Time Magazine* was in 1982. See Richard Cohen, "The Clock Is Ticking For the Career Woman: Biological Time Clock Can Create Real Panic," *The Washington Post*, March 16, 1978; Marilyn Fabe and Norma Wikler, *Up Against the Clock: Career Women Speak on the New Choice of Motherhood* (New York: Random House Inc, 1979); Sarah W. White, "The Baby Clock I: The Ticking Grows Louder At 30," *The Associated Press*, November 16, 1980; "The Only-Child Phenomenon," *The New York Times*, January 18, 1981; and John D. Reed, "The New Baby Bloom," *Time Magazin*e, February 22, 1982.

21 Gender difference management anxieties may be found in abundance in conservative and moralistic reflections on this period. See George Gilder, *Men and Marriage* (Los Angeles: Pelican Publishing Company, 1987) and William Jasper, "Perversion and Ignorance," *The New American*, April 11, 1988.

22 Michel Foucault, *The History of Sexuality, Vol. I: An Introduction* (New York: Vintage Books, 1980): 104.

23 Barbra Ehrenreich and Deirdre English, *For Her Own Good: 150 Years of the Experts' Advice to Women* (New York: Anchor Press, 1978): 28.

24 Ibid., 269-312.

25 John D'Emilio and Elisabeth B. Freedman, *Intimate Matters: A History of Sexuality in America* (Chicago: University of Chicago Press, 1997).

26 Coontz, *The Way We Never Were*, 187.

27 Ehrenreich, and English, *For Her Own Good*, 284-85

28 Coontz, *The Way We Never Were*, 192; D'Emilio and Freedman, *Intimate Matters*, 305-7.

29 Coontz, *The Way We Never Were*, 193.

30 Foucault, *The History of Sexuality*, 154.

31 Marsh and Ronner, *The Empty Cradle*, 211.

32 Lauren Berlant, *The Queen of America Goes to Washington City: Essays on Sex and Citizenship* (Durham: Duke University Press, 1997): 1.

33 Ibid., 5.

34 Marsh and Ronner, *The Empty Cradle*, 3-4.

35 Ibid., 228.

36 Ibid., *The Empty Cradle*, 208.

37 W. F. Pratt, W. D. Mosher, C. A. Bachrach, et al., "Infertility—United States, 1982," *The Morbidity and Mortality Weekly Report* 34, no. 14 (1985): 197-99.

38 Margaret J. Sandelowski, "Failures of Volition: Female Agency and Infertility in Historical Perspective," *Signs* 15, no. 3 (1990): 475-99.

39 Marsh and Ronner, *The Empty Cradle*, 255.

40 Ibid., 247.

41 Ibid.

42 Federation CECOS, D. Schwartz and M. J. Mayaux. "Female Fecundity as a Function of Age: Results of Artificial Insemination in 2193 Nulliparous Women with Azoospermic Husbands," *The New England Journal of Medicine* 306 (1982): 404.

43 Ibid.

44 It is important to note that even without undermining the scientific validity of the research findings or questioning their objective status, there is still room for examining the circum-

stances in which particular issues appear as needing scientific research. For an extended discussion on this topic, see Arnold I. Davidson, *The Emergence of Sexuality: Historical Epistemology and the Formation of Concepts* (Harvard: Harvard University Press, 2002): 5. Nevertheless, the validity of the research quoted herein was later questioned. See, for instance, J. Bongaarts, "Infertility After Age 30: A False Alarm," *Family Planning Perspectives* 14, no. 2 (1982): 75-8 and Lynn Gray, *Human Reproductive Technologies: Products, Markets and Manufacturers* (Connecticut: Business Communications Company Inc, 2005): 14.

45 Coontz, *The Way We Never Were*, 183 (emphasis in original).

46 Marsh and Ronner, *The Empty Cradle*, 236.

47 Robin M. Henig, *Pandora's Baby: How the First Test Tube Babies Sparked the Reproductive Revolution* (New York: Houghton Mifflin Company, 2004): 206. For an articulation of the objection of conservative organizations to the IVF procedure, see Sacred Congregation for the Doctrine of the Faith, "Donum Vitae: Instruction on Respect for Human Life, Sacred Congregation for the Doctrine of the Faith, 1987," *United States Conference of Catholic Bishops*, http://www.nccbuscc.org/prolife/tdocs/part2.htm.

48 Henig, *Pandora's Baby*, 12.

49 Robertson, "Assisted Reproductive Technology," 911.

50 Gray, *Human Reproductive Technologies*, 28.

51 Nicole Richardt, "Feminist discussion on IVF in the USA," *Biomedical Ethics* 1, no. 2 (1996): 38-44. Also available online at http://www.izew.uni-tuebingen.de/bme/96010204.htm.

52 For discussions of the influence of government regulation on scientific research, see analysis of developments in HIV research: Luc Montagnier, "A History of HIV Discovery," *Science* 298 (2002): 1727-8 and Emily Martin, "From Reproduction to HIV: Blurring Categories, Shifting Positions," in *Conceiving the New World Order: The Global Politics of Reproduction*, ed. Faye D. Ginsburg and Rayna Rapp (Berkeley: University of California Press, 1995): 256-69. On the influence of supply and demand on knowledge production, see Critical Art Ensemble, "Eugenics: The Second Wave," *Ctheory.net* (1998), http://www.ctheory.net/text_file.asp?pick=101.

53 This is not to claim that particular medical treatments are not sometimes needed in order to extract the eggs or the sperm or that the re-implantation procedure in the womb does not require medical intervention. However, one does not need to address the source of the fertility deficiency in order to perform IVF, one need only provide the conditions for the treatment in which it might succeed.

54 For the claim that, once the IVF treatment became so profitable, treatments which could address and cure conditions which cause infertility were under-funded or abandoned altogether see Critical Art Ensemble, "Eugenics."

55 Michael Fox, a reproductive endocrinologist, claimed in the year 2000 that, currently speaking, infertility clinics are treating subfertile couples and not infertile individuals: "We know that a significant proportion of patients who are not pregnant after one year will achieve a pregnancy with continued attempts. Therefore, patients are most commonly considered subfertile and not sterile. Therapies used to treat infertility are thus designed to shorten the interval to pregnancy in this group." Michael Fox, "Age and Infertility: The Biological Clock: Fact or Fiction?" *Jacksonville Medicine* May (2000): 210.

56 Marsh and Ronner, *The Empty Cradle*, 183; Richardt, "Feminist Discussion," under "Feminist Position on the IVF."

57 Garance Franke-Ruta, "Creating a Lie: Sylvia Ann Hewlett and the myth of the baby bust," *The American Prospect* 13, no. 12 (2002).

58 A comprehensive report of the assisted reproductive technology industry assigns women's

perceptions of their biological clock as a significant factor influencing the growth of the industry. The report states that while data which was published in the popular media might have been less than accurate, it still attributes importance to women's beliefs "that their biological clocks were not only ticking away, but also somehow running down." Gray, *Human Reproductive Technologies*, 14.

59 Coontz, *The Way We Never Were*, 187.

60 D'Emilio and Freedman, *Intimate Matters*, 305.

61 Berlant, *The Queen of America*, 4-5.

62 For instance, an article covering Ronald Reagan's first presidential campaign, published in *The Washington Post* in 1980, states that "To many he represents a world where men were men and women were in the kitchen." See "The First Salvos; Reagan's Main Street; Ronald Reagan Takes Over and Takes Aim," *The Washington Post*, June 5, 1980.

63 In addition to the operation of the biological clock as a norm which is discussed below, the concept of the biological clock has a significant role to play in other types of debates, such as the moralistic debate and the demographic debate. In this paper, I focus on the normative operation of the biological clock while elsewhere I discuss the complex role which is assigned to it in other types of debates. Merav Amir, "The Emergence of the Biological Clock of the Female Reproductive System as a Mechanism for Social Regulation," (M.A. thesis, Tel Aviv University, 2005).

64 Foucault, *Discipline and Punish*, 304.

65 Ibid.

66 Since the construct of the biological clock assumed heterosexuality, lesbians were categorically excluded from the range of the operation of this power configuration during the 1980s. However, as the gay and lesbian struggle to receive acknowledgment of their familial arrangements on the basis of their resemblance to "normal" families from the state and from the public at large, to a certain degree, the range of validity for the biological clock expanded to include them as well.

67 See Hillary Frey, "The Rules of Attraction," *The Nation*, July 5, 2004.

68 On the importance of these years for the career development of women, see Anna Fels, *Necessary Dreams: Ambition in Women's Changing Lives* (New York, Anchor, 2005): 213. Much debate on the implications of the apparent constraints on the lives of young professional women who are university graduates grew out of two articles which were published in *The New York Times*: "The Opt-Out Revolution" (October 26, 2003) and more recently: "Many Women at Elite Colleges Set Career Path to Motherhood" (September 20, 2005). These articles claim that young mothers face impossible decisions and are unable to reconcile the demands made on them by their professions and their parenting responsibilities. Although not discussed in these articles, it is apparent that these dilemmas are faced primarily by women and not by their male partners, due to the unequal load of parenting responsibilities imposed on women, both in terms of the labor divisions in the house and the emotional responsibility of the mother for the well-being of the child. For further discussion of this topic in light of such publications see Kathleen Gerson, "Understanding Work and Family Through a Gender Lens," *Community, Work & Family* 7, no. 2 (2004): 163-178.

69 This familial arrangement was far from being statistically normal either in the latter quarter of the twentieth century or in any other historical period apart from the 1950s. For an extensive discussion of this topic see Coontz, *The Way We Never Were*, 188.

70 Nancy Gibbs, "Making Time for a Baby," *Time Magazine*, April 15, 2002. For an extensive

criticism of Hewlett's work, both on the conceptual level and on the methodologies of data analysis see Franke-Ruta, "Creating a Lie."

71 For an elaboration of the role of "awareness" in the regulatory operation of the biological clock, see Keating, "And Sarah Laughed," 10.

72 See Larry Nolte, "Call No Man Father: The Attack On Fatherhood," *This Rock Magazine* 8, no. 10, (1997). Also available online at http://www.qadas.com/~carolann/483.htm.

73 For the historical contextualization of the infiltration of conceptual frameworks of the market into the context of relationships, see Ehrenreich and English, *For Her Own Good*, 283. For an example of the implications of this viewpoint for gender discourse, see Rachel Greenwald, *Find a Husband After 35 (Using What I Learned at Harvard Business School)* (New York: Ballantine Books, 2004).

74 The full list of do's and don't's, including the hairstyle remarks, can be found at Greenwald, *Find a Husband.* Additional partial lists may also be found at Lesley Stahl, "The Biological Clock," *CBS News Online Edition*, August 14, 2003, www.cbsnews.com/stories/2003/08/14/60minutes/main568259.shtml; Sherly Hayden, "Tough Reasons You're Still Single," *Cosmopolitan* 15, no. 9 (1998); and C. F. Jackson, "Black Professional, Educated, and Self-reliant Woman—Why Am I Still Single?" *Sage Heart*, October 15, 2004, http://sage-hearts.com/dating-advice/Black-professional,-educated,-and-self-reliant-woman-why-am-I-still-single.html.

75 For recent examples see Sumiko Oshima, "Stopping the Biological Clock: The Brave New World of Delayed Motherhood," *The Japan Times*, December 13, 2000 and Kendall Powell, "Age Is No Barrier...," *Nature: International Weekly Journal of Science* 432 (2004): 40-2.

76 Lesley Stahl, "The Biological Clock" and Anne Newman, "The Risks of Racing the Reproductive Clock," *Business Week*, May 5, 1997.

77 See note 55 above.

78 See Barbara Adam, "Within and Beyond the Time Economy of Employment Relations: Conceptual Issues Pertinent to Research on Time and Work," *Social Science Information* 32, no. 2 (1993): 163-84 and Leccardi, "Rethinking Social Time: Feminist Perspectives."

79 Emily Martin, "The End of the Body?" *American Ethnology* 19, no. 1 (1992): 121-2.

80 Ibid. See also Emily Martin, "The Egg and the Sperm: How Science Has Constructed a Romance Based on Stereotypical Male-female Roles," *Signs* 16 (1991): 485-501.

81 Keating, "And Sarah Laughed," 6. For a more elaborated discussion about the biological clock as linear time, see ibid., 9, 17.

82 For a comprehensive analysis of economic time as linear time in the capitalist logic, see Mellor, "Women, Nature."

83 Even that of gay men. For instance, see "Andrew, Dec. 8, 1997," *Gay Gaze*, (1997), http:/gaydaze.com/gdindex.htm.

84 David B Grusky, "The Past, Present, and Future of Social Inequality," in *Stratification: Class, Race, and Gender in Sociological Perspective* ed. David B Grusky (Boulder: Westview Press, 2001): 3-51.

85 Robin Silbergleid, ""Oh Baby!:' Representations of Single Mothers in American Popular Culture," *Americana: The Journal of American Popular Culture* 1, no. 2 (2002), available online at http://www.americanpopularculture.com/journal/articles/fall_2002/silbergleid.htm.

86 See Carol Stack, *All Our Kin: Strategies for Survival in a Black Community* (New York: Harper & Row, 1974).

87 For a discussion along these line concerning female fertility, see Margarete J. Sandelowski,

"Failures of Volition: Female Agency and Infertility in Historical Perspective," *Signs* 15, no. 3 (1990): 475-500 and Marsh and Ronner, *The Empty Cradle*, 113.

88 See Cynthia R. Daniels and Janet Golden, "Procreative Compounds: Popular Eugenics, Artificial Insemination and the Rise of the American Sperm Banking Industry," *Journal of Social History* 38 (2004): 5-27; Michelle Stanworth, "Reproductive Technologies and the Deconstruction of Motherhood" in *Reproductive Technologies: Gender, Motherhood and Medicine* ed. Michelle Stanworth (Cambridge: Polity Press, 1987): 10-35; Donna J. Haraway, *Simians, Cyborgs, and Women The Reinvention of Nature* (New York: Routledge, 1991); and Critical Art Ensemble, "Eugenics."

89 For an extensive discussion on non- and anti-normative temporalities, see Judith Halberstam, "Queer Temporality and Postmodern Geographies," in *In a Queer Time and Place: Transgender Bodies, Subcultural Lives* (New York: New York University Press, 2005): 1-21.

90 Elizabeth Grosz, *Time Travels: Feminism, Nature, Power* (Durham: Duke University Press, 2005): 177.

Marx and Deleuze: Money, Time, and Crisis

Matteo Mandarini

> *One can't think about the state except in relation to what lies beyond it [au-delà], the single world market, and in relation to what lies this side of it [en-deçà], the levels of minorities, becomings, and the "people." Beyond the state it's money that rules, money that communicates, and what we need these days isn't a critique of Marxism, but a modern theory of money as good as Marx's that goes on from where he left off.*
>
> —*Gilles Deleuze*[1]

> *Money will permit us to understand how surplus value is consolidated in social command; how to command crisis is the normal situation of capital.*
>
> —*Antonio Negri*[2]

The culture-industry continues to serve up, in an ever-increasing proliferation of introductions and commentaries, an insipidly apolitical Deleuze. That some of his solo works might permit such a reading is, perhaps, possible, but that even his writings with Guattari should suffer such a fate tells us plenty about the academy's willingness to ignore anything that might smack of Marxism or that cannot be simply reduced to the politics of difference, warmed-over multiculturalism, or "radical" pluralism.[3] What I wish to focus on here is Deleuze's call for a "modern theory of money"; at the same time, I hope that my reworking of such a theory will also provide a "critique of Marxism" or, at least, of a certain Marxism. Such a critique, I contend, is a critique from *within* Marxism that does not seek to leave Marxism behind.

The relation between Marxism and poststructuralism is a complex one requiring serious consideration, which it has yet to receive. The conviction that underpins this article is that both Marxists and poststructuralists are mistaken in seeing themselves as coming from antithetical theoretical traditions. Structuralists and poststructuralists have all too often failed to adequately conceptualize their own historical-theoretical roots in Marxist theory's attempt to confront orthodoxy, whether this be in the form of Stalinism itself or, more generally, determinism and dogmatism.[4]

This article will interweave a *pars destruens* challenging what Antonio Negri has called the *metaphysics of value* ascribed to a certain Marx and a *pars construens* focusing on a re-ontologization of the notion of time. By refusing the principle of synthesis and rationalization, i.e., value, we shall see money in the immediacy of its command structures, in its role as *correlator* coming from the outside, rather than as a quantifier of an abstract substance embodied in commodities and subject to a rational distribution in the service of equilibrium.[5] This effects a rupture of the closure of capitalism (and of Marxism as "the science of Capital") that reveals the anti-systemic temporal heterogeneity of the system, the hemorrhaging of totality into a multiplicity of temporal practices.

Monetary-Forms and Value

The concept of value is one of the forms of "socially valid"—hence "objective"—thought of bourgeois economics.[6] Undoubtedly Marx was at times beguiled by its seductive logic, although he also fought against it. Nevertheless, the concept of value has operated as a *rationalization* of economics such that it is seen as the common substance present in all productive activities and common to all commodities, as the materialization of *abstract labor*, as the abstract principle of a rational distribution of labors within the different sectors of production, and as that which ordered the "deployments of power (or really determine[d] its prices, subdivisions, and hierarchies)."[7] *Marx's analysis of value might thus appear to advance the theory of capitalist equilibrium beyond the apparent anarchy of production.*[8] The parallel with the history of philosophy's attempt to naturalize right is reproduced with the attempt to naturalize capital: the abstraction, "value," plays the role of rational foundation at the heart of concrete reality—it exists as theological principle. Further, it operates a moralization of economics, constraining it within a bourgeois logic of legality. Value is understood as expropriated from the "rightful owners." Revolt, the taking of power, is then seen as a reestablishment of natural justice. This is the transfiguration of the pre-modern schema of natural law into the bourgeois one of "the ego and his own." The future comes to be defined either in terms of the persistence of an inflicted wrong, a contradiction between social production and individual ownership, or a justice-to-come where concrete and abstract harmonize within the rightful, natural order of communism. It is imperative that this schema which views revolution in terms of *right* be subverted. Otherwise, the future is captured within the past, as a development of its own fixed *logos*. Marx was aware of the danger. In the rest of this paper I will be concerned with mapping precisely such a move beyond the metaphysics of value to be found within Marx's *Capital*.

Value comes not at the beginning but at the end. It is always a resultant space of overdetermined command. Commodity circulation begins on the margins, a practice of alliance rather than exchange, although as the ties grow stronger exchange proliferates and feeds back into the relations within each social grouping.[9] From this time forth, certain goods become produced *for* exchange, their commodity status gains a certain autonomy as a differential plane is formed from their encounter, which deterritorializes them in gaining a certain consistency as exchange proliferates.

1 **a** commodity **A** = **c** commodity **C**, where an exchange is singular, contingent, and produced through a random groping between aleatory factors. A positive difference arises as a result of this practice of exchange, of this encounter: *the form of value*. The difference between commodity **A** and commodity **C** is the condition for the exchange, but it only occurs through the confrontation of the two in a social exchange relation in which the commodity sought is presented as an equivalent—the equivalent form to which one's own commodity is relative. The exchange relation divests **A** and **C** of their qualities and manifests itself as a quantitative difference within a qualitative equivalence. Although the exchange is still motivated by a desire for **C** over **A** (and vice versa), the process of exchange must place the goods into a relation of quantitative differentiation whereby an exchange can be determined "objectively" in a manner which satisfies both parties. Marx describes this process as the displacement of *use-value* by *exchange-value*. The passive synthesis of difference produced by the encounter between commodity **A** and commodity **C** gains, however, little consistency and is consumed in the exchange, thereby being unable to feed back into production itself.[10] Although from the perspective of a social practice it is the search for the "equal" in an exchange which dominates the *differential*, it is only on the condition of the emergence of a consistent differential field, with its a-signifying elements marking the singular nature of each differential relation, that equality may arise, serving to reterritorialize difference on its deterritorialized plane. This difference is of a different order from that of bodies and their relations; it arises in their interstices, at the limit of each but only in relation to bodies. It exists in relation to a set of *incorporeal transformations* which exist as the produced "presupposition" of the linkage of the a-signifying elements of the differential plane to a set of more or less deterritorialized practices.[11] So, in the practice of a simple exchange there is, first, a relating of two heterogeneous goods—a process that divests them of their qualitative aspects, determining each merely in its quantitative difference from the other. Each good is placed in a position of equivalence with the other such that the two elements are subject only to a quantitative difference and/or equivalence with one another. Once an exchange has taken place, apart from a redistribution of commodities that has occurred, further transformations are undergone: an incorporeal transformation of the object received into property, setting it into a whole complex of other practices of consumption (legal, religious, assigned obligations, responsibilities, demands of production, etc.). Further, in selling your

calf, you have sanctioned the incorporeal transformation of calf into meat. You have not killed the calf, but by your exchange the calf is condemned. The set of incorporeal transformations to which these goods are subject form the variables of the given societal assemblage and are coded into a particular semiotic regime as a set of practices then attributed to the bodies.

2 **a** commodity **A** = **c** commodity **C** *or* **b** commodity **B** *or* **e** commodity **E** *or* **d** commodity **D** *or* .... Here we are at a stage where commodity exchange has become increasingly dominant. A series of exchanges, actual and virtual, produce *as an effect* the expansion of the differential plane, the plane of the form of value, of the passive synthesis of difference between commodities in the exchange relation. As increasing numbers of goods cease to be related through qualitative difference, difference-in-itself progressively gains consistency on a plane of its own. It ceases to be the effect of a contingent encounter, where relative and equivalent forms are the effect of a single exchange; each commodity now stands in a social relation with the "whole world of commodities" so that, in any one exchange, difference points beyond the particular towards a whole series.[12] The previous practices involving negotiation, a tentative groping, have become increasingly standardized and fixed, forming the warp of the assemblage. The differential plane of a-signifying elements is more formalized. The elements constitute a series of intersubstitutable units, hierarchically ordered, systematized in accordance with a whole set of equivalencies, etc. A whole syntax is generated and expands throughout the assemblage. Nevertheless, difference (the plane of the value-form) maintains only a relative autonomy for the following reasons:

i It is always incomplete and dependent, as difference—always the effect of a passive synthesis of the series of exchanges—is vulnerable to modification since the chain "is liable at any moment to be lengthened by a newly created commodity, which will provide material for a fresh expression of value."[13]

ii Each difference is partial and fragmented, revealing no univocity of ground. Difference remains (re)territorialized by the machinic assemblage of bodies.

3 **z** commodity **Z** = **a** commodity **A**
c commodity **C**
e commodity **E**
g commodity **G**
n commodity **N**

All differentiation is expressed in terms of a single commodity-equivalent "excluded from the ranks of all other commodities"[14] to which all commodities relate in different magnitudes and which enables them to relate to one another proportionately. The value-form (differential plane) has gained maximal consistency by being assigned a content of its own. Having always been the result of commodity exchange, it now has a commodity of its own to differentiate.[15]

Capital as Means of Semiotic Pilotage

I have tried to avoid speaking of value itself. In part this is simply to show how the "simple commodity form is … the germ of the money-form"[16] and to describe the relation of commodities to money without passing by way of the apparently more abstract notion of value. More importantly, I wish to describe the progressive autonomization of a plane of difference generated as a passive synthesis from the plane of commodity exchange that will then allow for a delineation of how value is produced by means of a *correlation* between the *formalization* of a plane of difference (monetization) and the *formalization* of a plane of circulation and of production (regulation and discipline). Such a correlation should be understood as a regulative regime, coming from without and submitting a set of "relative contents" to a form of expression which determines them. The interaction between these planes subsumes difference under unity, in that "a specification on any one level automatically calls forth a homologous specification on another."[17] With monetization, the plane of difference gains a consistency, a thickness, a content proper to itself, producing a double pincer of expression and content (as we shall see).[18] In fact, the monetary plane of difference only exists in the various degrees of consistency that the level of commodity circulation produces through the *intensity* of its circulation or to the extent that a specific content is withdrawn and appropriated by the field of monetary difference—reterritorializing on its deterritorialized plane—so that a consistent monetary plane or stratum is able to form. *For value is*—as I hope to demonstrate—*what results from the processes of homogenization and capture of labor-power by means of the correlation* and *conversion produced by the circulation of commodities in alignment with the monetary plane.*[19]

The reason for this form of "derivation" or synthetic approach to the structurations of the socio-economic body of capitalism is to avoid the pitfalls of reductionist Marxism, in which Marx is understood to reduce all phenomena to the productive relations between persons determined "in the last instance" by the development of the forces of production.[20] To reread *Capital* in such a manner as to truly integrate the historical analyses enables one to reintroduce the question of change—of the radically new—into a reconceptualization of capitalism. Whereas much of *Capital* reads as an analysis of a completed, totalized economic system, the consideration of its fractures, the autonomy of processes and their produced correlations, enables one to deal with system and anti-system, i.e., *the process* of production of homogenization of a differentiated, heterogeneous space and the synchronic relations established between the elements.

Nevertheless, the usefulness of an approach that attempts to grasp the relative autonomy of planes would appear to block any possible derivation of value from quantification of expended labor-power, which was surely the task of the labor theory of value. More importantly, it stands in the way of an explanation of how labor-power can be understood as the source of value. The result would be a failure to distinguish between price and value that, in turn, would mean crisis could no longer be understood in terms of inconvertibility.[21] This criticism, however, presupposes the already homogenous nature of the system, so that crisis, as an element immanent to capitalism, would only be understood as effectively developing from laws inherent to its functioning: crisis would be a fully costed sub-function. The radically new would not be new at all, merely a development within the same element. I wish instead to proceed from the presupposition of originary heterogeneity, to view the differentiation of planes and elements as a process with emergent effects produced by operations proper to each, and, only then, to attempt to think their intersection, correlation, and segmentation. Laws do not pre-exist and determine the space, predetermining the elements that are produced. Laws arise from the passive syntheses, the unanticipated effects that either deterritorialize the elements of the assemblages or territorialize the whole by folding over the plane on which they were produced, establishing specific correspondences, procedures of distribution, a centralizing or hierarchical form, as well as specific organizational practices. Correlations between the planes are engendered, produced by relations lying outside the elements they relate, though allowing something to circulate between them, conjugating the segments of each plane.[22] According to this understanding of socio-economic articulations, the homogeneity of the capitalist ideal is a *project* guided by a number of processes on and between the various planes whose effects must be constantly reproduced. I want to argue that *crisis is the possibility of non-conversion*, of incommensurability: a scrambling of the codes.

> What capitalizes capital is semiotic power. … What specifies it historically is that it only tries to control the different components which come together to maintain its processual character. … [I]t is first of all and continuously a *mode of evaluation* and *technical means of control* of the power arrangements and their corresponding formulations.[23]

I will approach the question of originary heterogeneity through a discussion of the mechanism by which a correlation between the regulated planes—labor-power/production and monetary differentiation—is produced. This may appear a strange procedure, to discuss a relation prior to the elements of that relation. However, this the manner in which Marx proceeds in *Capital*: although both elements are present from the beginning, labor-power is defined in terms of its value-forms (at least initially), hence as domesticated, whilst money is revealed in its process of composition/domestication, such that there is an asymmetry. Moreover, the element which correlates the terms operates a change in the terms related. Any other procedure would tend to segment too rigidly the space as an origin and disguise the immanence of the relations to one another. Elements will be seen to exist in their relationality not independently, but on a plane of exteriority that does not predetermine the relations or the elements. Finally, the terms labor and labor-power are also only apparently given at the beginning; they emerge in a different form through historical analyses, which reveal them as processual and emergent, and do so precisely in relation to the parallel formalizations of elements of circulation.[24] The correlation comes to be formed between the differential plane of money emerging as an effect of commodity circulation and the formalization of a plane of production in terms of quantities of labor-time. As discussed above, the differential plane emerges from the machinic relations between bodies and passes through various degrees of deterritorialization, initially highly dependant on the level of deterritorialization of the machinic assemblage, only gradually gaining a consistency of its own.[25] It is only when the differential plane was given a content of its own, enabling it to reterritorialize the element of exchange (e.g., gold) upon its own deterritorialized plane, that it gained sufficient consistency to form a (relatively) autonomous monetary plane able to intersect the plane of production on its own terms (or at least potentially so). In fact, the distinction between the planes of exchange, of production, and of money can emerge only through such autonomization-effects. Nevertheless, such autonomy is only relative. What we discover is the emergence of a new assemblage with different distributions of content and expression, of bodies and a-signifying elements, and a different correlation established between its segments and flows, its local power centers and coded elements. The correlation, however, is a project, a process that requires the circulation of an **X** that perpetually (re)produces the correlation by means of the formation of an "equivalent." The "equivalent" must operate as a bridge, an instance of communication between the planes. It must take a certain amount of labor-time to produce (hence be able to circulate on the plane of production as a commodity) and it must be homogeneous and divisible without changing in nature (and so be able to circulate in quantitative form on the differential plane).[26] In other words, the monetary assemblage arises through the machinic assemblage of bodies withdrawing a specific content from the plane of production and a collective assemblage of enunciation that formalizes a differential plane of expression with its a-signifying elements—situated in reciprocal relation with the plane of content. This is the emergence of a new assemblage: the monetary body—monetary a-signifying regime.

> Precisely because content, like expression, has a form of its own, one can never assign the form of expression the function of simply representing, describing, or averring a corresponding content: there is neither correspondence nor conformity. The two formalizations are not of the same nature; they are independent, heterogeneous.[27]

Various commodities play the role of correlator at different times, depending on the relative deterritorialization of the differential plane and the relative degree of homogenization of elements on the plane of production. In Marx's day it was gold. The correlator tends, however, to lose any qualitative determinations which would enable it to flee its assigned role. It becomes an "occupant without a place" on the plane of production, where commodities are doubled by their monetary expression—so that everything appears double (worker/wages, commodities/prices, etc.)—and an "empty place" on the differential plane, always circulating elsewhere.[28] There is a distribution of excess and lack between the series (occupant without a place and mobile empty place) which is the condition of re-alignments between the series in "perpetual relative displacement."[29] Without money operating as this paradoxical element, the originary heterogeneity would block any potential negotiation of the emergent systematicity (unless another element took its place, operating in another manner, actualizing another form of systematicity). Money is then subject to strategic interventions by power centers (states, central banks, the World Bank-I.M.F. complex) by means of which varying antagonistic conditions are negotiated and the series re-aligned. Lack and excess are then distributed in accordance with the alterations in the conditions of the system in order to maintain specific correlations.[30] Though unable to eliminate heterogeneity, capital operates a form of pseudo-homogenization through the extraction of (relative) constants and the autonomization of specific correlations. It is because (monetary) difference is an effect of commodity circulation/exchange, a result of a passive synthesis but not subject to it (it operates in the gaps, the interstices), that it is able to gain an autonomy and a consistency of its own—that it can be intersected and fixed by the circulation of a commodity **X**, which gives difference a content of its own whilst this content is able to operate as a circulating "equivalent" on all planes, producing correlations and communications.

A commodity appears under capitalism in two forms:

1 as a definite quantity of (socially necessary) labor-time—its *Value*;

2 as a variable quantity of monetary value which it may appropriate in exchange—its *value-form* or price.[31]

The value-form can be seen as an "effect" of value and its overdetermination, but value can be said to exist *only* in its effects, its modes of existence, its variety of forms. It is immanent to them, though the "effects" pass through degrees of deterritorialization, gaining consistency and autonomy, or the effects are reterritorialized across whichever plane takes it up.[32] Elements and planes communicate in accordance with their different degrees of deterritorialization: e.g., the commodity-form communicates with the money-form in terms of velocity of circulation and the degree of deterritorialization of property relations. Value (labor-time determination) is the site of overdetermination. The heterogeneity of this site (both with regard to elements and relations) means that crisis, rupture, and incommensurability are originary: "It is this disequilibrium that makes revolutions possible."[33] The question, then, is one of the production of homogeneity, of correlation and conversion, so that power can indeed be said to be defined by that which escapes it.[34]

It is the double nature of commodities—which enables them to intersect the plane of difference whilst keeping to their own plane—that allows Marx to say:

> Money as a measure of value is the necessary form of appearance of the measure of value which is immanent in commodities, namely labour-time. … The price or money-form of commodities is, like their form of value generally, quite distinct from their palpable and real bodily form; it is therefore a purely ideal or notional form.[35]

In fact, both commodities and money are elements of a machinic assemblage of bodies—though both are also subject to intervention from a collective assemblage or semiotic monetary regime. This latter operates by inserting elements into the interstices of the machinic body, parceling-off relations, interminglings, and mixtures. In other words, the semiotic monetary regime operates by segmenting the flows of bodies, correlating the various segments and flows: a flow of labor for a monetary segment (the wage); an expanding monetary body recoded in terms of price variation (inflation), investment, and/or interest rate increases; a flow of finance money segmented into reserves, corporate budgets, etc. The correlation does not, therefore, block the relative autonomy proper to each realm so that, for example,

> although price, being the exponent of the magnitude of a commodity's value, is the exponent of its exchange-ratio with money, it does not follow that the exponent of this exchange-ratio is necessarily the exponent of the commodity's value.[36]

In other words, the value relation operates between, on the one hand, a commodity and the labor-time (socially) necessary to produce it and, on the other, between the commodity and its monetary expression in quite autonomous ways. It is this internal split within value, its multiple composition, which can produce the imbalances within it:

> The possibility, therefore, of a quantitative incongruity between price and magnitude of value, i.e., the possibility that price may diverge from the magnitude of value, is inherent in the price-form itself. This is not a defect, but, on the contrary, it makes this form [price-form] the adequate one for a mode of production whose laws can only assert themselves as blindly operating averages between constant irregularities.[37]

This correlation is not carried out once only. The exteriority of the relations to their elements means that vigilance is required to maintain and enforce the correlation. This can only be carried through by the disciplining and formalizing processes distributed across each plane. Although it is important not to cloud the distinction between, for example, price and value, any attempted logical deduction of the form: socially necessary labor-time → value of commodity → expression in a commodity acting as universal equivalent: gold → in turn determined by labor-time necessary for its production, fails to grasp the autonomy of the segments and the differing distributions of contents and expression that are produced independently—both logically and historically—and that would otherwise result in a simple reduction to essence.[38] It is precisely because the planes are autonomously produced that there is "an essential lack of correspondence,"[39] that correlations can be produced and be subject to asymmetries and imbalances. The differential plane folds back over commodity circulation, deducting an element and producing it as a content of its own. This element is then allowed to circulate as a substitute, a simulacrum or double of the commodities. It circulates on all planes simultaneously, though taking on different forms on each plane in accordance with the varieties of segmentarity they encounter, in accordance with the various forms of content and expression they are taken up by.

The process of correlation is extremely complex because elements intervene from outside the apparent simplicity of the surface of exchanges: all heterogeneity is overlain with a homogenous—*axiomatized*[40]—surface: wages, circulating monetary quantities, all phenomena faithfully mirrored in their price—no perplexity, no disguise, a representative monetary democracy.

Just to fill in some of the things I have passed over briskly: money exists in two forms: as *measure of value*, it is determined in a complex negotiation with the quantity of labor socially necessary to produce the commodity in which it is materialized (e.g., gold), and it is differentiated on its own plane through quantitative specification of a representative—money of account; as *means of circulation*, it is quantitatively overdetermined by the price and quantity of the commodities in circulation, and the velocity of its exchanges.[41] As price is in turn determined in a complex negotiation between the monetary expression of the socially necessary labor-time required for the commodity's production ("social necessity" indicating the intervention of demand and supply factors as well as level of "development" of productive forces and, crucially, the degree of regulation within the labor process itself), it presupposes money as measure of value. It is money as equivalent or measure of value that enables the *correlation* across the planes of money-in-itself, circulation, and production, although it is the circulation of money which enables *communication* and *conversion*.

Different agencies emerge on the different planes as the abstract-machine of capital is specified, concretized in a proliferation of assemblages that maintain the correlations, regulate the elements of each plane of specification, and enable the continuing conversion.[42] Therefore, there are a number of variables, each operating on a plane with its own consistency, its own stratification procedures, its own formalizations of specific contents (bodies) and expressions (a-signifying elements), but which are made to intersect at certain critical points by an element effectuating an incorporeal transformation amongst the elements of the correlated planes. A number of factors come to overdetermine the relations and elements: price stability is *overdetermined* by the level of productivity, level of development of organized labor, growth of the economy, velocity of the circulating medium, etc. The quantity of the means of circulation is *overdetermined* by "the sum of the prices of the commodities divided by the number of times coins of the same denomination turn over,"[43] as well as credit demands for investment, etc. And both of these sites of overdetermination depend upon the relative stability of monetary value, which in turn depends upon the organization and segmentation of the plane of production, the circulation of commodities, etc. These orders of dependency are not causal. They depend on effective regulation of planes and a correlation produced through the incorporeal transformations that enables the intersection and conjugation of series. Rigidity of causal dependency would problematize notions of strategic modification between the assembled planes. It is precisely the heterogeneity of elements and relations which enables the plasticity of the capitalist axiomatic.

Crisis and Convertibility

Some further qualification, or rather, clarification, is required concerning the direction of "determination": from production to circulation, or circulation to production. An example: in the sixteenth and early seventeenth centuries, the huge increases in gold from the newly discovered territories of the Americas produced massive price inflation. Is this not an example of increased prices following upon the growth of the money supply? It is sufficient to clearly distinguish between the two forms of money Marx speaks of—money as measure of value and money as means of circulation—to reveal the complexity and overdetermination of correlations and interventions across planes. For Marx's position is quite consistent with the fact that—and in fact implies precisely that—an increase in money as the measure of value produces an increase in prices (inflation). For example, if there is an increase in gold so that its production time falls, there is a decrease in its value. As prices are the representatives of a commodity's value expressed in gold, a fall in the value of gold (due to the reduction in production time, e.g., a discovery of easily mined gold deposits)[44] will be represented in a general price increase, i.e., an increase in the gold represented by the price of the commodity. The amount of money as a means of circulation—i.e., enabling the price to be realized in an exchange—will have to increase in line with price increases (or circulation will have to speed up, the number of commodities diminish, etc.). Price increases in turn vary in accordance with the reduction in production time (and hence reduction in the cost) of gold. We have, therefore, inflationary pressures as a result of changes in production, and trade, and communication, and…, and…, and…, and…. I have already discussed the need to evade the metaphysics of the traditional "labor theory of value," which tends to create a future society within the "interiority" of capital, a form of economic preformationism. This is the case also for the role of the gold standard, where its *function* as real essence of the monetary function has diverted attention from its role as disciplinary element in the regulation of money. Whilst it is most certainly true that at various times in history the money-form has orbited around gold, the monetary semiotic and gold have never coincided; rather, gold is called on to engender specific tactics for *convertibility* and *conversion* across monetary registers and economic sectors. It is due precisely to the plasticity and consistency of the monetary semiotic that it is able to adopt and be adopted by different techniques that enables it to transform the forms of its interventions. When the money-form was tied to gold, transformations in gold production and circulation would produce effects upon the money-form, for the two forms would be specified reciprocally. However, each phenomenon is overdetermined by factors proper to planes exterior to their own. Each plane requires stratification procedures of its own so that any correlation must come from outside, albeit producing a reciprocal specification on the inside, enabling the emergent unity to arise by pragmatically negotiating a path through the variables in order to produce a "noise-free" communication. As we can see from the example of the discovery of the Americas, a number of aleatory factors intersect, producing a number of effects on the various planes, each one coping with the new events in accordance with the assemblages it is able to mobilize: expansion of trade followed upon the repression and organization of production of the colonial people and/or export of ones own population; the rise of prices at home meant exacerbation of popular unrest until wages were allowed—or forced—to rise with prices, though away from home (Spain) wages struggled to do so; price increases and the lag in wages produced high profits for commerce and early industry, proving a strong incentive to invest, and hence to the growth of early capitalism; the influx of gold was able to finance increasing military expansion and reverse or reconfigure political allegiances; piracy and smuggling increased, as did counterfeiting, thereby provoking the Dutch Republic to form the first central bank; etc. Paradoxically, the emergence of correlation, the paths they establish, and the assemblages which aim to stabilize the structured heterogeneity, rather than producing balance, enable the exacerbation of feedback across the planes, with the correlates just as frequently allowing destabilizing elements to travel across planes and assemblages.

As is clear, the two forms of money have drastically altered over the last hundred years, passing through increasingly critical thresholds of deterritorialization. It was still obvious, for example, in Marx's day that the correlation between money as value and commodities had to pass through production-time. The monetary stratum was prevented from fully deterritorializing production by reterritorializing it upon gold production. Thus, the monetary stratum was only as deterritorialized as its gold reserves (as the eventual conclusion of John Law's banking endeavors demonstrated). Increasingly, as commodity circulation expanded to form what Alliez and Guattari have called Integrated World Capitalism (IWC), so did the money-form.[45] It gained increasing consistency as gold reserves became ever more restrictive on the expansion of production, the freedom of financial institutions, and the requirements of national and global governmental institutions.

On August 17, 1971, U.S. President Nixon decided to allow the dollar to float free from gold, actualizing the autonomy of the monetary plane—in actual fact simply acknowledging a *de facto* state of affairs which enabled the distributed agencies (state-forms) to make themselves adequate to this event, producing a modification in the axiomatization of correlations in such a way that, in the words of Antonio Negri, "[e]very relative parameter of certainty of values was thereby dissolved."[46] In other words, monetary value ceased to be aligned with the conditions of (re)production. This deterritorialization of monetary-value by de-linking money from production increasingly dissociated the planes and thereby provoked the emergence of new forms, new agencies, new axioms by which correlations were produced and maintained, as well as a transformation of political demands. This involved both a maximization of regulation on each separate plane and a deregulation of their correlation. This did more than mark a new distribution of expression and content on the economic planes:

> In such a way the residual pathetic illusions of socialism were swept away—as were the possibilities of trade-unionism: in other words, the project of hooking up and reconnecting salaries, and the conditions of reproduction, to criteria co-determined by progress, development, value—this truth of theirs, the bosses, slammed it into your face, rudely but realistically.[47]

Therefore, inconvertibility is always present and is perpetually reproduced. It is the zero point of noncorrelation, of non-communication: the exteriority of relations. The velocity of circulation enables the emergence of the complex unity around which simple commodity exchange must circulate: the "identity" of sale and purchase (C-M-C)—the commodity/money "identity" produced through the autonomization of specific "motor-sensory" procedures. As circulation slows down, inconvertibility emerges. The elements fall back to their own planes, reterritorializing on consumption and finance. From the heart of the assemblage, from within the stratified elements and relations, sale and purchase have an "opposite yet mutually complementary character."[48]

> The two processes [sale and purchase] lack internal independence because they complement each other. Hence, if the assertion of their external independence proceeds to a certain critical point, their unity violently makes itself felt by producing—a crisis.[49]

The unity is an effect of correlation. However, it folds back over forming a new plane or stratum by deterritorializing the correlates and reterritorializing them across the monetary plane,[50] producing one as a plane of content the other as one of expression. A sale is also a purchase and vice versa, for a commodity is transformed into money at the same time as money is transformed into a commodity: instantaneous incorporeal transformation.[51] The formation of a new assemblage always proceeds by taking the most deterritorialized element and folding it back over, producing a new plane of expression for one of content—as Marx describes in the movement from the simple and isolated form of value to the money-form. From within the articulated double-pincer (expression/content), the whole movement, the circulation of elements, looks as though

> both the money and the commodity function only as different modes of existence of value itself, the money as its general mode of existence, the commodity as its particular or, so to speak, disguised mode. It is constantly changing from one into the other, without becoming lost in this movement; it thus becomes transformed into an automatic subject.[52]

The heterogeneity of elements is overlain by the homogeneity of filiation—the process is read through its emergent element and totalized. The product (money) folds back over and endlessly repeats its genesis, distributing elements and relations in accordance with a formalization proper to its own plane. This does not prevent the elements from continuing in a different form on their own plane, in accordance with immanent processes of mutation, or from remaining subject to different formalizations (different distributions of content and expression).

Although Marx views the problems of the circulation of money as symptoms of processes occurring on the plane of production, this does not mean that Marx views determination to operate in a single direction, blocking nonlinear phenomena:

> It should be mentioned in passing that it by no means follows, from the fact that the popular ascription of stagnation in the process of production and

> circulation to an insufficiency of the circulating medium is a delusion, that an actual shortage of the circulating medium resulting from, say, bungling government interference with the "regulation of currency" may not for its part give rise to stagnation.[53]

One reason for the frequent misreadings of Marx on this and other questions, which frequently result in the ascription of linear and equilibrium models to Marx, is the difference between his method of inquiry and method of presentation.[54] *Capital* operates by means of a series of ever-expanding "snapshots," each exhibiting a number of different actors and elements, interrelations, and emergent effects and becomings that are produced from the assemblage. The limited nature of each *tableau* produces an antagonism, a crisis (as a symptom of the heterogeneity of the elements and the attempted homogenization) that demands a widening of the view. At each stage, the introduction or emergence of new elements mutates the nature of the assemblage. In the first part of *Capital* the elements drawn from the chaos are: commodities, the agents of exchange, value, value-form, and a number of related concepts. Some of these were already present from the beginning, others emerged *en route*. We find these elements engaged in a set of stratified relations in a working assemblage, with heterogeneity at its heart, and crisis as its possibility. A set of rules of thumb, pragmatic procedures, axiomatized "trick[s]"[55] emerge as ways by which the consistency of the stratified assemblage can be maintained. However, these rules of thumb already indicate the rupture of the delimited field or snapshot by pointing towards agencies of anti-production proper to each assembled stratum, each deploying the capitalist axiomatic in accordance with its own forms of realization, by which the variables are negotiated and the correlations established and maintained.[56] In short, *Capital* operates by a progressive accretion that transforms the assemblage as new elements and relations emerge. It is this processes of accretion that I have attempted to describe—one which reveals the emergence of equalization, the production of homogeneity out of heterogeneity, which is perpetually reworked by its internal differential elements.

Time and Correlation

> *If we look at the whole process from the point of view of its result, the product, it is plain that both the instruments and the object of labour are means of production and that the labour itself is productive labour.*
>
> —*Karl Marx*[57]

Labor is productive in relation to the product which marks the completion, the limit or threshold, of the *productive process* or cycle. Beyond this point, the product is appropriated on another plane that withdraws it from production and feeds back into it in the form of monetary returns. Productive labor is determined in terms of the limit that marks the recoding of the product in terms of price,[58] although it is already appropriated as productive labor through capital investment at the beginning of the cycle: price is unrealized capital; it is in this sense that the end of the productive cycle is already its recommencement: "Products are therefore not only the results of labour, but also its essential conditions."[59]

Time is the primary form of appropriation, of intersection—the "common substance." Price acts as a matrix across which relations and elements are distributed in temporal segments proper to each plane. The determinations of socially necessary labor time (the social average time around which production—and productive labor—fluctuates) are all subject to translation into specific temporal segments and thresholds marking conditions of profitability: "technical machines" and labor-power must operate at a particular degree of intensity—i.e., a definite number of articles must be produced within certain temporal limits; there must be no more than an average waste-time in the form of waste of means of production. Raw materials themselves are, for Marx, elements that have "already undergone some alteration by means of labour"[60] and, hence, are correlated with a certain quantity of labor-time—as with the instruments of labor. Moreover, Marx's stress on the *quality* of labor and raw materials when determining social necessity is itself recoded in terms of temporal segments: e.g., skilled labor is concentrated time of training and different quality of goods are understood as that involving more or less production time to reach an "average," which is again determined temporally—e.g., the role of soil quality as a standard operates as a temporalization itself, determining the labor-time required for cultivation, etc. It is important to note that although the time of correlation appears as homogenous and univocal, this is the *effect* of the axioms of correlation. Indeed, various heterogeneous practices have temporalities of their own, which are the times of their constitution and operation—this only allows a functional reduction of these temporalities. It is this heterogeneity which capital must manage through its axiomatic. In the words of Antonio Negri:

> Therefore, [capitalism] is negation of the real time which is experienced as antagonistic, or rather, it is a reduction within a *formally dialectical* schema: the cycle and cyclical development, the market and the plan—that is, in the cyclical development, *time* is configured in the form, and follows the criteria of the ordering of economic *space*, as reversibility of all the points, as circulation, as money.[61]

What capitalism produces is an ideal time ("*tempo ideale*"),[62] the abstract time of *modernity*, through the displacement of the multiple heterogeneous presents of practice, by a formal *presentness* of universal convertibility.

Conducts of Time

Time is the element here. Closely following Hume's analysis, Deleuze maintains that our originary relation to time is not to the notion of succession but to the succession of independent "perceptions" in the *connective synthesis* of the imagination.[63] The repetition of instances or cases in a connective synthesis changes nothing in the object but only in the mind. For the synthesis of successive perceptions is not carried out *by* the mind but *in* the mind (*passive connective synthesis*). In other words, something *new* is produced in the mind by this contraction or synthesis, a difference is allowed to emerge from the repetition in the contemplating mind which determines an affective space from the encountered difference, a difference which comes to be coded in the mind.[64]

> [The imagination] contracts cases, elements, agitations or homogeneous instants and grounds these in an internal qualitative impression endowed with a certain weight [difference as the e/affect of an encounter].[65]

This *contraction* of the series of independent perceptions constitutes the time of the affective lived present of the subject.[66] The foundational productive passive synthesis organizes a milieu *as its expressed product*, a lived vibratory block of space-time, qualified as a *habit* defined by a "periodic repetition"[67] of contracted cases and elements, interweaving material and perceptual characteristics, in which one is affected and acts. The resulting emergent space of practice is to be understood as a "conduct *of* time."[68] Between the process of composition—the passive connective synthesis (the synthesis of production)—and its functioning (the produc-ed/ing habits and affects) there is no difference, for there is but one synthesis at work: "primary production: the production of production."[69] Nevertheless, a difference subsists between the contracted, synthesized differences and their "free state." Only the contracted habit of the present is actual. The past and future emerge from retentions and anticipations pertaining to the lived present. The present is constituted by the contraction of material and perceptive elements precipitating a milieu one inhabits, which in turn spawns pasts and futures as repetitions, dimensions of this contracted habit of the present. The picture is even more complex. Deleuze allows for the multiplication of contemporaneous presents as a function of the multiple coexisting passive connective syntheses, contemplations, or contracted habits/practices:

> the contraction implied in any contemplation always qualifies an order of repetition according to the elements or cases involved. It necessarily forms a present which may be exhausted and which passes, a present of a certain duration which varies according to the species, the individuals, the organisms and parts of organisms under consideration. Two successive presents may be contemporaneous with a third present, more extended by virtue of the number of instants it contracts. The duration of an organism's present, or of its various presents, will vary according to the natural contractile range of its [passive syntheses].[70]

The task is to think of variable accords or various compositions between milieus in terms of lateral temporal relations which are not successive but multi-dimensional.

For capital it is always a case of negating the heterogeneity of the consistent practices (conducts *of* time), substituting for them the zero-time of its analytic spatialization (e.g., ideal time-of-circulation=0). The connective syntheses also contract together other syntheses as machine parts, forming further connective syntheses and milieus as products, "continually producing production, … grafting producing onto the product."[71] It is a question of practice, in that the contractions constituting the present(s) distribute the elements and relations for potential spaces of action and for further productive syntheses. There is a practice *of* contraction, where the genitive marks a non-linearity: contraction is the condition *of* practice, whilst practice is itself a contraction. The "*of*" marks a point of constitutive ontological ambiguity.

Capital seeks to operate, in effect, as a *reserve of time*, an accumulation or capture of time which proceeds by the *parcelization* of time. Temporal segments are formalized differently on each plane.[72] Capital operates by axiomatizing correspondences between the conducts *of* time on each plane, its task aided by a thorough regularization or disciplining of practices.[73] Nevertheless, the formalizations and segmentations proper to each plane operate under exigencies emerging on those planes, e.g., social stabilization, profitable production, monetary stability, etc.

Thus time only exists in the variety of its forms, of its practices, but it is able to operate as the element in which correlation appears, i.e., in which it is produced in the form of temporal *parcelizations*. Time is commodified and marks a criterion of reversibility in circulation, for appropriation takes a set of elements proper to each plane and correlates (axiomatizes) them, enabling a displaced representative (money) to circulate the various planes performing de- and reterritorializations, de- and re-codings. Money dominates the processes of appropriation through the uniqueness of its role. It emerges as an effect of the circulation of heterogeneous products and labors and, therefore, circulates on this plane, but it gains a consistency on a plane of its own—with its own logic. It is immediately multi-planar and autonomous. Value exists only in the variety of its forms, and these forms can be further determined in terms of temporal parcelizations on each plane and across all planes at once by the multi-planar aspect of the monetary-forms. Appropriation produces correspondences across planes, generating different effects according to the planes intersected. For example, in Chapter 8 of *Capital*, "Constant Capital and Variable Capital," we see how the different elements are formalized or appropriated according to formalizations proper to each plane. On the plane of production, technical machines operate as a form of expression proper to content segmenting labor in a variety of ways, by subjugating it to their own breaks, stoppages, variable speeds, etc., formalizing a stratum of expression proper to a flow of labor-power/time that they parcel out, divide up and distribute. On the monetary plane, the technical machines consist in a homogenized set of contents taken up by the form of monetary expression, contributing to the expansion of the monetary body by a parcelization into a set of discrete temporal moments. Another example: the rate of surplus value measures not only the ratio of capital inputs into labor to capital generated by the investment (s/v), but also the degree of (formal or real) subsumption of labor to capital. As Marx argues, "surplus-value is in the same ratio to variable capital as surplus labour is to necessary labour."[74] Both ratios "express the same thing in different ways" or, rather, as appropriated on different planes—monetary or productive. Different processes produce effects which differ according to the planes upon which they occur, by which they are taken up—partly dependent upon the nature of the correspondences produced between the distinct formalizations, partly in spite of those correspondences.

Value and surplus-value, constant and variable capital, necessary and surplus labor, etc. are markers of segmentation of the various flows—of labor, of money, of goods—and elements of cross-referencing (e.g., value correlated with necessary labor, surplus-value with surplus labor) whereby the diverse procedures of appropriation across planes are produced. Or, rather, these different categories are effects/signs of the overdetermined formalization of elements and relations—generalized reversibility—on the various planes upon which processes of correlation supervene. These "signs" are "representations" (as in the title of *Capital,* Chapter 9 § 2: "The Representation of the Value of the Product by Corresponding Proportional Parts of the Product") that can be termed "ideological" in that they are effects generated through the process of cancellation of the heterogeneity of their production/genesis through the correlation to which they submit in cross-referencing. *Yet they are elements of concrete material production.* These "signs" are sufficiently consistent that they can fold over, describing routes to the expansion of production, paths to re-routing profits, markers to increase surveillance, signals for balancing-out the inter-planar exchanges, etc. The correlations produced by the monetary plane's emergence from the circulation of commodities, its deduction of an element (e.g., gold) to advance its consistency, through which it charts and intervenes in processes occurring on other planes (through correlating segments)—these operations reveal the process of interiorization of heterogeneity: i.e., the production of the analytic of capital, of capital as tautology, and the process of the reduction of temporal heterogeneity by the ideal time of capital's automated reversibility. There is no longer a need for a schematism between signs-systems and material flows. The exteriority of heterogeneous elements remains. The correlations are produced so as to carve out an interior. Once the correlations are produced (not once and for all but through a careful and continuous negotiation between heterogeneous formalization procedures on each plane, through an axiomatic of functional tricks), homogeneity/representation-effects supervene in the correspondences between the aligned planes, and "recognition effects" are able to further regulate and survey the elements on the various planes.

From the Critique of Money to the Critique of Power

Within the machinic distribution of bodies at the stage of real subsumption, where the whole of society becomes fully integrated, a loop produces effects across the whole socio-productive body. This is IWC. But why view value immediately in its monetary form? How is it that value as money leads directly into production? Does not this attempt to reduce value to the variety of its forms betray a naiveté alien to Marx?

> If a theory of value is given, can it be given outside of an immediate reduction to the theory of money, of the capitalist organization of exchange, of exploitation? ... Money has the advantage of presenting me immediately the lurid face of the social relation of exchange; it shows me value right away as exchange, commanded and organized for exploitation. I do not need to plunge into Hegelianism in order to discover the double face of the commodity, of value: money has only one face, that of the boss.[75]

By cutting out the derivational form (commodity production → value → surplus-value), excising the mediating role of value except in the forms in which it is given, the possibility of synthesis is removed, and we are left with heterogeneity, antagonism, and the proliferation of assemblages by means of which the heterogeneous is organized and submitted to procedures of command, surveillance, and re-alignment. *Value is extended into an immediately social relation*: the social averaging of labor, which operates a specific set of correspondences and correlations between the plane of production and that of circulation, instigating procedures of domestication and regulation internal to the productive process through the set of incorporeal transformations distributed throughout the assemblage, capturing elements and relations of production in a series of affects on the monetary plane—which, in turn, has its own semiotization procedures.

> The theory of value, as it has existed so far, is simply an allusion to money as a concrete representation of the social mediation of antagonism. Value will be defined through average labor, through *socially necessary labor* in the sense in which money is defined in this framework. "What determines value is not the amount of labour time incorporated in products, but rather the amount of labour time necessary at a given moment." But, if one looks more closely, the definition of necessary labor is a definition which is already social.[76]

To say "determines" is too strong. As we have seen, the monetary form of value has both a content and expression of its own, such that effects on the plane of production produce affects on the monetary plane of a different nature (and vice versa). Nevertheless, the form of value is correlated with the productive process in terms of the degree of command over the labor process. Negri goes on to quote Marx again:

> The *market value* is always different, is always below or above this average value of a commodity. Market value equates itself with real value by means of its constant oscillations, never by means of an equation with real value as if the latter were a third party, but rather by means of constant non-equation of itself (as Hegel would say, not by way of abstract identity, but by constant negation of the negation, i.e., of itself as negation of real value).[77]

"Real value"[78] is described here as a constant emerging from the continuous variation of market value or price. The "constant" is constituted through extraction from a set of variables in continuous variation. "Market value" operates by a continuous oscillation between the degree of command over the labor process and the over-determination of prices.[79] Hence, although there is a relative autonomy of planes, homologies are produced by a complex negotiation of different formalizations and appropriations proper to each plane.

It is not, then, that "value" is too abstract as a concept; rather, it is not abstract enough. In operating by the establishment of constants, it is unable to grasp the continuous variation of variables and their relations from which the constants are extracted.[80] What the expansion of value into its variety of forms does is lead us from exchange to money, and from money to the regulation of the process of production—not as a derivation but as the constitution of an immanent space of politico-economic control.

Conclusion

Much more could be said about the monetary plane, especially about the distribution and proliferation of collective assemblages of enunciation—in the form of central and world banks, the I.M.F., the W.T.O., speculative bodies (e.g., stock markets), etc.—and the impact of computerization/digitalization of financial institutions on the increased consistency and deterritorialization of the monetary body. I hope, however, that the space has been opened for precisely such an analysis.

Most importantly, what this return to Marx—if this is what we want to call it—reveals is not so much the continuing veracity of a systematic body of knowledge, the truth of a continuing actuality which it reveals, but the existence of a real *problematic field* that continues to condition a mutating actuality. As Deleuze argues, the virtual conditions of a conditioned actuality do not resemble that actuality—they are of a different nature.[81] They continue to operate by perpetually re-virtualizing, de-stratifying, and re-stratifying a changing reality which they differentiate. Yet Marx shows how, with capitalism, the actual is ever more tightly subsumed by its virtual conditions. Marx discovers a "true problematic" which continues to condition the contemporary systematicity of capital, which, throughout its mutations, returns—ever more closely—to its virtual differential core in order to renew and reconfigure itself in a perpetual negotiation, a continuing redistribution and coercive reappropriation of the heterogeneous series which compose it. But as we approach the core, the space for an alternative set of conducts of time can be glimpsed, opening a space for inconvertibility, for crisis, for a communist practice of time. ▪

....

1 Gilles Deleuze, *Negotiations*, trans. Martin Joughlin (New York: Columbia University Press, 1995), 152 (translation modified).

2 Antonio Negri, *Marx Beyond Marx*, ed. Jim Fleming, trans. Harry Cleaver, Michael Ryan, and Maurizio Viano (New York: Autonomedia, 1991), 40.

3 Manuel De Landa's tediously monotone appropriation of Deleuze and Guattari at least has the virtue of conceding—however unhappily—that the two thinkers "seem to preserve their own stratum, Marxism." *A Thousand Years of Nonlinear History* (New York: Zone Books, 1997), 331 n. 7. This is something that all too many commentators pass over in silence. There are some important exceptions to this situation: see, for example, the work of Jason Read, Nicholas Thoburn, Eugene Holland, and Michael Hardt.

4 Deleuze, Guattari, Badiou, Rancière, Lyotard, Derrida, even Foucault, not to mention Althusser—who of these seminal figures of the poststructuralist turn did not have a productive, long-lasting relationship to Marxism?

5 See Michael Hardt and Antonio Negri, *The Labor of Dionysus: A Critique of the State-Form* (Minneapolis: University of Minnesota Press, 1994), 8.

6 See Karl Marx, *Capital: A Critique of Political Economy*, vol. 1, trans. Ben Fowkes (New York: Penguin, 1990), 169.

7 Michael Hardt and Antonio Negri, *Empire* (Cambridge, MA: Harvard University Press 2000), 354. See also this earlier statement of Negri's in *Marx Beyond Marx:* "The theory of value, as a theory of categorical synthesis, is a legacy of the classics and of the bourgeois mystification which we can easily do without in order to enter the fields of revolution" (23).

8 See, for example, the misuse throughout the Marxist tradition of Marx's "reproduction schema." For a discussion of this, see Ernest Mandel, introduction to *Capital: A Critique of Political Economy*, vol. 2, by Karl Marx, trans. David Fernbach (New York: Penguin, 1978), 31-38 and Roman Rosdolsky, *The Making of Marx's Capital*, trans. Pete Burgess (London: Pluto Press, 1977), part VII, chapter 30.

9 See Marx, *Capital*, vol. 1, 182, as well as Gilles Deleuze and Félix Guattari, "Savages, Barbarians, Civilized Men," in *Anti-Oedipus*, trans. Robert Hurley, Mark Seem, and Helen R. Lane (Minneapolis, University of Minnesota Press, 1990), 139-271. To begin with, exchange plays an extra-economic function of alliance. When, however, the effects of this form of exchange hit a certain critical threshold, they feed back into the interior, linking exchange to production (and its relations) and drawing alliance into an economic function. A threshold is hit which modifies qualitatively the practices themselves.

10 This is what Marx calls the simple or isolated form of the appearance of value. For his discussion of this relation, see Marx, *Capital*, vol. 1, 139-154. The various forms emerge as different thresholds of relative deterritorialization are reached. On the notion of a "passive synthesis," see Gilles Deleuze, *Difference and Repetition*, trans. Paul Patton (New York: Columbia Press, 1994), 70-128.

11 For a discussion of "incorporeal transformations" see Gilles Deleuze and Félix Guattari, *A Thousand Plateaus*, trans. Brian Massumi (Minneapolis: University of Minnesota Press, 1987), 80-83.

12 This is what Marx calls the total or expanded form of value. See Marx, *Capital*, vol. 1, 154-57. The phrase "whole world of commodities" appears on 155.

13 Ibid., 156.

14 Ibid., 162.

15 This is what Marx calls the money-form, although it involves passing via the general form that I do not need to discuss for the purposes of this essay. On the money-form, see ibid., 162-63; for the general form, see ibid., 157-62.The extent to which these monetary forms can be considered to be historically determined is open to question, and it is not a question I want to confront here. It is sufficient that these forms be *temporally* defined, i.e., determined by passive synthesis understood in terms of specific *temporal conducts* (a notion to which I shall return), whether or not they can be ordered chronologically.

16 Ibid., 163.

17 Georges Dumézil, cited in Deleuze and Guattari, *A Thousand Plateaus*, 352.

18 With the notion of the "double pincer" I am referring to Deleuze and Guattari's discussion of "double articulation" in Deleuze and Guattari, "10,000 B.C.: The Geology of Morals," in *A Thousand Plateaus*, 39-74.

19 Though this will be qualified below by indicating that, strictly speaking, it is the *value-form* which reterritorializes labor, for value exists only in its variety of forms (price, wage, profit, etc.).

20 In effect, the economy here operates as an essence, such that change can only be predicated on the transformations of the economic base. Even classes—and their struggles—are seen purely as functions of these economic laws, functionally subsumed to the *telos* inscribed in their development.

21 This is an aspect of the critique Marx directs against "time-chits," both in Karl Marx, *Grun-*

drisse, trans. Martin Nicolaus (New York: Penguin, 1973) and Karl Marx, *The Poverty of Philosophy*, trans. H. Quelch (New York: Prometheus Books, 1995). See also Étienne Balibar, *The Philosophy of Marx*, trans. Chris Turner (New York: Verso, 1995), 61.

22 Of theoretical importance both here and in what follows is the thesis of the externality of relations to their terms, which Deleuze derives from the philosophy of David Hume. See Gilles Deleuze, *Empiricism and Subjectivity: An Essay on Hume's Theory of Human Nature*, trans. Constantin V. Boundas (New York: Columbia University Press, 1991), 101-4.

23 Félix Guattari and Eric Alliez, "Capitalistic Systems, Structures and Processes," in Félix Guattari, *Molecular Revolution: Psychiatry and Politics* trans. Rosemary Sheed (New York: Penguin, 1984), 275.

24 For an example of such a historical analysis, see Marx's analysis of the working day in the first volume of *Capital* (340-416).

25 Historically, difference was always reterritorialized upon a particular commodity used for exchange, which had the dual role of element in an exchange and use-value external to its purely economic function—e.g., the use of tobacco as money in Virginia, a function it maintained for two centuries, far longer than the gold standard. See John Kenneth Galbraith, *Money: Whence it Came, Where it Went* (London: Penguin, 1977), 48-50.

26 I have simplified somewhat, as the planes are at least three: differential monetary plane, plane of circulation (of commodities and money as medium of exchange), and plane of production.

27 Deleuze and Guattari, *A Thousand Plateaus*, 86.

28 On the "occupant without a place" and the "empty place," see Gilles Deleuze, "Sixth Series on Serialization," *The Logic of Sense*, trans. Mark Lester and Charles Stivale (New York: Columbia University Press, 1990), 36-41.

29 Ibid., 39.

30 For example, variations in "structural" unemployment at different degrees, inflationary variations, differences in intensity of production, varieties of taxation, interest rate changes, etc. These correlations are maintained by series of axioms.

31 "Each commodity 'counts' simultaneously as a fraction of the total stream of income deriving from the total product and as a fraction of the total doing involved in producing the total product." Bruce Roberts, "The Visible and the Measurable: Althusser and the Marxian Theory of Value," in *Postmodern Materialism and the Future of Marxist Theory*, ed. Antonio Callari and David F. Ruccio (Hanover: Wesleyan University Press, 1996), 198.

32 For example, wage, profit, interest, rent, etc. Negri's discussion of causality in relation to Spinoza and Althusser is important in this respect. Antonio Negri, "Notes on the Evolution of the Thought of the Later Althusser," in *Postmodern Materialism and the Future of Marxist Theory*, 51-68. See esp. 61.

33 Deleuze, *The Logic of Sense*, 49.

34 "When we talk about banking power, concentrated most notably in the central banks, it is indeed a question of the relative power to regulate 'as much as' possible the communication, conversion, and coadaptation of the two parts of the circuit. That is why power centers are defined much more by what escapes them or by their impotence than by their zone of power." Deleuze and Guattari, *A Thousand Plateaus*, 217.

35 Marx, *Capital*, vol. 1, 188, 189.

36 Ibid., 196.

37 Ibid.

38 For example, the economic as essence, labor as its humanist correlate. On this point, see

Louis Althusser and Étienne Balibar, *Reading Capital*, trans. Ben Brewster (New York: Verso, 1979).

39 Deleuze, *The Logic of Sense*, 39.

40 On the notion of "axiomatics," see Deleuze and Guattari, *Anti-Oedipus*, 240-262.

41 There is a third determination of money, which may perhaps be called finance money; it is the object of speculative investments. This flow is segmented by an increasingly mobile and flexible axiomatic; by the increasing contraction of monetary onto temporal flows, time itself becomes both the tool and the object of speculation. This third form may be seen as a mutation of the first form (money of account) or as an instance of this first form at a particular degree of deterritorialization and autonomization, although more needs to be said about this.

42 Central banks are one of these agencies proper to the monetary sphere, which aim to maintain the convertibility of money as measure of value with money as means of circulation.

43 Marx, *Capital*, vol. 1, 216.

44 For the sake of clarity, I assume that all other relevant variables remain constant, crucially that the production time necessary for the production of other commodities remains the same as prior to gold's fall in value.

45 For the conceptualization of Integrated World Capitalism, see Guattari and Alliez, "Capitalistic Systems, Structures and Processes"; Félix Guattari, "Plan for the Planet," *Molecular Revolution: Psychiatry and Politics*, trans. Rosemary Sheed (New York: Penguin, 1984), 262-272; and Félix Guattari and Toni Negri, *Communists Like Us: New Spaces of Liberty, New Lines of Alliance*, trans. Michael Ryan (New York: Semiotext(e), 1990), 47-74.

46 Antonio Negri, *Pipe-Line. Lettere da Rebibbia* (Turin: Einaudi, 1983), 130 (my translation).

47 Ibid.

48 Marx, *Capital*, vol. 1, 200.

49 Ibid., 209. See also Marx, *Grundrisse*, 197-8.

50 This is not the subsumption of one correlate to the other, for the correlates are both commodities and means of circulation. The two are reterritorialized across money as measure and differentiator of command.

51 "They are defined only by their mutual solidarity, and neither of them can be identified otherwise. They are defined only oppositively and relatively, as mutually opposed functives of one and the same function." Louis Hjelmslev, *Prolegomena to a Theory of Language*, trans. Francis J. Whitfield (Madison: University of Wisconsin Press, 1969), 60, cited in Deleuze and Guattari, *A Thousand Plateaus*, 45.

52 Marx, *Capital*, vol. 1, 255.

53 Ibid., 218, note.

54 See Karl Marx, "Postface to the Second Edition," *Capital*, vol. 1, 102.

55 Marx, *Capital*, vol. 1, 216.

56 Agencies of anti-production are not alien to production. They are elements of redundancy proper to each assembled plane that operate by maintaining specific correlations and producing incorporeal transformations. Cf. Deleuze and Guattari, *Anti-Oedipus*, 7-8.

57 Marx, *Capital*, vol. 1, 287.

58 This recoding does not transform the material properties of the product. It substitutes itself for it whilst allowing it a continued existence on other planes.

59 Marx, *Capital*, vol. 1, 287.

60 Ibid., 285.

61 Antonio Negri, "The Constitution of Time," *Time for Revolution*, trans. Matteo Mandarini (New York: Continuum, 2003), 107.

62 Ibid.

63 "Wherever we have no successive perceptions, we have no notion of time, even tho' there be a real succession in the objects. From these phænomena, as well as many others, we may conclude, that time cannot make its appearance in the mind, either alone, or attended with a steady unchangeable object, but is always discover'd by some *perceivable* succession of changeable objects." David Hume, *A Treatise of Human Nature* (Oxford: Clarendon Press, 1987), 35. Cf. Deleuze, *Empiricism and Subjectivity*, 92-6 and Deleuze, *Difference and Repetition*, 70-79.

64 The fundamental modification which Deleuze initiates, is the substitution of "sensitive plate," "passive synthesis," "recording surface," etc. for "mind" in order to displace the centrality of conscious perception by what he calls the "primary sensibility" of "organic syntheses," so that any encounter produces a sign, an affect. This is also in order to rigorously determine a difference in kind between the connections on the plane of immanence and the produced synthesis. See Deleuze, *Difference and Repetition*, 70-3.

65 Ibid., 70.

66 By "subject" we should merely understand the emergent point-of-view on the "world," defined precisely through the *practice "of"* difference-contraction. ("Of" is to be understood here "in the two senses of a genitive belonging both inside and outside the concept." Eric Alliez, *Capital Times: Tales from the Conquest of Time*, trans. Georges Van Den Abbeele [Minneapolis: University of Minnesota Press, 1996], xv.)

67 Deleuze and Guattari, *A Thousand Plateaus*, 313.

68 See Alliez, *Capital Times*, and Gilles Deleuze's "Foreword" to that volume (xi-xiii).

69 Deleuze and Guattari, *Anti-Oedipus*, 7.

70 Deleuze, *Difference and Repetition*, 76-7.

71 Deleuze and Guattari, *Anti-Oedipus*, 7.

72 For example, the time of circulation is overdetermined by the time of production, the size and velocity of the money supply, interest rates on borrowing—short or long term, etc.; the time of production is overdetermined by the efficiency of technical segmentation of labor, the intensity of surveillance of the labor-process, the degree of organization of labor, the mobility of labor, the size of the industrial reserve army, etc.

73 Heterogeneous practices have heterogeneous temporal consistencies, whereas the capitalist axiomatic always realizes itself in a particular domain with its own *model* of realization (determined by the assemblages which stratify it). Thus the axioms will differ in accordance with the assemblages composing a social formation. Nevertheless, "the difference and independence of the axioms in no way compromise the consistency of an overall axiomatic." Deleuze and Guattari, *A Thousand Plateaus*, 465.

74 Marx, *Capital*, vol. 1, 326.

75 Negri, *Marx Beyond Marx*, 23.

76 Ibid., 29. The embedded citation is from Marx, *Grundrisse*, 135. Value is "determined" by the degree (of efficiency) of the exploitation of labor, i.e., the efficacy of command and regulation structures within the productive process.

77 Marx, Grundrisse, 137, cited in Negri, *Marx Beyond Marx*, 29.

78 Where "real value" is defined as the average socially necessary labor time, i.e., the degree of disciplining of (social) labor, over a set period of time.

79 Prices are overdetermined by: the rate of exploitation or control of the production process, both generally and in particular sectors (e.g., gold production); the quantity and velocity of

the circulating medium; the quantity of commodities in circulation; currency speculation; interest rate shifts; security of investment; political equilibrium; etc.

80 "Anything but a metaphysics of value! Marx leaves that to his predecessors, and too often as well to those who follow him." Negri, *Marx Beyond Marx*, 29.

81 For a succinct determination of the "problematic" as "the reality of the virtual," see Deleuze, *Difference and Repetition*, 280-1.

Grief Time: The Crisis of Narrative in Don DeLillo's *The Body Artist*

Rachel Smith

Biopolitical theory has been instrumental in contributing a rare quality of hope to contemporary life. This is no small accomplishment; our current moment has been marked by a profound theoretical and practical hopelessness. This new optimism has emerged primarily out of the development of various concepts of *potentiality*, or of productive possibility already immanent to structures of labor, politics, and ontological experience in general. The political task is thus reoriented away from the project of imagining what could reside outside of the various systems that govern contemporary life and toward the possibility that lies unexpressed inside those systems. Implicit, then, in these potentialities, are new ways of thinking about futurity. Significant work has already begun on a project of destabilizing traditional conceptions of politics as determined by the sum total of history, undermining linear assumptions about narrative, and contributing to a concept of the *to-come* that is not bound by the discursive rules of the past.[1]

Potential, located in the present state of things, opens up the future for new forms of radical action, commonality, and life. However, if the future is open, it is empty both of the constraints of the past and of the habitual forms of action that protect and insure us a safe passage from day to day, decade to decade. There is thus a temporal dark side to potentiality: once the future is no longer assumed to be automatic, life itself can no longer be imagined as safe, predictable, or continuous. Just as there is always death inherent in life, there is always loss inherent in potential. Just as the recognition of that potential leads to optimism in light of possibility, it also leads to grief in the face of loss. How can we come to terms with this grief at the heart of hope? Furthermore, can we conceive of grief itself as a site from which potential life can emerge?

The Body Artist I: Narrative and Time

Don DeLillo's *The Body Artist* poses these questions within the temporal constraints of a novel, albeit a novel that pushes against its own narrative structure in substantive ways. In *The Body Artist*, the event of a death creates a temporal and sensory rupture that necessitates the construction of new life in the face of its instability and emptiness. However, the novel shows that the awareness of this emptiness does not automatically lead to the production of new forms of engagement. Though the future *is* exposed by loss as a kind of restless void, the pain that accompanies the process creates a kind of pausing, a life within the rupture, before a new life can be constructed. This grief-life resides on the border between life and not-life. It is a blank spot, a white space before the capacity to act. In so being, it is both a dangerous moment of emptiness and the material of radically productive potential. *The Body Artist* links grief to time, and in doing so enacts it as an ontological rather than a psychological state. It produces the grief-void that is often understood as radically subjective, but does so by constructing grief as a material state of being rather than an emotional experience belonging to a particular subject. In doing so, the novel renders grief common, and thus potentially politically productive.

After her husband Rey's suicide, the novel's central character, Lauren, immediately recognizes the problem of grief as connected to the problem of time. She passes the days mechanically, compulsively attached to markers of time such as ferry schedules and breathing exercises. Her plan to "organize time until she could live again"[2] rests on a disassociation between life and time, as if time proceeds regardless of whether or not a life moves it forward. However, this assumption is called into question by the appearance of a strange young man in Lauren's home. He has no name or identity, he speaks through citation, and even his physical appearance is washed out and ageless. His lack of stable subject position is linked to his lack of capacity to distinguish between past, present, and future. As a result, he relives past and future moments as others, becoming them through speech and gesture. After he becomes Rey in this manner, Lauren looks to this possibility of stopping time, of living perpetually in a group of always-present and palpable simultaneous moments, as a way of life that could allow her to avoid leaving the dead behind. Confronted by the possibility of living in co-existent presents without moving into the future, away from Rey and into his absence, Lauren experiments with giving herself over entirely to grief. As she allies herself with the young man, Lauren literally scrubs layers off of her skin, bleaches her hair, and de-pigments herself to the point where she becomes "colorless, bloodless and ageless."[3] As she connects the young man's capacity to live in overlapping temporal states with an inability to experience time as a stable fabric of normative duration, she too rejects both identity and narrative in favor of retreat, pausing and stretching the present until it encompasses past and future.

However, this pausing threatens to become stasis. This is apparent in the young man, who cries in his room late at night, "alone and unable to improvise, make himself up."[4] While pushing forward against the unknown and resisting narrative conceptions of time is vital to innovation and production, bivouacking oneself in the void hinders ethical action just as much as traditional complacency does. This is the danger of abandoning signification and subjectification entirely. Life must exist through means other than either total rejection of normative experiences of time, narrative, and subjectivity or complacent participation in the status quo. *The Body Artist*, however, appears to offer these two options for possible ways of living through loss—either to "organize time" or to "[s]ink lower. … Let it bring you down. Go where it takes you."[5] The problem of grief in the novel is the problem of anchoring an active life in an abyss of meaninglessness. The temptation to dive into that abyss and make a home there is linked with the presence of the dead in that place; there time does not pass, life does not push forward, and subsequently the living and the dead can coexist.

It is this empty center, where signification and subjectification fall away, where all that is left is stammering, wailing, and despair, that the young man inhabits in *The Body Artist*. Despair, as it is materialized in the character of the young man, is essentially this stopping in the interstice, the refusal to allow time to pass into action, the inhabiting of the void for its own sake. For that reason, while he disrupts habit, his presence ultimately threatens nihilism and suicide. At the same time, for Lauren, he is a catalyst for creative manipulation of temporality through art. Becoming the young man aesthetically—by altering her body, speaking in his voice, and eventually constructing a performance piece (her body-art) in which she lip-synchs to the conversations she has recorded with him—is, for Lauren, somewhere between capitulation to narrative norms and capitulation to despair. In this way, it embodies the ambivalence at the heart of grief. While her work is a failure in that it does not and cannot stall time completely,[6] in becoming art it refuses to reside in total absence of action and instead throws itself out upon the world. The creative work mirrors the process of grief in that it emerges out of something inarticulable and yet insists that it must speak, even if that speech is like the young man's: incoherent, high and squeaky, and cluttered with disjunctive tenses.

Lauren's art is necessarily a failure in this sense, but the failure itself is deeply important. As Giorgio Agamben suggests, the very act of attempting to communicate and failing at that attempt exposes the communicative medium in all of its potentiality. The gesture toward communication "is, in this sense, communication of communicability. It has precisely nothing to say because what it shows is the being-in-language of human beings as pure mediality."[7] Thus, means and ends are detached from one another in gestural work. The attempt to say becomes more important than the communication of one thing or another. In this way, by pausing the linear progression of narrative time, grief provides the obstruction to communication in Lauren's piece that allows it to point towards the struggle to communicate and the impossibility of containing time, affect, and the body entirely within a single narrative system. However, gesture is not akin to nihilism. The performance of the attempt is as much a gesture toward the relentless pursuit of life as it is the performance of the impossibility to communicate. Hence, grief in *The Body Artist* is a deeply ambivalent state of being, producing detachment from everyday life on one hand and a vigorous commitment to it on the other.

Of course, DeLillo's work is, in this way, itself a gesture. When the novel finally pushes Lauren out into the world, the narrative suddenly surrenders to expectations of the novel form that it otherwise resists until the final page. In the final paragraph, just as Lauren opens her bedroom window to feel "the flow of time in her body, to tell her who she was," she is also given a psychological history for the first time. Suddenly, the phrase "[h]er mother died when she was nine"[8] drops into the text almost as a non sequitur. While the novel resists attributing grief to the emotional life of a single subject until the final lines, in order to put Lauren back into life, the form of the novel requires that she be put back into narrative, and thus the material and ontological state of grief must become "her grief," comfortably contained within a subject.

Hence, the novel is restricted by its own structural constraints and ultimately succumbs to the narrative temporal requirements of the novel form. The ambivalence of the void cannot be maintained in the novel because the void cannot be articulated until it is comfortably codified. However, while DeLillo's novel fails, its very failure points to the value of the attempt to keep the tension between the void and action dynamic, to communicate the places where speech falls away and point to the necessity of regaining words.

Good Grief

Biopolitical theory has provided a basis for rethinking the binary between private states (emotions and affects) on one hand and public states (labor and politics) on the other. From Paolo Virno's work on the politics of cynicism and opportunism to Michael Hardt and Antonio Negri's analysis of affective labor, the production of affects is a central concern of biopolitical thought. However, this consideration has been limited in several ways. First, having freed affects from the constraints of the psychological disciplines, many biopolitical theorists simply reinstate the affects exclusively in the realms of labor and political economy. For instance, while Virno states that "[w]ith the expression 'emotional situation' I do not refer, let it be clear, to a cluster of psychological tendencies, but to ways of being and feeling so pervasive that they end up being common to the most diverse categories of experience (work, leisure, feelings, politics, etc.),"[9] his analysis of these emotions is concerned primarily with their implications for wage labor. Similarly, while biopower, according to Hardt and Negri's analysis of Foucault, is "expressed as a control that extends throughout the depths of the consciousness and bodies of the population—and at the same time across the entirety of social relations,"[10] the analysis that follows focuses on the manner in which biopower changes the conditions and meaning of labor and politics rather than examining the ways in which formerly personal aspects of life emerge as political forces.

The most notable exception to this trend has appeared in recent work that attempts to extend the significance of love beyond the confines of the couple form and into the political sphere. Hardt and Negri argue in *Multitude* that love can be understood as the constitutive force of the multitude, a position Negri examines further in *Time for Revolution*. The central argument of the book is a temporal one. Negri argues that time does not consist of a predictable linear path, but is instead an unpredictable series of ruptures that constitute creative production. Time progresses only through the construction of a "to-come" that emerges out of a direct confrontation with time as restless and immeasurable. Thus, the future does not occur automatically, and the present is always on the brink of a great void to be filled only with the immanent production of the lives within it. Negri, drawing from classical sources, terms this production of the to-come out of the confrontation with the void of time "*kairòs*." He explains, "*kairòs* is the instant, that is to say, the quality of time in the instant, the moment of rupture and opening of temporality. … *Kairòs* is the modality of time through which being opens itself, attracted by the void at the limit of time, and it thus decides to fill that void."[11] Ordinary linear spatializations of time territorialize the to-come by constructing a concept of "the future" which is nothing but the sum total of past events. *Kairòs*, according to Negri, is the "power to experience temporality" itself, freed from these metaphors. This liberation of the to-come catalyzes creative action precisely because the lack of durational future allows for the construction of love, since "love is not infinite but eternal, not measure but immeasurable, not individual but singular, not universal but common."[12] Love requires the immeasurability and eternality of time to be exposed in order to exist.

In the text, Negri begins to address the second limitation that has heretofore constrained biopolitical articulations of emotion: the avoidance of concepts of pain. The influence of Spinoza on biopolitical theory often leads to analyses that focus only on the joyful emotions, those that augment the capacity for action, since "as long as the mind thinks of those things that increase or assist our body's power of acting, so long is the body affected in ways that increase or assist its power of activity."[13] Therefore, ethical philosophy in a Spinozan sense should itself be joyful, or as Gilles Deleuze argues, "[e]thical *joy* is the correlate of speculative affirmation."[14] Despite this, Negri is aware of a necessary passage from the recognition of the immeasurability of time and the affirmative power of love. He defines the state of being that is most open, most exposed to the immeasurable, and thus most ready to be filled with the full force of love, *poverty*. He explains, "When he appears before us, the poor person is naked on the edge of being, without any alternative."[15] And yet, Negri almost instantaneously moves the state of poverty away from deprivation, pain, or sadness. He argues, "The poor person is then not someone constituted by pain, but is *in reality* the biopolitical subject. He is not an existential trembling (or a painful dialectical differentiation): he is the naked eternity of the power of being."[16] Finally, though the poor are confronted with the total openness of time, and thus total loss of meaning, and though their very bodies teeter on the edge of existence, the very concept of poverty, according to Negri, "excludes that of death in as much as, in order to live, the poor have already overcome death. The poor have put death behind themselves: the common is exalted by this realization."[17] The potential inherent in the recognition of the essential ambivalence of the openness to the immeasurable, the simultaneous potential and pain, promise and danger, is thus glossed over into a thin utopianism in Negri's argument.

When Spinoza argues that "a free man thinks of death least of all things, and his wisdom is a meditation of life, not of death,"[18] he does so to persuade thought away from sadness, which, in contradistinction to joy, limits our power to act. However, to contemplate contemporary politics is to be confronted with the corporeal realities of pain and death, and to engage with the destruction of meaning is to engage with loss. Hence, the contemplation of joy and love must include the contemplation of loss or grief. The term *grief* has yet to be invested with biopolitical significance, despite its potential to embody the myriad ambivalent states of pain that emerge from engagement with life. While grief is the affective state of having-lost, it is not synonymous with sadness or despair, nor does it lead automatically into the state of joy or love. It is the ambivalent state of in-between, the durational pause between the habitual participation in the status quo and the capacity for creative production in the world. Grief is imbedded in the body; it is the condition of dismantling stable structures of meaning.[19] Its biopolitical potential emerges from the following aspects of the concept:

1 *Grief is temporal.* Grief has the temporal quality of *pausing*. It interrupts the habitual action-reaction circuits of life by intervening on the level of the brain and the body. For this reason, it delinks time from its mediating spatial structures and exposes its indeterminacy and discontinuity. When Deleuze argues that the beginning of the time-image in cinema is contingent upon a situation which "does not extend into action," which "makes us grasp … something intolerable and unbearable,"[20] he implicitly links time and grief. The shock of grief is the shock of time; the disruption of movement and spatial relations results in the direct exposure of time. However, this exposure of time does not automatically extend into action. There is a pause in the void before action can occur. This pausing is a necessary temporal addition to the concept of *kairòs*. The rupture, the leaning off into the void, itself has duration, and as such involves pausing or stretching out the delay between perception and action, interpretation, and engagement. The pausing of grief, the shattering of the capacity for action, renders this temporality visible.

2 *Grief is not limited to a subject/object relation.* The psychoanalytic understanding of grief as a subjective pathological condition limits its expression to an alienated individual experience and thus constrains its potential as a site for the production of forms of political resistance. While recent theoretical works have successfully politicized Freud's work on mourning and melancholia, pointing to the centrality of loss in politics of war, colonization, and race,[21] the corresponding project of politicizing the inevitable pain at the heart of biopolitical concepts of potentiality requires a distinct conceptual vocabulary that acknowledges the need to free affective concepts from psychoanalytic subjective and temporal constraints. Thus, grief is understood as a non-subjective force that is the inevitable consequence of potentiality. It does not belong to a subject but is a material force contingent upon the lives that produce it.

3 *Grief emerges out of an event or moment of rupture.* The cloaking of the restlessness of time in narrative and spatial metaphors is not simply a philosophical misconception; it is a precondition for the survival of the sociopolitical status quo. The immeasurableness of productive power in the futureless present is a threat to regimes of control precisely because it is always immanent within those very control structures. The stakes are high for maintaining the

illusion of the future as predictable, certain, and already-present. Therefore, the unveiling of the instability of time cannot occur without a catalyst, an event, or a rupture that points to the immeasurability of time itself. Even if it does not take the form of a death event, the very definition of a rupture suggests that something changes dramatically, and thus something is lost, the world changes, a life no longer seems consistent, predictable, and safe. In the loosest sense, then, all ruptures are grief-producing. Recognizing this ambivalence in the disruption of control mechanisms, Gilles Deleuze and Félix Guattari point to the inevitable difficulty of moving beyond ordering strata: "in the absence of strata we no longer have forms or substances, organization or development, content or expression. We are disarticulated. … How could unformed matter, anorganic life, nonhuman becoming be anything but chaos pure and simple?"[22] Thus, disarticulation and chaos are never easily negotiated. However, their very difficulty makes them potentially productive.

4 *Grief is ambivalent.* Grief is always *between* one form of life and another, the before and the to-come. It unsettles because it marks the end of something, but in so doing, it points outside of itself toward an unknown to-come. Grief also always vacillates between *acceptance* (reterritorialization of the event) and *despair* (total deterritorialization in the wake of the event). While it can settle in either of those states, once it does it ceases to be grief. Grief itself is the refusal to accept and the refusal to be destroyed, the uncertainty that one can go on and the continuance of life in the face of that uncertainty. In this sense, it insists upon the difficult posture of the body on the brink of choice and the resistance to categorization that makes corporeal life both so difficult to theorize and so useful to theoretical discourse as such. The undecidability on the brink of decision should not simply resolve into the sum total of a rational cause/effect analysis, nor should it result in a blind jump into the unknown. The ambivalence that vacillates between acceptance and despair must resolve into *belief* that is neither rational-habitual nor chaotic-suicidal. This irrational will to construct links with a painful and essentially meaningless world can emerge only from the corporeal insistence that one go on despite so much evidence to the contrary. This is the direct consequence of Spinoza's conatus, which insists that "each thing, in so far as it is in itself, endeavors to persist in its own being."[23] This desire is not rational in that it does not necessarily conform to any prior categories of whether that being is good or bad. Rather, "we judge a thing to be good because we endeavor, will, seek after and desire it."[24] The very insistence upon life when that life is indeterminate, meaningless, and painful suggests that we judge life to be "good" despite all evidence. This irrational belief can only be conveyed through the body, as the material of life that exceeds narrative categories of knowledge at the same time as it persistently anchors life in the world. For that reason, only the living body can encompass the ambivalence necessary to both destabilize categories that constrain us and continue to engage in the world that is always marked by those constraints.

The Body Artist II: The Word and the Body

What does it mean to construct this body through language, particularly through the narrative language of a novel? Must we understand the body produced by a novel as always less than a body, contained within language and thus lacking that excess that calls narrative categories of time into question? While *The Body Artist* performs the insufficiency of the narrative form to allow for corporeal ambivalence on a macro level, it also performs a productive tension between words and bodies on a micro level, and points to a potential role for narrative in theorizing the relationship between knowledge and belief, the word and the body.

Words and the body are often portrayed as opposing forces in *The Body Artist*. This occurs, for instance, in the passage that immediately follows Rey's death. It begins with a view of the highway:

> Everything is slow and hazy and drained and it all happens around the word *seem*. All the cars including yours seem to flow in dissociated motion, giving the impression of or presenting the appearance of, and the highway runs in a white hum. … Then the mood passes. The noise and rush and blur are back and you slide into your life again, feeling the painful weight in your chest.[25]

Here, words allow for a withdrawal from corporeality into a space of simile. Things become signifiers, pointing elsewhere beyond their own concrete role in the world, and, as words become detached from action, time slows down. When "you slide into your life again," it happens through a reconnection with the body, "the painful weight in your chest." Hence, the "seeming" that requires a word-center is opposed to "life," which relies upon a body-center. Here, again, the body is associated with grief, anchoring ambivalent attachment to experience through pain and its connection to life.

Grief in the novel exposes this fraught relationship between words and the body. As Lauren attempts to shed her subjectivity entirely, she paradoxically begins to narrate her own experience: "She thought in words sometimes, outright and fully formed."[26] She even begins to give herself instructions, directly attempting to shape her experience through narrative: "Sink lower, she thought. Let it bring you down. Go where it takes you. … Sometimes she thought in these motive forms, addressing someone who wasn't quite her. … I am Lauren. But less and less."[27] Ultimately, when the moment comes for Lauren to choose between the infinite stopping-in-the-void of despair and the acceptance of life (here, figured as a return to narrative forms of subjectivity and time), this dissociative discourse returns with a vengeance and shapes the final episode of the novel.

In the final pages of the novel, Lauren resolves her flirtation with different forms of temporal experience into an absolute certainty that Rey is alive. She climbs the steps to their bedroom, knowing that "Rey was intact, in his real body, smoke in his hair and his clothes."[28] In the movement from this ambivalence to the certainty that Rey is present, narrativity exceeds the limits of corporeal belief. She is already aware of this abstractly before the scene plays out: "She knew how it would happen, past the point of playing it through, because she refused to yield to the limits of belief."[29] It is at this point that the language of the novel switches from a description of physical sensation to a series of dissociative directives which emphasize the shaping power of narrative. This transition from corporeal belief to narrative knowledge is essentially the transformation of a sensation into a knowable certainty. This produces tension immediately between the body and words: "Once she steps into the room, she will already have been there, now, at night, getting undressed. It is a question of fitting herself to the moment."[30] At this point, the novel begins to produce two Laurens, one who is physically present with Rey in the room, who "will already have been there, now," and the other who narrates the scene without looking, who tells herself what she will see if she looks into the bedroom.

This splitting becomes increasingly apparent as Lauren refuses to look into the room, "aware of the look on her face."[31] Again and again, this awareness of her own face stops her from physically joining in on the story that she tells of Rey and Lauren alive and together in the bedroom just beyond the doorway where she stands:

> But before she stepped into the room, she could feel the look on her face. She knew this look, a frieze of false anticipation. … She stood a while, thinking into this. She stopped at room's edge, facing back into the hall, and felt the emptiness around her. That's when she rocked down to the floor, backed against the doorpost. She went twisting down, slowly, almost thoughtfully, and opened her mouth, *oh*, in a moan that remained unsounded. She sat on the floor outside her room. Her face still wore a decorative band, a trace across the eyes of the prospect of wonders. It was a look that nearly floated free of her so she could puff her cheeks, childlike, and blow it away.[32]

In this passage, belief exceeds the constraints of the narrative Lauren attempts to impose and becomes a visceral reaction, an unsounded moan, a corporeal awareness of the emptiness that narrative cannot contain. The look on her face, of which she is persistently aware because she is narrating her own presence in the story, becomes merely an aesthetic accoutrement that signifies nothing more than her own capacity to shape the world in words, to make things *seem*. However, there is nothing *seeming* in the physical decision to look into the room and find it empty. Her body twists, she moves slowly but not purposefully as she falls, and then, "thinking into the blankness of her decision, … she worked herself up along the doorpost, slowly, breathing completely, her back to the fluted wood, squat-rising, drawing the act over an extended length of time."[33] This movement, which echoes her body-art in its conscious gesturality, arises out of a "blankness," a total corporeal commitment to the action in and of itself. This belief that emerges out of the body, rather than being imposed upon it, leads her to the empty bedroom that has no trace of Rey. Here, the body is in some sense ahead of the narrative shaping of the world in words. This physical engagement with the room leads her to see that "[s]he'd known it was empty all along but was only catching up."[34] Again, the limit that corporeality interposes resists narrative withdrawal into description and insists upon an engagement with the world, with loss, and with the postures of the body. Thus, the tendency for the "rational" to detach itself from the body through the process of signification is undermined through the confrontation with the demands of corporeal life.

Circulation and the Cultural Politics of Time

The Body Artist performs the insufficiency of language from the level of the letter to the level of the arc of narrative. While the novel ultimately exposes the weakness of narrative, capitulating when it is faced with the need to propel the pausing of grief into action, the negotiation of the word and the body constructs a productive tension that takes the body beyond the word. However, this body is itself constructed in language, and thus the novel does have a role in offering a theoretical model of the body, even if that role is fraught with perpetual tension. Constructing the body in novels allows for the parallel construction of radical temporalities out of ambivalent corporeal states, grief being just one such state.

While these temporalities are pivotal in and of themselves for the role they play in opening up the future, the fact that they are constructed in cultural media is vital for that role to be a political one. Cultural works, such as novels, circulate. They move between readers, constructing social networks and commonalities to constitute what Michael Warner defines as *publics*: not national or spatial publics, but "the kind of public that comes into being only in relation to texts and their circulation."[35] In doing so, they construct more than just discourse or relationships; they construct modes of being, forms of life, and a shared connection to the world that they bring into existence. Furthermore, they are a challenge to dominant publics, "those that can take their discourse pragmatics and lifeworlds for granted, misrecognizing the indefinite scope of their expansive address as universality or normalcy."[36] And yet, their challenge occurs on a different register than that of formal politics. Cultural works can play with ontological assumptions, construct and deconstruct temporal and affective states, precisely because they are not works of political theory. This allows them to skirt around what is, according to Warner, the greatest danger to "counterpublics" that threaten the status quo: that "they enter the temporality of politics and adapt themselves to the performatives of rational-critical discourse."[37]

Hence, grief itself is not a political force, but the construction of temporalities of grief in cultural products that circulate *is*. A text that circulates a temporal experience of grief has the possibility of producing the ontological conditions of corporeal belief without the concrete loss of an object. This is not to say that grief becomes, in this sense, detached from anguish or instability, but rather that grief becomes a temporality of instability and pain rather than the concrete experience of a lost object. Thus, a state that is understood to be prohibitively private and individual becomes public, common, and potentially political. If political control functions in part by restricting the perceivable openness of the future, then the circulation of competing temporalities in the form of cultural products has potentially far-reaching political consequences. In this way, the politics of time suggests a role for cultural works that exceeds explicit political content. Temporalities are constructed through the very formal qualities of these works, and, through their circulation, a public challenge to the dominant narrative experience of time can evolve. That ontological formation is itself a potentially radical force in contemporary political life. ▪

....

1 See in particular Elizabeth Grosz, *Time Travels: Feminism, Nature, Power* (Durham: Duke

University Press, 2005); Giorgio Agamben, *The Time that Remains: A Commentary on the Letter to the Romans*, trans. Patricia Daily (Palo Alto, CA: Stanford University Press, 2006); and Antonio Negri, *Time for Revolution*, trans. Matteo Mandarini (London: Continuum, 2003), among others.

2 Don DeLillo, *The Body Artist* (New York: Scribner, 2001), 37.

3 Ibid., 103.

4 Ibid., 90.

5 Ibid., 116.

6 She tells an interviewer: "'It ought to be sparer, even slower than it is, even longer than it is. It ought to be three fucking hours.'" Ibid., 106.

7 Giorgio Agamben, "Notes on Gesture," in *Means Without End*, trans. Vincenzo Binetti and Cesare Casarino (Minneapolis, MN: University of Minnesota, 2000), 59.

8 DeLillo, *The Body Artist*, 124.

9 Paulo Virno, *A Grammar of the Multitude*, trans. Isabella Bertoletti, James Cascaito, and Andrea Casson (Los Angeles: Semiotext[e], 2004), 84.

10 Michael Hardt and Antonio Negri, *Empire* (Cambridge, MA: Harvard University Press, 2000), 24.

11 Negri, *Time for Revolution*, 152.

12 Ibid., 193.

13 Baruch Spinoza, *The Ethics: Treatise on the Emendation of the Intellect; Selected Letters*, ed. Seymour Feldman, trans. Samuel Shirley (Indianapolis, IN: Hackett, 1992), 111.

14 Gilles Deleuze, *Spinoza: Practical Philosophy*, trans. Robert Hurley (San Francisco: City Lights Books, 1988), 29.

15 Negri, *Time for Revolution*, 194.

16 Ibid.

17 Ibid., 197.

18 Spinoza, *Ethics*, 108.

19 Several works of trauma theory have examined the world-destroying and word-destroying power of traumatic experience. Among them are Cathy Caruth, *Unclaimed Experience: Trauma, Narrative, and History* (Baltimore: Johns Hopkins Press, 1996); Shoshanna Felman, *Testimony: Crises of Witnessing in Literature, Psychoanalysis, and History* (New York: Routledge, 1992); and Elaine Scarry, *The Body in Pain* (Oxford: Oxford University Press, 1986). My concept of grief begins from a similar assertion, that the dismantling of forms of signification should be thought of in terms of loss. However, grief, as I conceive of it, is distinct in its immanence to processes of world-making. Grief is productive; it has a central political function in dismantling habitual forms of perception and opening the future to creative action.

20 Gilles Deleuze, *Cinema 2: The Time Image*, trans. Hugh Tomlinson and Robert Galetta (Minneapolis: University of Minnesota Press, 1997), 18.

21 See Judith Butler, *Precarious Life: The Power of Mourning and Violence* (New York: Verso, 2004); David Eng and David Kasanjian ed., *Loss: The Politics of Mourning* (Berkeley, CA: The University of California Press, 2003); and Julia Kristeva, *Black Sun: Depression and Melancholia*, trans. Leon S. Roudiez (New York: Columbia University Press, 1989), among others.

22 Gilles Deleuze and Félix Guattari, *A Thousand Plateaus: Capitalism and Schizophrenia*, trans. Brian Massumi (Minneapolis, MN: University of Minnesota Press, 1987), 503.

23 Spinoza, *Ethics*, 108.

24 Ibid., 109.

25 DeLillo, *The Body Artist*, 31.

26 Ibid., 113.
27 Ibid., 116-7.
28 Ibid., 121.
29 Ibid., 122.
30 Ibid.
31 Ibid., 123.
32 Ibid.
33 Ibid., 124.
34 Ibid.
35 Michael Warner, "Publics and Counterpublics," *Public Culture* 14:1 (Durham: Duke University Press, 2002), 50.
36 Ibid., 88.
37 Ibid., 89.

Matisse and the Becoming-Life of Art

Eric Alliez and Jean-Claude Bonne

How can we define what appears to us as the untimely singularity of Matisse? Through the radicality and daring of his break with art, to the extent that the latter is both inscribed and made in a history and as a history which is that of the (continuous) evolution or the (discontinuous) succession of the diverse forms of the Art-Form—of Art inasmuch as it is defined by Form. This is a history that has constantly (re)written itself in function of the (supposedly) most advanced state of art, thinking itself as the overcoming (of the limits) of a prior moment, a history whose modernist formalism has conceived of itself as the final finality (painting brought back to its essence in the optic of pure pictoriality/planeness). Fauvism (1905-1906) signals a break with this finalized history and, beyond, with the very idea of a History (of art) whose "grand narrative" is built on the idea of a finality that would dialectically orient each of its moments, like so many stages on the way to a conquest or unveiling of its ultimate truth (at the point of identification of the *material* and the *essential*). What opens up then is a new, non-historico-dialectical idea of the temporality of and in art, the operation of which Matisse will not cease delving into in terms of *a becoming that does not produce, that shows nothing but itself, in the events to which it gives body.* So that with fauvism it is becoming that *gives matter* to art—and that *exposes* itself as such—by freeing the Outside (the multiplicity of forces) which, up to that point, had been caught up in representation, enclosed in a Form (the Art-Form).

In so doing Matisse de-monstrates, like no one else before him, the plastic reality of time and the temporality of the event in art—in accordance with a movement which, in each of his works, is so little to be conceived in the image of a "given/giving" (implicating the teleological essence of art) that it dismisses the ideality of the *image* itself in favor of the "consciousness of the forces that one employs," when one moves, "pushed by an idea that one only truly knows to the extent that it develops itself in the procession of the painting."[1] Far from any "reporting" of the mental image, its necessity is a function of the impossibility of a difference/*différance* between conception and its *realization*. Or again: in the absence of a "break between thought and the creative act,"[2] no conception is worthwhile unless it can *(make a) surface* [*faire surface*] in full immanence, through a continuous becoming wherein the principle of composition can only be perceived together with what it composes. It must be emphasized that this processual materialism is at the antipodes of the post-romantic exasperation to which some have sought to reduce fauvism.

In landscape painting, for example, the emergence of this other temporality can be caught in the act. Whether descriptive or sublime, the classical and romantic landscape inscribes itself in the Art-Form of Art, it is the fabulation [*mise-en-récit*] of a view: it encourages a trajectory of the gaze that situates the elements of the landscape in relation to one another in a spatially and temporally coordinated ensemble (these elements are subordinated to a natural locus, at a given time and place, for a determinate point of view which is the one of the spectator "at the window"). History is the development-unveiling of a spatial form, or rather of the formal totality of a space, in a time that makes one perceive without itself being perceived as such (reduced as it is to a *psychological extension*). In turn, each landscape painting is situated in a history of landscape painting whose moments are defined in relation to one another in variable teleologies, depending on whether the accent is placed on the evolution of themes (the variability of perceptions and feelings of nature ...) and/or on that of the manners of painting and the succession of "styles" (realism, impressionism, post-impressionism, cubism, figurative abstraction ...). The fauve "landscape" marks a twofold break with the story-landscape and, correlatively, with pictoriality conceived as the ultimate form of the Art-Form. It presents itself as a total *defenestration* of the Painting-Form, which it *deterritorializes* by making it pass from the aesthetic to the aesthesic.

In a fauve painting like *Landscape at Collioure* (1905, oil on canvas, 39 x 46.2 cm—The Museum of Modern Art, New York), the local/global confrontation of the groups of brush strokes and colored patches produces the disappearance/disparateness [*disparition/disparation*] of landscape *qua* identifiable or emotionally experienced *form* (in accordance with the impressionist and expressionist variants of the landscape). One can neither project a landscape nor project oneself into it as its spectator: perception becomes the deterritorialized agent of these colors-forces at play and in tension in a "landscape" that does not describe or narrate anything, that does not take form because it captures and ex-poses the *becoming-intense of a multiplicity comprising heterogeneous terms the relations of which compose a being of sensation, without either reducing or formalizing the elements in tension.* Its duration is no longer extensive (a spreading out of places in a succession of moments, constituting a beautiful totality) but entirely, and intensively, processual: a diagrammatization of all the forces that make the Painting-Form explode. If the painting does not by any means "structure" itself into the image of a landscape, neither can it be reduced to a pure "hedonist" play of colors for colors' sake, and even less, were that possible, to a purely "formal" abstraction—rather, (figurative and/or abstract) form is that which slips away and, in its place, we have colors-forces in a constant *vital* confrontation, colors-forces that *push beneath* forms [*en deçà des formes*] *and beyond the painting*, in the manner of *tensors*. The generalized tensitivity of space, which is thereby open to all the expressive matter of *duration* as well as to its plastic condition of real experience, results from its appropriation by the processuality of a vital energetics which replaces an aesthetics of forms composed—fixed—in (the closed) space (of Art). Matisse: "With me, color is a force. My paintings are composed of four or five colors that undergo mutual shocks, eliciting sensations of energy."[3] Farewell to the image, goodbye to the landscape, down with purism, long live the energetic "mechanics of the painting,"[4] which dislocates it in its Form in order to constitute a *sensational bloc of forces*.

We can observe this *forceful* dynamization of forms in a particularly remarkable fashion in the works where Matisse allows erased or stumped variants to transpire. The effect of this practice is to produce a metamorphic indeterminacy and tension between forms: this shifting does not aim to suggest an impression of successive forms or a form in movement within time, as in futurism, but rather expansively to open or to exfoliate the virtualities of form—dynamically to subordinate form to the power of the virtualities *that exceed it*. Not the oriented history of the Same (developing its identity) but the processuality of a becoming-other (alteration) that makes (the whole) work without the mandatory orientation towards its completion. (This is an essential question for the series in *Drawings: Themes and Variations*.)[5]

The break with the Painting-Form of painting and with its forms of historicity was only possible for Matisse because of the discovery with which he associated fauvism—the discovery that the painting involves the *construction* of colors in relations of forces whose *expressive* power is intrinsically vital, vital/vitalist and not purely pictorial. Regarding the deep expressivity of colors—which his contemporaries (Cézanne, Van Gogh, Gauguin) also sought, without managing to extricate it from every natural or supernatural mediation (that is, from the figurative or symbolic representation of forms)—Matisse understood and experienced that it could only be of an energetic nature: "It is necessary to return to the essential principles that made human language. It is then the *principles* which 'resurface', which take on life, which *give us life*. Paintings, which are refinements, subtle degradations, mixes devoid of energy, invoke beautiful blues, reds, yellows, matters that move *the sensual ground* of men. That is fauvism's point of departure: *the courage of recovering the purity of means*."[6] *Recovering the purity of means* has nothing to do with any purism whatsoever; on the contrary it means making a vital principle *resurface*, thereby "purifying" colors from any (purely) formal artistic finality, in order to give them over to their vitalist ontological power and engage them in a bio-aesthetics.[7] This "resurfacing" of the vital ground (irreducible to a hedonism), this becoming-sensible that carries with it an unprecedented "expressionism," is indissociable from its production as (chromatic) surface in an energetic constructivism for which *it is the differences in quantity of colors that underlie their quality*—in accordance with a principle repeatedly affirmed by Matisse. The differences in quantity that produce the vital quality of all the colored surfaces in relation to one another are indissociably intensive (they depend on the degrees of saturation of the colors) and extensive (they relate to their spatial properties: quantity of surface, form, orientation, mutual positions, and so on). Proceeding thusly through *"physically" non-formed matters* (and not through formed substances, pertaining to the order of representation) and *"semiotically" informal functions* (instead of figurative or abstract forms of expression that would in themselves be signifying), the "motor-diagram"[8] of forces *tends* to produce *at the very level of sensation* (for which quality is nothing other than contracted quantity) the identity Expression = Construction, to the extent that content and expression attain their highest degree of relativity, becoming the functives of a single function as well as the materials of a single matter (becoming *is* the becoming-indiscernible of content and expression). That is the very principle of this *fauvist chaosmosis* that we can characterize, following Deleuze and Guattari, as a "creative involution" or a constructive/constructivist involution, that is, as a "dissolution of form" that does not "turn into a regression into the undifferentiated"[9] because it is exercised in the process of assembling the heterogeneities put into play by the composition of an "abstract machine."[10] To the extent that "an assemblage is all the closer to the *living abstract machine* inasmuch as it opens and multiplies connections, and traces a plane of consistency with its quantifiers of intensity and consolidation,"[11] each "work" will show itself *within* the heterogenesis of an in-the-making that makes it "stand alone" through its intensive variations qua consistent multiplicity. (One should reread in this sense the "Notes of a Painter," from 1908—as the *making of* the whole work and the key to the permanent fauvism advocated by Matisse.)[12]

....

In the same period that Matisse was affirming the vitalist difference of fauvism, Bergson expounded (in 1904-1905) the conceptions that were to engender *Creative Evolution* (1907), after the philosopher had developed, in *Matter and Memory* (1896), that "metaphysics of matter," showing us, "advancing through concrete extension, *modifications*, *perturbations*, changes of *tension* or *energy*, and nothing else."[13] Starting from a "*pure* experience, which is neither subjective nor objective,"[14] Bergson profoundly renews the vitalist current's *consciousness of being*, letting himself be guided by intuition, which leads "to the very interiority of life," towards a single activity grasped in different directions by material energy and spiritual energy (differences in tension on the ground of a univocity of being as moving and living continuity). Oriented in the sense of creativity as the *élan vital of difference to the extent that it passes to the act*,[15] "*life in depth* [following the expression suggested by Lionel Dauriac] … designates what art makes us experience at certain moments, and what (true!) philosophy should make us experience continually."[16] Is it not in effect this "intention of life, the simple movement that runs through the lines, which links them to one another and gives them a meaning … that *the artist aims to seize by placing himself within the object through a kind of sympathy, lowering, by an effort of intuition, the barrier that space introduces between him and the model*"?[17] This formula could, to the letter, be signed Matisse. Reciprocally, Matisse's formula and above all its *movement*—"first form, then life; here form no longer counts"—responds *literally and intimately* to the movement of Bergsonian thought, inviting us to *pass* from the intelligence that takes "a stable view [on the real] that we call a form," to the intuition of the "fluid continuity" of life, for which "*there is no form*, since form is something immobile and reality is change." Thus, regarding living beings, we should say that "the very permanence of *their form is nothing but the outline* [*dessin*] *of a movement*."[18] It is this movement that Matisse invested in an *energetic leap* that frees it from Bergsonism's "historical" limits with respect to art. About Bergson himself (who prized above all Corot and Turner), one can indeed think that his "technical" conception—oscillating between mechanism and finalism—of the "requirements of the material on which [the artist] operates" and which would not be an instance of "creation itself"[19] (despite being an integral part of its *means* ...) prohibited him from practically raising aesthetic intuition to the level of philosophical intuition, because for him the fixation of artistic-individual forms necessarily means the interruption of the generative action of the forces of the élan vital. This was precisely the "Nietzschean" question of fauvism (which, in return, offered to the thought of the Great Noon a powerful alternative to the antagonism of romanticism and classicism): to displace this necessity so that creative force (re)invents *plastic art* as its own transformation in the *constituent* processuality of construction. It remains the case that even though Bergson still came up against said necessity and could only see an outlet for it in music, he nevertheless thought artistic creation as a *becoming*. We can adduce this formula from *Creative Evolution* by way of proof: "The completed portrait is explained by the physiognomy of the model, by the nature of the artist, by the colors mixed on the palette; but, even in full knowledge of what explains it, no one, not even the artist, could have predicted exactly what the portrait was to be, since to predict it would have been to produce it before it was produced, an absurd hypothesis that destroys itself."[20] That is the *first* reason for the overcoming, in fauvism, of the Painting-Form qua active critique of the *Art-Form* as a whole: carried out by what we call Matisse-Thought, it partakes in a *Nietzschean Bergsonism* (the Nietzschean wasp and the Bergsonian orchid) favoring the expansion of forces-forms in the art of life (vitalist de-formation of Art, to which Nietzsche gave the name of *aesthetic physiology*).[21]

....

This vitalist energetics will equip itself with a new *pragmatic* dimension by passing from the easel painting to mural painting, even if the expansiveness of Matisse's paintings after the fauve period will make them radiate on the wall like fulcrums of energy (with the exception of a phase of his work from the twenties). In Matisse, painting on the mural scale will take possession of space *otherwise*, no longer treating it simply as the place of irradiation but rather as the life milieu with which it must be dynamically articulated, *in order to vivify it* (according to Matisse's phrase). And this "decorative painting which is indivisible from [*faisant corps avec*] architecture"[22] will not only be conceived—architectured—*in function of the latter* ("site specificity") and depend on it, it will realize (itself), reciprocally, (in) its *mural* quality as an *(architecturing) function of architecture*. This double architectural function of mural painting reduces the easel painting to the private relation entertained with

Figure 1. Henri Matisse, *The Unfinished Dance*, 1931-1933. Oil on canvas, 341 x 394 cm (left), 351 x 498 cm (center) 335 x 391 cm (right). Pierre Matisse Estate, Musée d'Art moderne de la ville de Paris.

it by a contemplative gaze: "the painting circumscribed by its frame … cannot be penetrated without the attention of the spectator especially concentrated on it. … In order to be appreciated, the object must be isolated from its environment *(the opposite of architectural painting)*."[23] Moreover, the public dimension of architectural painting leads us believe in "the possibility of an art in common," to *dream* "of making painting into a collective thing," basing ourselves on the social dimension of architecture without falling into the fallacies of a "propaganda art." "Art for the people? Sure, if by people one understands the young minds who are not fixed in the art of a tradition. … I prefer ignorant students to students whose heads are filled with ancient truths …."[24]

The bio-environmental mutation of Matisse's work can be observed particularly well in the three large versions of *The Dance* from 1931-1933 (oil on canvas in three panels), a monumental decorative composition that Matisse executed on the occasion of a commission from Dr. Albert Barnes and which was intended for hanging in the great hall "filled with painted canvases" of Barnes's foundation in Merion, Pennsylvania. The form and dimensions of the three canvases that make up this composition, and which vary a little from one version to the next, are determined by the configuration of the site in which the work was to be placed—to wit, three spaces in the form of ribbed vaults 3.5 meters in height, rather dark to the extent that they stood beneath an archivolted ceiling, and above three French windows 6 meters in height and about 2 meters in width, situated on a single wall and giving onto a lawn. The ensemble—"made especially for the place … like a fragment of architecture"[25]—is more than 13 meters in length. The three parts of the work, widely separated by the archivolts, nevertheless communicate continuously beneath the latter.

The first version, undertaken in 1931, is called *The Unfinished Dance* (Musée d'Art moderne de la ville de Paris) because Matisse interrupted its execution (figure 1). Despite the simplification of the figures, their reduced volume, and the sobriety of the colors (a blue for the unfinished background, a grey for the bodies-without-flesh), this first composition is not yet, strictly speaking, mural, because it strongly retains something of the large painting. The (male or female) dancers are lightly modeled

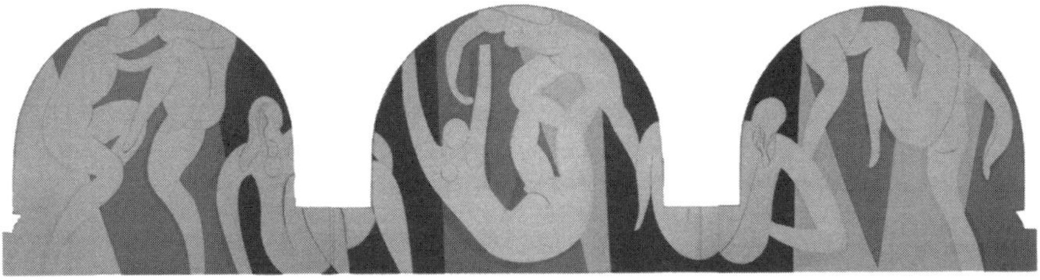

Figure 2. Henri Matisse, *The Dance (Merion)*, 1932-1933. Oil on canvas, 339.7 x 441.3 cm (left), 355.9 x 503.2 cm (center) 338.8 x 439.4 cm (right). The Barnes Foundation, Merion, Pennsylvania.

by a slight play of the brush that Matisse will more and more try to suppress in the two subsequent versions of *The Dance*. The dancers develop a series of postures that are both forcefully held and very contrasted—for example in the center a figure strongly juts forward, one arm outstretched and its legs split, whilst, above her, another stands on one rigorously vertical leg while horizontally projecting the other leg, bent at the knee. The composition arrays extreme positions while inviting us potentially to link the gaps between their postures because, to remain with the same example, the posture of the horizontally stretched figure could be seen as a forward projection of the figure overhanging it and because, in a general sense, the dancers are also stretched out towards one another. We are thus dealing with *the representation of a complex action whose (solely) rhythmic unity is entirely based on the gestural.* As in a classical painting subjected to the paradigm of *istoria*, this large composition *constructs in a purely internal way the spatio-temporality of a figured scene.* This spatio-temporality goes as far as annexing and subordinating architecture to itself in a representational mode—it "disarchitectures" it—since the space corresponding to the pendentives is treated as the quasi-theatrical frame of the scene. In some small sketches, Matisse even treats these surfaces as pillars of sorts, around which circles a rondo of dancers.

The second version of *The Dance* is the one that was placed at the Barnes Foundation (figure 2). Unlike the first, it has been defined as taking into account "site specificity" without being subordinated to it (as we shall see). The most striking difference between this version and the previous one is the appearance, in lieu of the grey background, of large oblique bands, ten in number, alternatively pink and blue (in the three lunettes of the arches, above the French windows) and black (between the arches, above the two spaces between the doors). These bands outline great chevrons of sorts that rhythmically and continuously articulate the entire field on which the eight dancers are cut out, dancers whose forms are more simplified and who are treated above all in grey flat tints. These bands constitute the most directly architectonic component of the wall between the arches. The chromatic combinations of the bands and their inclines—in other words their tempo—are attuned to the play of the dancers: the parts that are both pink and black, whose inclines are more oblique and more dynamic, correspond to the three couples engaged in a violent clinch [*corps à corps*] in each of the three lunettes, while the two black bands into which the pendentives fall back, which are more vertical and thus more static, correspond to the sitting nymphs who receive the falls of the arches. The work is already more mural to the extent that the internal rhythm of the triple panel no longer has the gestural autonomy that it possessed in the previous version, because the large colored bands can be doubly articulated with the rhythm of the dancers and that of the three French windows, the two spaces between the doors and the pendentives of the arches. What's more, the curves of the bodies situated at the two extremities of the composition and that of the upper body in the central panel echo the form of the arches. Above all, the blue, black, and pink of the bands, like the grey of the bodies, no longer draw their expressive power from the transposition of a landscape or a dance spectacle; on the contrary, "their frank contrasts, their decisive relations provide an equivalent of the hardness of stone and of the sharpness of the arches' nervure, conferring upon the work a great mural quality."[26]

Furthermore, it is by working in particular on the relation between the ambient light and the lighting of his composition that Matisse achieved the integration of his monumental decorative panel with the complex architectural environment with which he was dealing. The principal difficulty had to do with the contrast between the strong light coming from the windows and the twilight of the arched area set aside for the composition. Matisse explains that he "closely observed the particular lighting conditions," so that he was "led by the need to give his painting the visibility that the architectural arrangements refused it."[27] To "sufficiently destroy the action of the light from the two doors which could make his decoration impossible to see,"[28] Matisse had the brilliant idea of lighting the upper area, thereby provoking, thanks to the opposition of the black (anti-light) both to a muted pink and blue and to the white of the arches, a stronger contrast than in the lower part.

Thus the link between the interior and exterior of the composition is not limited to the relation between the triple decorative panel and the ribbed vaults that frame it; it also affects the ensemble of the wall, height and bay windows included—an ensemble whose architectural unity is carried out by the painting. Matisse underlines this fact: "The painting forms something like a pediment to these three doors ...—a pediment which finds itself in the shadows but must nevertheless, prolonging the great mural surface punctured by these three large luminous bay windows, itself maintain all its luminosity, and therefore its plastic eloquence (a surface in the shadow juxtaposed to a violently lit bay window without destroying the continuity of the surface), *the result of modern findings on the properties of color*."[29] Matisse makes the point even more precise: "*Therefore all my art, all my efforts consisted in changing apparently the proportions of this band* [i.e. the surface to be decorated]. *I arrived then, through the lines, through the colors, through energetic directions, at giving to the spectator the sensation of flight, of elevation, which makes him forget the actual proportions*, much too short to crown the three glass doors—with the idea always of creating the sky for the garden one sees through the doors." And to the interviewer who asked him "*Then really your painting has corrected architecture?*" "Matisse admitted that this had seemed to him imperative."[30] Far from submitting to the "frame," architectural painting shows itself to be inseparable from a *power of unframing* [*décadrage*] that opens the house-panel onto a plane of composition that affects the (changed, corrected) architecture at the same time as the painting (which is aerated, even aerial, in its absolute distance from the easel painting) for an inhabitant-spectator "on the verge of flying up into the air."[31]

The necessity of the work of architectural differentiation undertaken by Matisse goes together with two essential propositions, which presuppose one another:

1 *The principle of modernity*: "My painted surface is quite opaque and does not give the illusion of transparency of the stained glass window"; and

2 *The principle of construction*: "My vertical plane exists before anything else."[32]

Without this work of differentiation, Matisse remarks, "The mural painter today makes pictures, not murals."[33] He makes *images* that prolong the formalist illusion of the autonomy of the pictorial instead of constructing new *relations* that would involve (modified, de-essentialized, *muralized*) painting in a veritable becoming-other, simultaneously "social" and "cosmic." The reversal can thus be affirmed in bold characters: while ("today's") mural painter translates architecture into painting in order to sublimate the difficulties of an environment that is *a priori* hostile, isolating himself from the milieu and trying to concentrate the attention of the spectator on an image encircled in an "imaginary" frame, Matisse declares: "My aim has been to translate paint into architecture, to make of the fresco the equivalent of stone or cement."[34] This single great plane with its flat tints frees forces that detach the mural decoration from what Matisse now calls "the human element."

It is the Merion *Dance* that makes Matisse aware of the need for a more radical overcoming of organicity: "In architectural painting, which is at stake in Merion, it seems to me that the human element must be tempered, or even excluded." That is because "this painting must associate itself to the severity of a mass of stone. … What's more, the mind of the spectator cannot be halted by this human character with which *it would identify and which would separate it by immobilizing it from the great harmonious, living, and moving association* of architecture and painting."[35] The human must therefore recede in mural painting to the extent that the organicity of the figures both cuts them off from their environs and, in the same movement, invites the spectator to an *identification* with their humanity that *separates* him in turn, *by immobilizing him*, from the movement that should make of him the agent of the constructive association of the work to its architectural environs and to the "cosmic" (vital) opening of the latter—"in this case, it is the spectator that becomes the human element in the work."[36]

The human element—the female dancers—will be rendered in a *uniform grey* whose *mural quality* accounts for the inhuman adherence of the figures to the cement or stone—"The flesh grey between black and white, *like the walls of the room.*"[37] Matisse realizes here that the pictorial character of the brushstroke would betray through its mannerism the decorative spirit of the composition that he envisioned, and that it is therefore necessary to make the decision to escape it entirely, by materially distancing oneself from all the manners of painting, haunted as the latter is by a formalism that fixes it to its interiority. Impersonal, *non-pictorial* uniformity allows for the *equality* of "colors employed in all frankness [to] make it so that it is their relation of quantity that underlies their quality."[38] One-dimensional man, man without qualities, *the building painter* [*le peintre en bâtiment*] (charged by Matisse with the task of applying the definitive colors to the surfaces that he experimentally determined with the help of cutout gouache papers) can then make his forced entry in what was up to that point "the beauty parlor of civilization"—according to the lapidary formula of the philosopher John Dewey,[39] Barnes's advisor and Matisse's veritable intercessor in the United States.

Matisse would have liked for Barnes (who refused) to remove the two paintings placed on the walls between the French windows, in order to establish "the very clear separation that he … wanted to introduce between mural decoration and easel painting."[40] The mural composition was equally designed to "serve as a sky for the green landscape" which should have remained visible through the windows, thereby arranging a double compositional relation between the interior of the room and the exterior landscape (a decorative combination that already served as the theme—but only the theme—of numerous easel paintings). The integral environmental sense of the decorative (in the Matissean sense) is thereby verified, because it even affects nature *taken in the artifice of construction.* After the installation of the panel, Matisse verified the expansiveness of his composition: "It is a splendor of which one cannot have an idea without having seen it—because the whole ceiling with its arches lives through radiation and this effect extends to the floor itself. … When I saw the canvas hung, it detached itself from me, in order to belong to the building."[41]

The becoming-architecture of painting does not therefore imprison it in the "house," because the becoming-painting of architecture opens the "house" onto a universe that, from the inside, carries the spectator towards the "sky" that the dancers are drawn to, and—through the diffraction of the gaze dear to the decorative aesthetics of Matisse—opens it to a "vaster" space, which will soon be qualified as "cosmic." In a note from 1946, Matisse will write: "Having been gripped by the light … I spiritually [*en esprit*] escaped the small space that encircled my motif—the awareness of a similar space being enough, it seems to me, for the painters of the past—I therefore escaped the space found at the base of the painting's motif, in order spiritually to feel above me, above any motif, studio, even house, a cosmic space in which one would not feel walls any more than the fish feels the sea."[42] This "cosmic space" will open its doors to the inhabitant of the Sensation-House that incorporates the plan(e) of construction in a deterritorialization of the expression of the enclosed space. Architectural painting, Matisse thus underlines, "must give to the space enclosed in this architecture a whole atmosphere comparable to that of a beautiful and vast sunny undergrowth, which surrounds the spectator with a feeling of lightening in sumptuousness."[43]

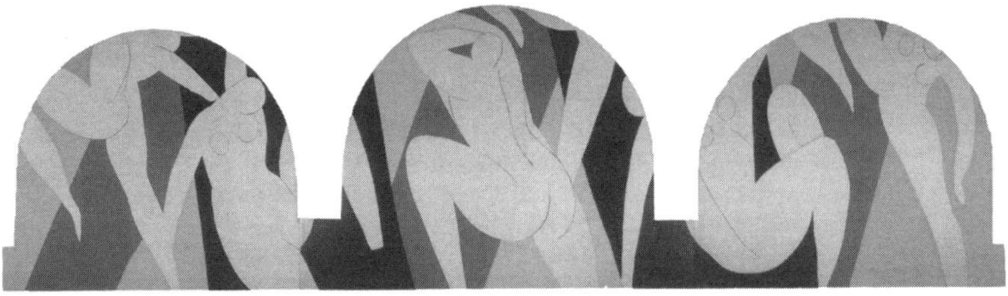

Figure 3. Henri Matisse, *The Dance (Paris)*, 1931-1933. Oil on canvas, 340 x 387 cm (left), 355 x 498 cm (center) 335 x 391 cm (right). Musée d'Art moderne de la ville de Paris.

In the Merion version, the composite architecture of the wall, with its French windows and its arches, the oblique bands of color and the facing dancers, thus begins to share a common spatio-temporality, but it too comes up against its limits. The great size of the pendentives and the reduced visibility imposed by the depth of the archivolts led Matisse to fracture the whole into three very distinct "centers of composition": each involves a couple of dancers whose attitudes differ from one panel to the next, as also differs the rhythm of the pink and blue bands which are associated with them. The spatio-temporal unity that Matisse tries to restore to the ensemble is of a narrative-descriptive type, as in the previous version. The three "scenes" are linked on the one hand by the seated nymphs, on the other by a gradual decline in the confrontations. In the middle scene, a dancer leaps above another in a circular dynamic that appears as the central nucleus or vortex of the composition, while the couples facing off in the panels framing it are constructed quasi-symmetrically on a general background constituted by a kind of sweeping fan of the colored bands, whose inclines are inverted from left to right. The couple from the panel on the right actually presents itself as a more advanced degree of the symmetrical ascending movement of the couple on the left; this intensification is also marked by the acceleration of the rhythm and the dramatization of the inclines of the colored bands (from left to right, one passes from three bands to four, then to five, and from a quasi-parallelism to bands that oppose one another, then intersect and interpenetrate). The ensemble of this arrangement [*dispositif*] confers on this version a certain orientation as well as a certain narrativity and a relative closure.

The leap into a space-time, into a *milieu* divested of any form of narrativity, breaking with any kind of historicity, is carried out in the last version, the so-called "Paris" version (figure 3). Finalized after *The Dance* of Merion and presented on its own (Musée d'Art moderne de la ville de Paris), this version functions independently of any "site specificity," like a paradigm of the inseparably architectonic and pragmatic (because non-contemplative) function of mural painting. The rhythm of this new composition, marked by powerful scansions, is more regular, as well as broader and more continuous. There are now only six parallel figures, instead of the eight differently oriented ones of the previous work. Their size has been enlarged in order to be proportionate to that of the bands. These bands of color form a periodic sequence of the three colors (pink, blue, black) whose sizes and inclines, almost parallel for a single color, undergo only slight variations. The blue bands link up with the black bands in a series of large dynamic chevrons in which are inserted the pink triangles, in accordance with a total, *all-over* partition that is strongly articulated but entirely open (neither totalizing nor totalizable, even relatively, as would be the case for any organic composition or historical structuring). The same thing can be verified with the nymphs. Their attitudes are no longer gesturally coordinated in couples composing a series of confrontations, which would be like the successive or alternating, dramatically arranged, figures of a single ballet. The exceptional architectural force of *The Dance* of Paris comes from the fact that the nymphs, becoming pseudo-bands, are no longer just engaged with one of their companions but instead directly with the monumental system of bands that themselves become pseudo- or trans-human/transhuman actors. This double, mutual becoming is neither an assimilation nor an identification to another becoming but rather a becoming-other, a vital intensiveness made superior as an effect of the crossing of heterogeneous realms. The only transitivity here is that of the composite rhythm in which the limbs of the dancers, alternately flexing and extended, diagrammatize the composition of forces by *assembling* [*s'agençant*] themselves onto the dynamic of the bands. Having fully become "bodies without organs"—since they are now fully open onto a rhythm that they share with the bands, without thereby merging with them—the figures are only embodied in a minimal silhouette that qualifies the action of the coloring-colored quantum of force exerted by the figures (all of them active) in the multiplicity of the forces at play. There is no longer either center or symmetry, beginning or end, progression or temporal development. There is absolutely nothing that could be considered under the notion of history, only a pure becoming as movement of differentiating repetition mobilizing the Outside, making this movement itself, outside of any representation and in its processuality, a *working* work [*une œuvre œuvrante*]. Correlatively, the gaze, snatched in and by this processuality, no longer needs to stop on each of the three represented "centers of composition" to grasp its singularity in relation to the others and its organico-temporal articulation with them. On the contrary, the apprehension of this construction—of which Matisse already said at the time of the Merion: "one will feel it rather than see it"[44]—takes place in an a-focal manner, as if in passing and as if accompanying a passage, in the smooth time that is given its rhythmic scansion by *The Dance*, inviting the spectator to *become* in turn a *vivified* actor of this intensive processuality qua inhabitant of the *mi-lieu*, the in-between—not the contemplator of a work of art in which the relation to the "exterior" is always mediated by an interiority, and dissolved into it.

....

It remained for Matisse to verify, by means of generalization, whether the decorative-pragmatic paradigm inaugurated by *The Dance* of Paris outside of any "site specificity" was also valid for works that take possession of a definite space in order to "vivify" it. This was made possible by the so-called paper cutout technique: great sheets gouached in advance by the anonymous hands of assistants are cut out with scissors by Matisse who, like a sculptor, incises color in the raw [*à vif*] into biomorphic form-forces, free from every imaging reference (whether figurative or abstract).[45] He then tacks these elements on the wall (of his apartment-studio), which allows the permanent readjustment of their form and their reciprocal positions in a continuous variation of assemblages. The work is carried out as an experience opened by a machinic force (*a sort of perpetual cinema*, to take up an expression of Matisse[46]) which invests the place in a free-direct manner by constructing within it a nomad space, a space whose nature is smooth, a-focal, *all-over*. It develops of its own accord, inventing itself at each instant, both assembled and aleatory, with no idea of a global organization. This art is less "popular" than the bearer of a "community to come" because it is the closest to *the means and forces of common experience, trans-formed by Matisse into a superior spontaneity that knows how to express the cerebral instinctiveness of his vitalism*. An art that *does not want* simply to accommodate (itself to) common experience but rather *forcefully to draw it* [*tirer de force*] outside itself (by conferring upon it not so "common" singular forces) towards a more highly intensive experience of the *life milieu that it installs* (but does not decorate in the *common* sense of the word). It is a matter of elevating without sublimating, that is of *augmenting* through intensification the sensible-cerebral quality of common life, rendering it the most singular possible in each "experience" (a superior pragmatism). The "finite" work (in the twofold sense of "finite") puts into continuous variation a mural (non-pictorial) space that is "de jure infinite, open or unlimited in all directions."[47] It does not cease to compose itself, to assemble itself, to processualize itself without ever making an (organic-organized) composition that would delimit through its Form the place of art.

We will only evoke here a particularly successful example, that of *The Swimming Pool* (The Museum of Modern Art, New York), executed in 1952 with cutout paper gouaches (figure 4). This composition presents itself in the form of a long panoramic frieze of blue paper gouaches glued onto a band of white paper of 71.7 cm by 16.43 m in length. Begun by Matisse for his own pleasure, irrespective of any commission (and thus a model of *free action*), it developed into successive panels (9 in total) that ended up going around the perimeter of a rectangular room in his apartment in Nice, with the exception of the openings that cut through the two narrowest walls. The apprehension by fragments of the entirety of the piece demands from the body of the viewer a complete rotation. The coupling of the varied movements and postures of the blue and white swimmers with the white band that runs along a continuous invariable axis determines a discontinuous succession, but one that is stretched and opened by *kinetic moments* (defined in relation to this axis of reference). The gaze passes through energetic moments which are simply contiguous but which are sustained by a continuous *vital* current that determines a powerful cut through space—a stretched flux, rhythmically mobilized by the bodies, for which the white band would serve as a kind of furrow. These trails, which re-launch energy by varying its accelerations and decelerations, its amplitude or intensity, do not

Figure 4. Henri Matisse, *The Swimming Pool*, 1952. Gouache on cut-and-pasted paper, 230.1 x 847.8 cm, 230.1 x 796.1 cm. Museum of Modern Art, New York. © 2006 Succession H. Matisse, Paris / Artists Rights Society (ARS), New York.

outline *a* trajectory: there are scansions and even some local concatenations but no imposed global direction (the figures are oriented in contrary directions). There is a becoming without either progression or temporal unfolding in this *post-pictorial* and *environmental* work in which we should look less for the silhouettes and limbs of the swimmers than experience the intensive modalities of the action of swimming in water and being carried along by it. The water *smoothes out* any organic differences in the bodies, making them into a fluid, elastic, deformable mass, open to a sensible and dynamic osmosis, which is that of an *active multiplicity*. The body stretches beyond itself, it slides, undulates, elongates itself, bucks and somersaults, composes a liquid body with the water, not following its natural articulations but in accordance with a shared rhythm, because the water in turn enters into a dynamic resonance with the body that stirs it, to the point of entering into a rhythmic and chromatic reversibility with it.

Élan vital of a white and blue undulation "that delimits nothing, that no longer defines a contour, that no longer goes from one point to the other, but rather passes between points, and does not cease conjugating the horizontal and the vertical, deviating the diagonal by constantly changing direction ...."[48] Mutant line making intensities circulate, abstract line, decorative line or rhythm, if it "knows how to take its place in the mind, in the brain of a sensing man," if it "takes place among the other things of our life."[49] The *fleet in being* of a rondo of water in the guise of the Line of Life where *nothing happens, but everything becomes* in the power of experimenting new vital forces/forms—beyond any form of interiority or exteriority. *Like some becoming, a little becoming in the pure, trans-historical state,* as Deleuze and Guattari put it, investing, through this opening of the common to heterogeneous processes of subjectivation, an entire biopolitics of creativity. ▪

Translated by Alberto Toscano. The Matissean "ground" of these pages is taken from a book co-signed by Eric Alliez and Jean-Claude Bonne, La Pensée-Matisse *(Paris: Le Passage, 2005). An earlier version of this text (already translated by Alberto Toscano) was the object of a presentation at the interdisciplinary symposium "Philosophies of Time and the Problem of History," March 16-17, 2005, organized by the Centre for Research in Modern and European Philosophy at Middlesex University.*

....

1 Henri Matisse, "Notes of a Painter on his Drawing," *Le Point*, no. 21, July 1939. Translated from the French text reprinted in Matisse, *Écrits et propos sur l'art*, rev. ed., ed. Dominique Fourcade, new revised and corrected edition (Paris: Hermann, 1972), 163. Unless stated otherwise, translations of the Matisse quotes in the text are by Alberto Toscano.

2 Matisse, *Écrits et propos sur l'art*, 47 n. 11, cited by André Verdet, *Prestiges de Matisse* (Paris: Emile Paul, 1952). It is necessary to have a vision of the global state at each moment: "Everything must be envisaged correlatively when the work is in progress" ("Notes de Sarah Stein," 1908, *Écrits et propos sur l'art*, 71); "I never know in advance what I will do" (comment from 1942 addressed to Jean and Henry Dauberville, *Écrits et propos sur l'art*, 47, n. 11).

3 This is the statement, from around 1942, made by the ever "fauve" Matisse to Pierre Courthion cited in Pierre Courthion, "Avec Matisse et Bonnard," *D'une palette à l'autre. Mémoires d'un critique d'art* (Geneva: La Baconnière Arts, 2004), 173.

4 The expression "mechanics of the painting" is *signed* Matisse.

5 Matisse, *Drawings: Themes and Variations* (New York: Dover, 1995); originally published as *Dessins: thèmes et variations* (Paris: M. Fabiani, 1943), with an introduction by Louis Aragon, "Matisse-en-France."

6 Matisse, "Propos rapportés par Tériade" (extracts from "Constance du fauvisme," *Minotaure* II, 9, 1936); *Écrits et propos sur l'art*, 128 (our emphasis).

7 While, to our knowledge, the expression "bio-aesthetic" appears only once in the work of Deleuze and Guattari—see Gilles Deleuze and Félix Guattari, *Mille plateaux* (Paris: Minuit, 1980), 622, n. 33—it is a notion whose determining importance is everywhere felt, to the extent that it involves a becoming-life of art which amounts to a politics of sensation. Not without a polemical intention with regard to the dominance of the Duchampian paradigm, we can say that this is the becoming-life of modern-contemporary art borne by Matisse, whose operation we have constructed under the heading of Matisse-Thought.

8 "To obey the intentions of [Matisse's] painting, I must subject myself to the 'motor diagram' that its form produces in my brain," writes Matthew Stewart Prichard, in a letter to Frances Burton-Smith from June 1914, quoted in Dominique Fourcade and Eric de Chassey, "Anthologie," in *Henri Matisse 1904-1917*, exhibition catalogue, February 25–June 21, 1993 (Paris: Centre Georges Pompidou, 1993), 499.

9 Deleuze and Guattari, *Mille plateaux*, 331. Involution, the motor of becoming, is just as opposed to the idea of regression as it is to those of "filiative evolution" or of development, which presuppose the continuity of forms, 291ff.

10 Ibid., 175-178 and 636-640. Starting from the idea that in a semiotic system (or at the level of the semiotic functioning of a system), expression and content "are in reciprocal presupposition ... because they are two faces of the same assemblage," Deleuze and Guattari call "abstract machine," "something that is even deeper" than this double face, to wit the plan(e) of the work whose assemblage is made of relations between all the forces (which are vital forces in Matisse) and where consequently there is no longer any formal distinction between the (formed) plan(e) of expression and the (formed) plan(e) of content. This single and underlying plane of immanence or consistency of all the forces is therefore more abstract, more radically deterritorialized than the formalist abstraction that bears only on the elimination of content. The machine is no less real for being abstract, in terms of the (ontological) reality of the vital forces of which it is the assemblage. It can also be called deterritorializing to the extent that it presides over the reciprocal deterritorialization of content and expression by investing them with its energy. Every movement of deterritorialization in effect comes down to "crossing a threshold" to attain "liberated zones of intensity where contents separate themselves from their forms."

11 Ibid., 639 (our emphasis).

12 See n. 2, above.

13 For Bergson, "Matter thus resolves itself into numberless tremblings, all linked by an uninterrupted continuity, all solidary with one another, and running in every direction like so many shudders," Henri Bergson, *Matière et mémoire*, in *Œuvres*, Edition du centenaire (Paris: Presses Universitaires de France, 1970), 337, 343. (In all the texts cited here, the italics are Bergson's.)

14 Bergson, Letter to William James, July 20, 1905, reprinted in Bergson, *Mélanges*, (Paris: Presses Universitaires de France, 1972), 660.

15 This is Deleuze's definitive formula in the article from 1956 entitled "Bergson, 1859-1941": "Élan vital is difference inasmuch as it passes to the act." Reprinted in Deleuze, *L'Île déserte et autres textes. Textes et entretiens 1953-1974* (Paris: Minuit, 2002), 37.

16 Bergson, Letter to Lionel Alexandre Dauriac, March 19, 1913, in Bergson, *Mélanges*, 990.

17 Bergson, *L'évolution créatrice*, in *Œuvres*, 645 (our emphasis).

18 Ibid., respectively, 645, 750, and 604 (our emphasis).

19 Bergson will elaborate this theme in the 1920s in "Le possible et le réel." See Bergson, *La pensée et le mouvant*, in *Œuvres*, 1134.

20 Bergson, *L'évolution créatrice,* in *Œuvres,* 500.

21 The "remarkably unexplored obscure domain [...] of Physiological Aesthetics" appears in §8 of the third essay of Friedrich Nietzsche, *On the Genealogy of Morals*, trans. Walter Kaufman and R. J. Hollingdale, ed. Walter Kaufmann (with *Ecce Homo*) (New York: Vintage Books, 1989), 111-2.

22 Matisse, Letter to Simon Bussy, March 7, 1933, *Écrits et propos sur l'art*, 140, n. 4. Unless otherwise noted, all other letters from Matisse are from this collection.

23 Matisse, Letter to Alexandre Romm, March 17, 1934: 148, our emphasis.

24 Respectively, these declarations are made to Fels (1929), Zervos (1931), and Lejard (1951). Matisse, *Écrits et propos sur l'art* , 120, n. 78.

25 Matisse, Letter to Alexandre Romm, January 19, 1934, *Écrits et propos sur l'art*, 145.

26 Ibid.

27 Matisse, "Répertoire 6" around 1946, quoted in Jack D. Flam, "Histoire et métamorphoses d'un projet," in *Autour d'un chef d'œuvre de Matisse, les trois versions de la Danse Barnes (1930-1933)* (Paris: Musée d'Art Moderne de la Ville de Paris, 1993), 56ff.

28 Ibid., 57.

29 Matisse, Letter to Alexandre Romm, January 19, 1934, *Écrits et propos sur l'art*, 144, our emphasis.

30 "Interview with Dorothy Dudley," extracts from "The Matisse Fresco in Merion, Pennsylvania," *Hound and Horn* 7, January-March 1934, reprinted in Flam, *Matisse on Art* (Berkeley: University of California Press, 1995), 110-111, our emphasis. The "work in situ integrates the site in which it takes place to as to avoid being deflected by it and … consequently tends to transform it," Guy Lelong, *Daniel Buren* (Paris: Flammarion, 2001), 40.

31 This is the famous passage from *The Birth of Tragedy*, §1: "Singing and dancing, man expresses himself as a member of a higher unity. He has forgotten how to walk and talk and is on the verge of flying up into the air as he dances…" Friedrich Nietzsche, *The Birth of Tragedy Out of the Spirit of Music* (London: Penguin Books, 1993), 17.

32 Matisse, Letter to Alexandre Romm, February 14, 1934, *Écrits et propos sur l'art,* 147.

33 "Interview with Dorothy Dudley," 109.

34 Ibid.

35 Matisse, Letter to Alexandre Romm, February 14, 1934, *Écrits et propos sur l'art,* 146-147, our emphasis.

36 Ibid., 147.

37 "Entretien avec Dorothy Dudley," *Écrits et propos sur l'art*, 140, our emphasis. Unless otherwise noted, otherwise cited in this article from the English version "Interview with Dorothy Dudley."

38 Letter to Alexandre Romm, January 19, 1934, *Écrits et propos sur l'art,* 146.

39 John Dewey, *Art as Experience* [1934] (New York: Perigee Books/Penguin Putnam, 1980), 344.

40 Matisse, Letter to Pierre Matisse, February 1934, quoted by Jack D. Flam, "Histoire et métamorphoses d'un projet," 74.

41 Matisse, Letter to Simon Bussy, May 17, 1933.

42 Note from 1946 in the margins of a manuscript by Aragon, published in Louis Aragon, *Henri Matisse, roman* (Paris: Gallimard, 1971), quoted in *Écrits et propos sur l'art*, 104, n. 59 (our emphasis).

43 Matisse, Letter to Alexandre Romm, 14 February 1934: 147.

44 "Interview with Dorothy Dudley," 109.

45 "Cutting out into color in the raw reminds me of the direct incisions of sculptors" [*Découper à vif dans la couleur me rappelle la taille directe des sculpteurs*], *Jazz* (Paris: Tériade, 1947), *Écrits et propos sur l'art*, 237.

46 "When I work, it is really a sort of perpetual cinema," statement quoted by Gaston Diehl, *Henri Matisse* (Paris: Tisné, 1954), quoted in *Écrits et propos sur l'art,* 152.

47 Deleuze and Guattari, *Mille plateaux*, 594.

48 Ibid., 621.

49 Interview by Louis-Bertrand Rayssiguier, June 29, 1949; published in Henri Matisse, Marie-Alain Couturier, and Louis-Bertrand Rayssiguier, *La Chapelle de Vence. Journal d'une creation* (Paris: Cerf, 1993), 212: "The first quality of a work must be decorative", and, Matisse adds, it is decorative if "it knows how to take its place …."

Deleuze's "Life" Sentences

Ian Buchanan

> *It would be naïve to think that the problems of life and death, love and the difference between the sexes are amenable to their scientific solutions.*
> —*Gilles Deleuze,* Difference and Repetition[1]

> *We are not physicists or metaphysicians; we must be Egyptologists.*
> —*Gilles Deleuze,* Proust and Signs[2]

While many commentators have observed the importance of "Life" to Deleuze's work, few have been prepared to say what its function in his work actually is, save for a couple of half-hearted efforts here and there to read it as the basis for a new form of ontology and/or ethics. Where it is considered, the general tendency is to treat it as either Deleuze's object, or rationale, for doing philosophy, making him either a "Life"-philosopher or philosopher-of-"Life." Consequently, "Life" has been accorded a metaphysical status by Deleuze's most serious critics in spite of the fact that that is an utter anathema to his whole project. If "Life" is to be freed from the isolation chamber of inverted commas I have felt it necessary to impose at the outset of this discussion, then it must be accounted for from within Deleuze's philosophy. In this regard, we can summarize ahead of time how things must be if they are to be consistent with Deleuze's philosophy: "Life" may be transcendent *in* his system of thought, but it cannot be transcendent *to* his system of thought.

Of the few commentators who have been prepared to state the function of "Life" in Deleuze's work, one may legitimately single out Giorgio Agamben as being the most influential.[3] He is also, I will argue, the most unreliable. Through a series of sleights of hand, Agamben attempts to position Deleuze's work on "Life" as his legacy, as his last great unfinished work that defines his philosophical project as a whole. Agamben's rationale for this reading is, I will show, a rich compost of coincidence and recondite word-sleuthing that is not finally convincing. His word-sleuthing, as I have called it, includes short disquisitions on the punctuation of the title of Deleuze's essay; thus, in addition to speculations on Ladino grammar, we get notes on significance of the colon and the ellipsis. As interesting as this is, it is of secondary importance, more rationalization than argument, and I won't dwell on it here. Suffice it to say, it is of a piece with Agamben's broader attempt to align Deleuze's conception of "Life" with his own interest in "bio-power" and its concomitant, "naked" or "bare" life, and create a space for a philosophy to come predicted by both Deleuze and Foucault and realized by none other than Agamben.[4]

Agamben's essay opens as follows:

> By virtue of a striking coincidence, the last texts published by Michel Foucault and Gilles Deleuze before their deaths have at their centre the concept of life. The meaning of this testamentary coincidence (for what is at issue in both cases is something like a will) goes beyond the secret solidarity between two friends. It implies the statement of a legacy that clearly concerns the coming philosophy, which, to make this inheritance its own, will have to take its point of departure in the concept of life toward which the last works of both philosophers gesture. (Such, at least, is the hypothesis guiding this inquiry.)[5]

It is the final parenthesis that primarily concerns me.

Agamben wants us to believe that because Deleuze's short essay entitled "Immanence: A Life ..." is his last known piece of work, it can be treated as a last will and testament.[6] He corroborates this claim with the coincidental fact that Deleuze's friend Michel Foucault also happened to present as his last published work a short disquisition on "Life."[7] Both produced these pieces when they were dying: Foucault presumably corrected the proofs of his piece (actually a modification of something written, as Agamben himself notes, several years earlier in 1978 as an homage to his mentor Georges Canguilhem) from his hospital bed at La Pitié-Salpêtrière, while Deleuze must have composed his, if indeed this is when he wrote it (we don't actually know for sure), at a time when already mortally ill, and thoughts of suicide were perhaps weighing on his mind. But two coincidences do not create a truth. There is nothing in the texts themselves to suggest that it is anything but a coincidence that these essays happened to be the last thing either Deleuze or Foucault worked on, and it is certainly *nothing but a coincidence* that these essays happened to be the last both Deleuze *and* Foucault happened to work on.

Agamben reinforces the illusion that "Immanence: A Life..." can be treated as a bequest note with the further prestidigitation of captioning this essay—as well as an indeterminate number of Deleuze's other works—as "late Deleuze." However, neither a specific date corresponding to a particular life event, such as the diagnosis of a fatal illness, say, or perhaps a decisive encounter such as Deleuze describes his meeting with Guattari as being, nor a specific work, save for this final piece, is offered to give substance to this delicious phantasm of a "late Deleuze." Consequently, the effect of its usage is rhetorical rather than analytical. But one only has to survey the vast literature on Foucault to see the insidious effects such distinctions as "early" and "late" can have on the reception of an author's oeuvre. It is noteworthy in this respect that Deleuze himself felt it necessary to weigh in against the idea that there is such a thing as a "late" Foucault, if by that we mean there is a rupture or return in his work as many scholars have said of the second and third volumes of *The History of Sexuality*.[8] Deleuze's own ethos of taking an author as a whole would in any case preclude him from taking this approach to a body of work.

But having said that, it is obviously not the case that Deleuze himself was in principle averse to using the description "last work," or "late work," although for him it always refers to projects that were cut short by an untimely death or were knowingly too large for a single life to accommodate. He was even willing to consider his own work in this way, describing the questions with which *What is Philosophy?* opens as perhaps being the kinds of questions that only old men could ask.[9] Such references obviously give body to the illusion of the testamentary. In this respect, it is advisable, I would suggest, to treat Deleuze's own use of such phrases as "last work" (as he says of Fichte and Main de Biran in the essay in question) in the manner of Edward Said's concept of "late style."[10] This describes a certain confidence to experiment that writers and artists attain when they sense they are in their twilight years, rather than a maudlin concern for legacy. However, that being said, if we concede that there is such a thing as a "late style" in Deleuze, which I suggest might be dated with the writing of his final collaboration with Guattari, we still cannot take the leap that such work is by its very nature testamentary.

Agamben's forced association of this essay with the author's death has the effect of making it seem that in those lonely hours before he took the fateful decision to end his life all Deleuze could have been thinking about is his life and by extension his philosophical legacy. The step from this assumption and the decision to read "Immanence: A Life…" as a suicide note evinces no pause or hesitation from Agamben, although it should because the textual evidence offers little support for his interpretation. If anything, it reads more like an attempt to sketch out a new project. It is conclusive in the way only an untested hypothesis can be. This would not trouble Agamben, of course, since in his lights it is precisely its preliminary and indeed peremptory nature that confirms his opinion that it is a bequest of a work to come. It is Nietzsche's arrow waiting to be fired again by an eager new mind. Still, if we grant Agamben that this is indeed one last gesture to secure a legacy, we nonetheless cannot share his confidence in thinking that Deleuze's intent here is to promulgate "Life" as either the essential substance of his life's achievement or even his fantasized gift to future generations of a work still to come.

It is telling, I think, that of these two alternatives, Agamben chooses the latter, more speculative option. Only the worthy, though, will benefit from this gift. "To assume this legacy as a philosophical task," Agamben stipulates, we shall have to pass through two trials: first, modern philosophy will need to reconstruct its genealogy so as to distinguish between what might be termed the immanence phratry and the transcendence phratry; then, it will need to undertake a genealogy of the very term "Life" to confirm what Agamben states we already know, namely that it isn't a medical or scientific notion, but a philosophical, political, and theological concept.[11] But by treating it this way as an impossible/sought after object, Agamben transforms "Life" into a "Thing" in the Lacanian/Žižekian sense of that word. It turns "Life" into an empty form or vessel in need of content. This gives "Life" an unwarranted spectral cast, making it a philosophical equivalent of Derrida's "hauntology": it lives in what might be, rather than what is, or has been. In this manner (as with all ghost stories) that which was left undone outgrows in significance that which was actually done, thus supplanting the actual philosophical concept with a phantasmatic other.

But this just begs the question: is "Life" Deleuze's primary focus or concern? Agamben's claim that "Life" defines Deleuze's philosophical legacy rests on the conviction that "Life" is the specific focus of this essay, but from the very first sentence—"What is a transcendental field?"—Deleuze makes it clear that it isn't. His concerns are elsewhere. So if it is a matter of legacy, which remains an open question, then it isn't "Life" that defines that legacy. In some senses, his last work takes up the task that by rights belongs to his first work. Yet such questions are always the most arduous, and it is undoubtedly for this reason that Deleuze reserved them for his later years. Knowing where to start is always difficult, Deleuze says, because one has to start with one's presuppositions.[12] In contrast to the presuppositions of scientists, which have a purely objective character and can be eliminated via the rigors of scientific method itself, philosophical presuppositions are as much subjective as they are objective. Objective presupposition refers to those concepts which our attempts to define something—"man," let's say—explicitly presuppose. In Descartes's case, to use Deleuze's own example, he did not want to define "man" as a rational animal because that would presuppose a certain agreement as to the meaning of the concepts of rationality and animality, both of which are obviously troublesome.

Of course, the form a presupposition may take is not always so blatant as this. Deconstruction thrives on discovering less obvious forms of this conceptual dependency and has consequently enhanced our sensitivity to its myriad presentations. Sometimes, though, as Judith Butler's work has shown, we can forget all about the existence and operation of presupposition and allow a naturalized—i.e., non-conceptual—form, like "sex," to stand uncontested as the point of definition for a concept, like "gender," and thereby convince ourselves it is grounded in the true. What Butler shows is not that "gender" presupposes "sex," but that they presuppose each other, an instance of what Deleuze and Guattari call mutual or reciprocal presupposition.[13] A similar process is at work in the case of "Life," which some readers want to match with a non-conceptual, naturalized form called life, using all the resources of scientific description to conjure a nonsubjective vitalism of genes and innumerable subatomic particles to give it legitimacy.

By subjective, then, Deleuze means presuppositions of "the everybody knows" and "no one can deny" variety—"sex" is one such example, "Life" is clearly another. Both are terms whose meaning flourishes independently of philosophy in the tumultuous realm of "opinion."[14] Everybody knows and no one can deny there is a biological life that thrums along regardless of what the philosophers and political scientists say about how life ought to be lived or is lived. We at least have that, we seem to be saying. Caught between the double pincers of objective and subjective presupposition, it might seem that philosophy can never truly begin because it can never find an authentic point of departure:

> [If] it is a question of rediscovering at the end what was there in the beginning, if it is a question of recognising, of bringing to light or into the conceptual or the explicit, what was simply known implicitly without concepts—whatever the complexity of this process, whatever the differences between the procedures of this or that author—the fact remains that all this is still too simple, and that this circle is truly not tortuous enough.[15]

"We would do better to ask," Deleuze continues, "what is a subjective or implicit presupposition?"[16] Its form is that of common sense in its philosophical variant. In philosophy, the one thing "everybody knows" and "no one can deny" is that "thought has an affinity with the true; it formally possesses the true and materially wants the true. It is in terms of this image that everybody knows and is presumed to know what it means to think."[17] This image of thought, as Deleuze refers to it in the abstract, is not only true of this or that philosophy but the general condition of philosophy as a whole. That is to say, it is not a particular trait of one philosophy and not another, of Kant or Hegel, say, and not Nietzsche, but common to western philosophy as a whole, at least since Plato. Deleuze's anti-Platonism, his famous desire to overturn Platonism, which is such a persistent theme in the literature on Deleuze, can be traced to this one essential claim: thought does not naturally yearn for truth, and therefore philosophy cannot begin from this presupposition.

Deleuze's concept of the "image of thought," first proposed as an attempt to explain the artistic rationale of Proust's writing and later developed into a fully fledged concept in *Difference and Repetition*, follows from this claim that thought doesn't naturally long for truth. It is an attempt to name and begin to theorize presupposition as something like the philosophical equivalent of predisposition. That is, it theorizes our acquired, but innately functioning, sense of what thought ought to look like and tries to explain our preference for certain types of argument over others as the consequence of a cultivation of philosophical habit rather than the product of ratiocination.

For Deleuze, there is no more pernicious nor persistent habit of thought than the one he refers to as the "natural illusion," which traces problems from propositions—"we operate upon unknown quantities as if they were known: this is how we pursue the hard work of reducing problems to propositions capable of serving as cases of solution."[18] Those readers of Deleuze who act as if biological life is in fact a "known known" (to use Rumsfeld's barbarous phrase) are clearly prey to this illusion. If we assume the biological is the living and that "Life" is merely the abstract form, we effectively treat "Life" as the solution to the problem of what distinguishes the biological or organic from the inorganic. This treatment does not yield an affirmative understanding of "Life"; it simply positions it as an ineffable something other, which lands us right back in the realm of metaphysics. Deleuze's main objection to both Hegelian dialectics and Freudian psychoanalysis is its willingness to accept explanations relying on such heterological devices. His insistence on a philosophy of surfaces, rather than heights and depths, is precisely directed against the deployment of "an ineffable something other" as a means of solving the problem of how to begin.

However, the point not to be missed here, as the leading exponent of the philosophy of "an ineffable something other" Slavoj Žižek likes to say, is that for Deleuze "Life" is neither the originating question nor the terminating answer to his inquiry. Deleuze doesn't ask, "What is Life?"; he asks, "What is a transcendental field?" and answers—admittedly with some difficulty—that it is a pure plane of immanence. He then proposes to call the immanence of this pure plane of immanence "Life." "Life" answers the question of what constitutes the immanence of immanence. It can only be understood in its Deleuzian sense—it has other senses, of course—insofar as it is enveloped within its originating question, not as its terminating answer but as its motivating force: without its question, the answer is hollow. "Life is the immanence of immanence, absolute immanence: it is complete power, complete bliss."[19] What begins as the answer to a complex question seems to trail off into a flight of fancy. But in a sense, it is this flight of fancy that provides the best clue as to the meaning of "the immanence of immanence" because it is only in such a system that universals like "complete power" and "complete bliss" are thinkable. The actual world does not permit such notions because there are too many prevailing counterforces that could and would disrupt the completeness of one's power or bliss. But in a virtual world these counterforces can be set aside.

The thinkability of "the immanence of immanence" is an issue that directly concerns Deleuze. I said above that Deleuze answers his question—"What is a transcendental field?"—"with some difficulty" because the transcendental field, as Deleuze conceives it, is not immediately available to thought; or, rather, the form in which it becomes available to thought, or appears to be thinkable, is already somewhat less than purely immanent, which is to say already grasped as transcendent to something. "Must we then define the transcendental field by a pure immediate consciousness with neither object nor self, as a movement that neither begins nor ends?"[20] The problem with this formulation, and the reason we cannot use a pure immediate consciousness as our theoretical anchor point, Deleuze continues, is that "the relation of the transcendental field to consciousness is only a conceptual one."[21] He means by this that consciousness without some form of reflection could not be visible in the transcendental field—in a related footnote, he cites Bergson to the effect that it is like trying to see a beam of light reflected back onto its source. Consciousness, Deleuze writes, "becomes a fact only when a subject is produced at the same time as its object, both being outside the field and appearing as 'transcendents.'"[22]

As we've noted already, Deleuze doesn't ask, "What is Life?." This is not his question. But neither does he ask, "What is a pure plane of immanence?," which it should be noted still would not have brought us to the answer "Life." That requires the further question, "What constitutes the immanence of the immanence of the pure plane of immanence?." But in fact Deleuze doesn't ask this question either. He moves (without pause) from asking "What is a transcendental field?" to telling us that a transcendental field is a pure plane of immanence and from there to stating that the immanence of this pure plane of immanence is "Life." If we are confused by this apparent non-asking and non-answering of questions, it is because we expect questions to lead to answers and answers to extinguish questions.

The foregoing is reminiscent of the scene from Lewis Carroll that Deleuze uses to exemplify Frege's paradox of the proliferation of verbal entities. Poor Alice is confounded by the Knight who announces that the name of the song he's going to sing is "Haddocks' Eyes" only to qualify, when Alice bemusedly replies "Oh, that's the name of the song, is it?" that no, that is what the *name* of the song is called. The song's name in fact is "The Aged Aged Man," but it is called "Ways and Means"; the song *is* "A-sitting On A Gate."[23] At which point, Alice gives up, completely bewildered. The song is "A-sitting On A Gate," its name is "The Aged Aged Man," it is, however, called "Ways and Means," but its name is called "Haddocks' Eyes." Alice's problem is that she can never seem to pose the right question to get the answer she's actually seeking. The song has a name, but it is called something else; the song's name is one thing but called another; and so on. Our confusion above, by contrast, arises from the fact that "Life" is apparently given in answer to a question not yet asked, the effect of which is that since we do not know the nature of the question, we cannot grasp the answer as answer.

Our philosophical heritage does not prepare us for the possibility that answers are not simply the missing pieces of a puzzle-question that, once supplied, neutralize that question completely but extra-beings with a vitality and substance of their own. By the same token, conditioned as we are by a mathematical viewpoint, we find it practically impossible to see that questions are not products of lack—they do not arise from the perception of lack but correspond to the real movement of the unconscious itself. At issue, as Deleuze argues in *Difference and Repetition*, is the image of thought itself. Deleuze himself nominates this concept, the image of thought, and the corresponding discussion of it as "the most necessary and the most concrete,"[24] and yet its significance does not seem to have been understood by many of Deleuze's commentators, least of all by those who pursue a course of trying to validate Deleuze's questions with answers drawn from scientific sources. What Deleuze wants to do in this chapter is first of all overturn the calculus of problems, that is, the misapprehension that problems arise from lack and that answers supply a missing plenitude. This is what he means when he says he wants to overturn Platonism; this is the specific version of the dialectic he objects to. In Deleuze's view, the dialectic is precisely a calculus of problems, but when it traces its problems from propositions, it loses its power. A philosophy sensitive to the dynamic relation between question and answer, problem and solution, such as Deleuze's own, should accordingly be referred to as dialectical.[25] Deleuze aims, then, to install a new image of thought that does not demand that ideas and concepts be subject to a trial. His ideal is a form of thought without image, but such a form is, like "Life," essentially impossible to present.

What is obvious from the foregoing is that the distinction between biological life, whether the life of the author himself or life itself as a scientific given, and "Life" as a concept is exceedingly difficult to preserve. Constant references to Deleuze's own life do not help matters. The failure to attend to this obvious difficulty of presentation, to the rhetorical difficulty as well as the philosophical difficulty of presenting "Life" in its philosophical purity, has meant Deleuze's commentators have read him with one eye shut. It is as though they've been reading his words without any sense of his meaning. The insistence on reading him through the lens of biology is a symptom of this failure because it (knowingly?) goes against the grain of one of the key aims of the piece, which is precisely to enunciate a conception of "Life" that is not enveloped by its proximity to and inevitable confrontation with either bare life or sheer death.[26] The more biological life is foregrounded as the conceptual anchor point, the harder it is to see the nonpersonal form of "Life" Deleuze was in fact trying to theorize. It is not for nothing that Deleuze finds his examples in the work of poets, novelists, film-makers, and artists. In contrast to philosophers, they are content to put "Ideas" into the wind without a rope securely tying them to a grounding Idea. In other words, it is not just Deleuze's biological life that we must be wary of confusing with "Life": the notion of biological life by itself, shorn of all biographical associations, is, if anything, even more problematic because it is very difficult to break the habit of assuming that "Life" must at some point intersect with life in its commonest usage.

A final refutation of Agamben's focus on "Life" as the philosophical legacy of these two thinkers can be found, I think, in what was undoubtedly the most passionate intersection of their work, namely Deleuze's reading of a short extract from *L'Usage des plaisirs* (its ink barely dry, having been published only a month or so earlier) in place of a eulogy on June 29, 1984, in the courtyard outside the La Pitié-Salpêtrière mortuary to a crowd of several hundred gathered in mourning to view Foucault's body one last time before it was consigned to the earth in Vendeuvre-du-Poitou:

> What is the point of striving after knowledge [*savoir*] if it ensures only the acquisition of knowledges [*connaissances*] and not, in a certain way and to the greatest extent possible, the disorientation of he who knows? … What is philosophy today—I mean philosophical activity—if not the critical work of thought upon thought, if it does not, rather than legitimising what one already knows, consist of an attempt to know how to and to what extent it is possible to think differently?[27]

This passage could not be more in tune with Deleuze's own thoughts on the role of philosophy, as he would make definitively clear in his final collaboration with Félix Guattari, *What is Philosophy?*, published seven years later in 1991. We may infer, too, that if Deleuze himself were to articulate what he thought Foucault's singular legacy was, it would be the effort he made to think differently, not his concept of life. His book on Foucault, completed as an homage to an absent friend, makes this point abundantly clear. But lest we think it is a judgement he reserved for special cases, it needs to be observed that this was Deleuze's measure of all philosophies and philosophers. Perhaps the most compelling statement on this matter is to be found in his vivid description of Francis Bacon's practice of seemingly destroying his pictures. This, Deleuze argues, is what the artist needed to do in order to cancel out cliché, opinion, expectation, and the "givens," the countless images with which our media-soaked universe has flooded our consciousness. Beyond that, there are "psychic clichés just as there are physical clichés—ready-made perceptions, memories, phantasms" which must also be stamped out whatever cost.[28] Philosophers, too, must battle against cliché in its equally nefarious guises of presupposition and opinion, as Deleuze first argued in *Difference and Repetition*. In other words, it is not what Deleuze (or for that matter Foucault) has to say about "Life" with his dying philosophical breath but the effort to think differently about it that constitutes his legacy. We fail to see this if we put "Life" on a pedestal.

How, then, does Deleuze describe "Life"?

> No one has described what *a* life is better than Charles Dickens, if we take the indefinite article as an index of the transcendental. A disreputable man, a rogue, held in contempt by everyone, is found as he lies dying. Suddenly, those taking care of him manifest an eagerness, respect, even love, for his slightest sign of life. Everybody bustles about to save him, to the point where, in his deepest coma, this wicked man himself senses something soft and sweet penetrating him. But to the degree he comes back to life, his saviors turn colder, and he becomes once again mean and crude. Between his life and his death, there is a moment that is only that of *a* life playing with death. The life of the individual gives way to an impersonal and yet singular life that releases a pure event freed from the accidents of internal and external life, that is, from the subjectivity and objectivity of what happens: a "Homo tantum" with whom everyone empathizes and who attains a sort of beatitude.[29]

It is this description that Deleuze's commentators, including Agamben, who even troubles himself to read the original passage from Dickens, have been reading with one eye shut. Here we need to draw on all the resources of textual analysis to challenge Agamben's conclusion that Deleuze's attempt "to clarify the vertigo of immanence by means of 'a life' leads us instead into an area that is even more uncertain, in which the child and the dying man present us with the enigmatic cipher of bare biological life as such."[30] What is consistently overlooked, as much by Agamben as anyone else, is the fact that Deleuze's first, and by his own estimate best, illustration of "Life" is drawn from fiction. This does not invalidate it, by any means, but as Deleuze would himself be the first to admit, it does place certain interpretive obligations on us, which, to date, Deleuze's philosophical readers have avoided. That obligation, simply put, is to read it in context.

To begin with, no one has mentioned the humor of this passage, yet surely that is its most remarkable feature. The solemnity with which this scene and Deleuze's exegesis of it has been attended by Deleuze's commentators is completely misplaced. It is riotously funny! Deleuze, too, seems to miss the fact that the passage is a mordant satire of the manifold pieties and hypocrisies surrounding such notions as charity, forgiveness, and rebirth. He shows no interest in its ironic intent. But having said that, I am also tempted to think he did not miss its irony, his own mischievous sense of humor finding its best realization in a deadpan delivery. I can easily imagine Deleuze thinking of this scene in his last days and it bringing tears of laughter to his eyes as he contemplated the hypocritical way his philosophical bones would be picked over. Why else choose this passage? If it was only a matter of a scene depicting a character hovering between life and death, he could surely have pointed to other scenes in literature and film of a similarly exemplary kind. To my mind, Rutger Hauer's amazing death scene in *Blade Runner* offers an equally but, and this is precisely my point, quite differently valenced disquisition on "Life."[31] Is not our pity, our pathos, our concern, provoked in that scene by the sense that even cyborgs can contain a "spark of life"?

That Deleuze is quite willing to use literary references in this ironic fashion has already been demonstrated to us by Gregg Lambert, who shows the uncanny way Deleuze uses a discussion of Melville's *Bartleby, the Scrivener* to articulate his critique of Derrida.[32] That Derrida was cognizant of this critique and mindful of its subtle sting is confirmed by his eulogy for Deleuze, which quite explicitly tries to turn the tables on his philosophical rival and return Deleuze's message back to its sender. This in itself has to be seen as an ironic gesture—is not Derrida the one who has taught us to think messages never arrive at their destination? If Deleuze's choice of this particular scene from *Our Mutual Friend* is indeed indicative of his philosophical temper, if it is his way of characterizing himself, then I think it has to be said that Derrida was wrong to say Deleuze is (also) Bartleby. In this instance, the message definitely does not arrive. It is true Deleuze often states his personal preferences in the negative—he prefers not to travel, he prefers not to cut his fingernails, he prefers not to eat, etc.—but his conceptual persona, expressed in his philosophical works as an anarchic delight in treachery, is in fact nearer to that of the Rogue Riderhood, the man who thanks no one for saving his life.[33]

Although it describes a near-death scene, the charmless Rogue Riderhood pulled apparently drowned from the Thames, Dickens makes us laugh at our disregard for the living by juxtaposing it with our romantically inflated evaluation of life: "Neither Riderhood in this world, nor Riderhood in the other, could draw tears from them; but a striving human soul between the two can easily do it."[34] Even rough fellows, as Dickens describes the watchful denizens of the Six Jolly Fellowship Porters (the Thameside pub presided over by Miss Abbey Potterson, who only moments before, and unwitting of the events that were about to unfold, had been moved to pronounce that "Rogue Riderhood is a villain"), find themselves choking up at the prospect of a soul trapped between two worlds. But, when he revives, the rough fellows gathered round his bedside cannot bring themselves to feel joy at his resurrection, even though they had ardently longed for it moments before. His life doesn't seem worthy of it, and though they wouldn't go so far as to wish him dead, they nonetheless feel cheapened by his pulling through. As if in consolation for succeeding, the redoubtable Miss Abbey stands drinks for all the fellows involved in his rescue.

His daughter, too, gives in to the "sweet delusion" that her father will come out of his near-death experience cleansed, somehow purified, reborn even, thanks to his watery trial. And, for a brief moment, she allows herself to believe that he will be forever changed for the better. His lack of character, or rather his bad character, is further contrasted by the picture glass of her evident saintliness that Dickens constructs. Her beatific countenance makes Riderhood's roguishness seem all the worse since apparently he doesn't even have the good grace to spare his daughter's feelings. By the same token, if his daughter can be good, then we must say good can come of bad and Riderhood has no excuse for his lack of reform, but also his blood cannot be blamed for his bad character since that would have affected his daughter too. Our pity, which at first we extend to the near-dead man, is, as his life returns, steadily withdrawn and redirected towards his daughter. The "sweet delusion," not unsurprisingly, doesn't last past the first flicker of life returning to Riderhood's body although clearly the desire remains but becomes twisted and transmuted into bitter regret. Rogue he was, and Rogue he remains.

Humor, Deleuze says, is "an art of consequences and descents, of suspensions and falls."[35] We are moved to laugh first by the way hard hearts seem to melt not, as pity might demand, at the prospect of Riderhood dying but rather in view of some entirely metaphysical entity, "the spark of life." Their impious hearts soar with tender recognition of this sublime element—miraculously untainted by its vile possessor—with which they presume themselves to be blessed too, and momentarily they seem to ascend above their station. They hover like Angels in a rarefied air that isn't theirs to breathe. They have no qualms about judging the life of the victim unworthy of the "Life" they exalt. Meanwhile, Dickens twists his knife a little further by treating the slowness with which Riderhood come to life as an occasion further to confirm his bad character by describing him as "instinctively unwilling to be restored to consciousness of this existence," as though he were shirking work or duty rather than struggling against death![36] His spirit is lazy. The Angels are fallen, mocking creatures.

Our smirks become smiles and uproarious laughter once again, though, at the moment when these dutifully maudlin souls, the rough fellows, the Six Jolly Fellowship Porters, suddenly turn against pity and once more harden themselves. The Angels do not smile upon Riderhood's recovery but rancorously turn their backs. *Ressentiment* replaces the hopeful tender sentiments beating in their burly breasts but moments before. Our final laugh comes when Riderhood revives and not only displays none of the hoped-for transformations his sweetly deluded daughter dreamt might come to pass but quite uncharitably derides his saviors for failing to rescue his hat! If "Life" had lifted him up to the heavens, life itself brings him thudding back to earth. Deleuze's interest in this scene stems from the way Dickens elucidates a notion of life that does not depend on the actual possessor of that life—it is a moment of pure immanence. But the humor of this passage derives from the fact that the possessor of this life is deemed unworthy of the pure immanent form of life animating him. The pure immanent form of life is a height created so that Riderhood can be made to fall.

Perhaps the biggest laugh comes from the impossible, but utterly Dickensian, chain of chance and coincidence contained in the scene. The near dead Rogue Riderhood just happens to be brought to the very place where moments before he had been denounced. It is the one place where his life or death can be greeted with genuine ambivalence of feeling. Elsewhere, pity or indifference is all that could be had. To strangers, his life is bare life and nothing more. But at the Six Jolly Fellowship Porters where his reputation is established and his distraught, but hard put upon daughter is near at hand, Riderhood's fate extracts a very different kind of response. At first, it is met with surprise that the bedraggled figure is known; what appeared a bare life is suddenly transformed into "his" life. This is soon followed by the "bare" hope that "his" life will be saved; in this moment, the feeling for (if not the consciousness of) "Life" emerges and flutters its wings like an ethereal creature, temporarily canceling out all feelings for the quality of "his" life, but, as hope is rewarded, so "Life" and, indeed, "bare" hope start to recede, becoming, finally, dismay and resentment. If it had been strangers who revived him, they would not have known of Riderhood's poor character and would not have been in a position to judge him. So, the dialectical shift between "his" life and "bare" hope could not have occurred. Consequently, the pure immanent form of "Life" could not have been brought into view, at least not this particular modulation of it.

"Life" is reflected in the movement between "his" life and "bare" hope, and it is for this reason that I have argued that the passage as a whole needs to be read in context. Further to this goal, we need to shift our attention from matters of content to issues of form. As I've stated already, it is the formal device of coincidence that enables the humor. It brings about the necessary-but-improbable meeting of a dying stranger with fellows who know him well enough to recognize him and to have opinions as to his character. The whole passage can be described as utterly Dickensian because coincidence is one of Dickens's key formal devices. Indeed, one can scarcely think of a Dickens novel that does not rely on it, either for the farcical intricacies of his set-piece comic sketches or the dramatic irony of his denouements (the conclusion to *Our Mutual Friend* being an excellent case in point). His realism is concentrated in his "thick description" *avant la lettre* of the everyday life of Londoners, in particular, and the English more generally, of virtually every class. It does not, however, extend to his plotting, which has the hallmarks of the adventure novels he gently satirizes several of his characters for reading.

Coincidence can help us to understand Deleuze's concept of "Life" but only if we treat it as an abstract structure or, better still, an "abstract machine." Coincidence looks like a matter of chance, but this impression is false because in narrative there is never any chance that two characters who must meet might not meet. For instance, there was never any chance that Scottie wouldn't see Judy in *Vertigo* (1958) and discover that *his* Madeleine (i.e., not the *real* Madeleine) is still very much alive; by the same token, there was never any chance that Roger Thornhill wouldn't be mistaken for George Kaplan in *North by Northwest* (1959). In other words, Hitchcock's infamous McGuffin, the nothing that always leads to something, is anything but a simple matter of chance. It is no exaggeration, nor indeed denigration, to say Hitchcock's art is an art of the coincidence. But if it isn't a simple matter of chance, neither is it a straightforward case of necessity; for the encounter to be a true coincidence, there must always remain the possibility of it not occurring, of Scottie not seeing Judy, and of somebody besides Roger Thornhill being mistaken for George Kaplan. However necessary the encounters are between Scottie and Judy and Roger Thornhill and his alternate identity George Kaplan, it is equally true and indeed equally necessary that they remain improbable.

A true coincidence is a paradox, but there are many kinds of paradoxes each with their own special significance to what we are calling "Life." The coincidence is an inevitable encounter that seems to occur by chance. In this sense, one can't even say the encounter is "necessary" since, strictly speaking, there is nothing in either the terms of the encounter nor the situation of the encounter that guarantees it will take place. Anyone—at least any man of a certain age—who stood up at the precise moment George Kaplan was called to the telephone could have been apprehended as embodying that fictional entity; by the same token, given how busy the lobby is, if the observers had been differently positioned, they might not have seen Roger Thornhill but somebody else as George Kaplan. Yet if the story is to progress, the unlikely must happen and duly does. From nowhere, the name "George Kaplan" surfaces and abducts the body of Roger Thornhill. All at once, his pleasantly purposeless life, which to that point had been unfolding without much thought to the future, is seized by a fully formed totality whose place in the social grid is quite different from his own.

Scottie wasn't looking for Judy, yet he discovered her all the same; Roger Thornhill could not have contrived to be mistaken for George Kaplan even if he wanted to, yet it happened all the same. As viewers, we want these meetings to take place, albeit after the fact (as must be the case with *North by Northwest*), and know they must take place, but it is essential to our enjoyment of them that they remain contingent, accidents of time rather than accidents befalling particular characters. This is obvious in the second example—if Roger Thornhill was knowingly impersonating or pretending to be George Kaplan, the film would be completely different—but the same must be said for *Vertigo* too: it is because Scottie doesn't expect to find her that his discovery is shattering. Scottie wasn't looking for Judy because he didn't know she existed: every woman and of course no woman was Madeleine to him. To see Judy, he had to fail to see Madeleine, he had to realize that he had been deceived, that Madeleine was really Judy, and hadn't died as he had assumed. In effect, he never sees Judy, just Madeleine a couple of steps removed from her true self, easily correctible with the application of peroxide, costume jewelry, and a new dress.

Coincidence is comprised of two interlocking components: what, in *The Logic of Sense*, Deleuze calls a "mobile empty place" and an "occupant without a place."[37] The woman who was the Madeleine Scottie knew but not the real Madeleine wants to be known for who she really is, but she can only be known to Scottie in the guise of Madeleine. Her "lost" identity is an occupant without a place. Every woman is Madeleine, and no woman is Madeleine—Madeleine is always in excess; she is always the next woman in the series or the one we just missed. Scottie is always too soon and too late in his search for Madeleine. By contrast, Scottie's Madeleine is a mobile empty place. The true coincidence—that is, the true event of sense—in *Vertigo*, then, is not Scottie's discovery of Madeleine's real identity but rather the impossible convergence of the mobile empty place of Madeleine and the occupant without a place of Judy. At this moment, the first series—every woman and no woman is Madeleine—becomes the sense of the second series—Judy can only be known by Scottie as Madeleine and vice versa. The second series—Judy can only be known by Scottie as Madeleine—becomes the sense of the first series—every woman and no woman is Madeleine. Judy's loss of identity is confirmed at the moment when her true identity is discovered, as is Scottie's lack of real interest in her. That he was chasing a phantasm all along is confirmed when he asks Judy to assume that form for him. The truth of the situation serves only to fuel his fantasy-production. Coincidence brings together what had previously been separate but not in order to bring about their confluence. On the contrary, the distance between the two series remains indivisible: no woman, not even Judy, is Madeleine.

One can readily see that George Kaplan is a mobile empty place—everyone and no one is George Kaplan. By the same token, Roger Thornhill is an occupant without a place. The coincidence in this instance is that a louche character like Roger Thornhill, who is so ambivalent about his own identity as to hide behind the ridiculous, false acronym of R.O.T., should be captured by an empty space in such a way as to press him to forge a more concrete sense of himself precisely by adopting this other fictional persona. Roger Thornhill is more himself when he is George Kaplan than he ever was as R.O.T. Now, perhaps more fully than with the previous example, we see the full ambivalence of this system. As we discover early in the film, the "O" in R.O.T stands for nothing, the nothing that by his own estimate is Roger Thornhill himself. This "O" is obviously a mobile empty space. Meanwhile, the identity of George Kaplan lacks only a body to fulfill it and must be regarded as an occupant without a place. As the first series becomes the sense of the second, so in turn the second becomes the sense of the first, and so on in a clasp of mutual presupposition. In neither case, though, does the one answer the other in such a way as to cancel it out, as is evidenced by the fact that when the truth is discovered—when it is learned that not only is Roger Thornhill not George Kaplan but that George Kaplan never existed, it does not alter the course of events. The mobile empty space and occupant without a place do not complete each other; the one does not long for or lack the other. Rather, the mobile empty space and occupant without a place resonate together.

Coincidence is an art of the involuntary. In this respect, Deleuze's analysis of Proust's notion of involuntary memory is central to an understanding of his work as a whole because it is an analysis not only of the specific phenomenon of involuntary memory but the generality I am calling the art of the involuntary. For Deleuze, as for Proust, thought has to be produced and can only be produced via a violent encounter with a contingent object, the sign. Truth, Deleuze says, has to be betrayed. It isn't communicated; it is interpreted. It isn't willed; it is involuntary.[38] Insofar as they rely on the goodwill of thought and remain ignorant of the dark regions and forces of thought, truths are arbitrary, which is why Deleuze sets aside what he terms the "philosophical illusion."[39] The jealous lover and unfaithful beloved know more about truth than the philosopher because they are either constantly on the lookout for any sign that will give the truth away or similarly constant in their bid not to display any tell-tale signs. Moreover, the truth they seek cannot be met with equanimity; there is nothing idle or purely academic about it. No matter how well-prepared the intelligence is in advance of the revelation, the truth when learned will hurt. Intelligence, as both Deleuze and Proust insist, always comes afterwards, which is the second formula of Deleuze's anti-Platonism.

Our prejudice against coincidence in narrative can obviously be explained in psychoanalytic terms as a reality-principle-led reaction against gratification that comes too easily and too quickly. But perhaps there is another explanation to be had, one which takes us in the direction of what might be discouragement rather than disappointment, since what is at stake is our sense of the political rather than our personal pleasure. Coincidences remind us of the arbitrariness of the law and, more particularly, the uncanny way in which its many manifestations beset us and impose an ironclad necessity on that which we want to think of as open. They open up a gap between the river of time we think of as our life and the timeless black holes of the social institutions which punctuate it, creating countless gulfs and rifts. In this way, the use of coincidence in Dickens and Hitchcock recollects something Deleuze refers to as both Lévi-Strauss's paradox and Robinson's paradox.

Lévi-Strauss's paradox is:

> In whatever manner language is acquired, the elements of language must have been given all together, all at once, since they do not exist independently of their possible relations. But the signified in general is of the order of the known, though the known is subject to the law of progressive movement which proceeds from one part to another—*partes extra partes*. And whatever totalizations knowledge may perform, they remain asymptotic to the virtual totality of langue or language. The signifying series organizes a preliminary totality, whereas the signified series arranges the produced totalities.[40]

Robinson's paradox is:

> It is obvious that Robinson, on his desert island, could reconstruct an analogue of society only by giving himself, all at once, all the rules and laws which are reciprocally implicated, even when they still have no objects. The conquest of nature is, on the contrary, progressive, partial, and advances step by step. Any society whatsoever has all of its rules at once—juridical, religious, political, economic; laws governing love and labor, kinship and marriage, servitude and freedom, life and death. But the conquest of nature, without which it would no longer be a society, is achieved progressively, from one source of energy to another, from one object to another.[41]

In both cases, what is at stake is the unstable union of a fully formed virtual entity and an essentially unformed actual entity. The system of language rises up fully formed, and, in an instant, our inchoate vocalizations and gestures are rendered meaningful. The localizing of specific meanings or ranges of meaning attaching to particular sounds or gestures occurs much later and, indeed, is a progressive and ultimately arbitrary process. But, the irruption of meaning as the inescapable condition of all vocalizations and gestures occurs in an instant regardless of how delayed its appearance was. It is in this sense, fated. Similarly, when, by chance, Robinson happens upon Friday on his island and saves him from his fate at the hands of his attackers, it is as an "uncivilized savage" that he perceives him and, in this way, too, a fully formed virtuality captures an unfolding, unformed actuality, namely Friday's life.

How does this help us to understand "Life"? Deleuze's interest in the scene from *Our Mutual Friend* can be explained in terms of the Lévi-Strauss/Robinson paradox as follows: "Life" appears in the moment when the actual unfolding life of Rogue Riderhood is separated from the virtual—but fully real—judgements that society has passed on him and that he wears like a cloak. It presents itself as the possibility of those judgements being varied—it brings them to the surface, briefly, so they can see the light of day. At the surface, where there are neither heights nor depths, no standards by which good and bad can be judged, there is only life, not as it is lived, but as pure thought, a little ray of sunlight. The significance of this is witnessed in the next moment when, as Riderhood seems to regain his breath, thought retreats to the depths and resumes its deformed state as an admixture of principles, opinions, morals, and *ressentiment*. Deleuze's interest in this precise passage probably stems from the way it anticipates Nietzsche's critique of those philosophers who tear down God only to replace it with the false depths of the human, thereby putting Man in His place. Riderhood's rancour, his absolute ingratitude, which gives us our biggest laugh also stops us from being sentimental—our laughter signals that we would not want Riderhood to be different.

This passage has the quality of a primal scene for Deleuze. It adumbrates, at once, his method, his passion, and his politics. For Deleuze, the possibility of revolution resides in the disequilibrium between the progressive unfolding of social life and the solid state of its social rules. Revolutions that favor either one of the two poles of this paradox, either history as the progressive unfolding of social life or History as the always already written destiny of society, wind up making either the error of reformism or the error of totalitarianism. The former "aspires to promote or impose partial arrangements of social relations according to the rhythm of technical achievements," while the latter "aspires to constitute a totalization of the signifiable and the known, according to the rhythm of the social totality existing at a given moment."[42] The "make poverty history" campaign being waged by wealthy white nations today is an example of the former while neo-liberalism, the political doctrine of those wealthy white nations, is clearly an instance of the latter: a poverty alleviating campaign that does not address the iniquities of the system itself can only be so much window-dressing (the same must be said for current campaigns to inoculate the children of Africa against diseases they wouldn't have to contend with if they had clean water, adequate food, and decent housing; likewise, the attempt by the very rich to generalize a model of capitalism that has made them rich is painfully ignorant of the conditions of actual history—as many commentators have said, the only truly totalitarian system is that of the market).[43]

> The technocrat [i.e., reformist] is the natural friend of the dictator—computers and dictatorship; but the revolutionary lives in the gap which separates technical progress from social totality, and inscribes there his dream of permanent revolution. This dream, therefore, is itself action, reality, and effective menace to all established order; it renders possible what it dreams about.[44]

The gap between technical progress and social totality is the passage of pure thought—as Deleuze might say, only thought can grasp these two things in the abstract. Pure thought assumes its revolutionary form when, as Deleuze tirelessly argues, it forms its own problems, not as a function of an insufficiency of knowledge but as an imperative of the mind. A contemporary formulation of this idea is to be found in Fredric Jameson's concept of utopia—for him it takes the form of an impossible demand, such as the demand for universal employment, which, as soon as one tries to think through what it would take to make that happen, necessitates a radical shake up of everything that we had presupposed about both social life itself and the social totality underpinning it. On the one hand, it challenges us to rethink what economists call structural unemployment, that is, unemployment that the system itself deems necessary, whether to discipline the workforce or open up other avenues of realization elsewhere. On the other hand, it opens questions to do with the right to laziness and the implicit undesirability of most forms of labor.[45] Jameson's point, which is precisely Deleuze's point too, is that the demand itself is an "effective menace to all established order; it renders possible what it dreams about."

And, as Jameson argues, it does so precisely by bringing about what he calls a "suspension of the political." This should not be understood to mean it stops politics, but, on the contrary, it enables a renewal of politics precisely by opening up a gap between social progress and social totality in which two series can begin to ramify one another rather than impede and stall one another. Deleuze is constantly on the lookout for these moments, when the revolutionary gap—the mobile empty space and occupant without a place—makes itself felt. In the examples I have given above, what I have wanted to emphasize is the way that time seems to be put out of joint by coincidence and that, in turn, opens up a space for the "I feel" of a revolutionary politics. This, I take it, is what Deleuze means when he says desire invests the total social field. We don't respond to Dickens or Hitchcock because of the kitchen-sink Oedipal crises but because they put thought itself in motion. This is the importance of all the arts for Deleuze; it is why, in his later works, he would substitute the term "war machine" for what, in his earlier books, he simply called pure thought or thought without image. It returns in his cinema books under the heading of the "powers of the false." In his last work, it appears simply as "Life." "It suffices that we dissipate ourselves a little, that we be able to be at the surface, that we stretch our skin like a drum, in order that the 'great politics' begin."[46] ▪

For Martin Fuglsang.

....

1 Gilles Deleuze, *Difference and Repetition*, trans. Paul Patton (New York: Columbia University Press, 1994), 129.
2 Gilles Deleuze, *Proust and Signs: The Complete Text*, trans. Richard Howard (Minneapolis: University of Minnesota Press, 2000), 92.
3 See, for instance, John Rajchman's prefatory remarks to the posthumous collection of Deleuze's essays entitled *Pure Immanence: Essays on a Life,* trans. Anne Boyman (New York: Zone Books, 2001). Rajchman reads this essay, as Agamben does, as both a comment on the state of philosophy today and an outline of a program of work for a philosophy to come, and, in the process, imbues Deleuze's work with the force of a messianism he was himself always at pains to resist.
4 Giorgio Agamben, *Potentialities: Collected Essays in Philosophy*, trans. and ed. Daniel Heller-Roazen (Stanford, Calif.: Stanford University Press, 1999), 238.
5 Ibid., 220.
6 Gilles Deleuze, "Immanence: A Life," in *Pure Immanence: Essays on a Life*, trans. Anne Boyman (New York: Zone Books, 2001), 25-33. The original French publication is: Gilles Deleuze, "L'immanence: une vie … ," *Philosophie* 47 (1995): 3-7.
7 Michel Foucault, "Life: Experience and Science," in *Aesthetics, Method, and Epistemology*, ed. James D. Faubion (New York: Free Press, 1998), 465-478.
8 For the three interviews Deleuze gave on Foucault following the publication of *Foucault*, see Gilles Deleuze, *Negotiations, 1972-90*, trans. Martin Joughin (New York: Columbia University Press, 1995), 83-118. Deleuze acknowledges that Foucault's work underwent a profound shift in the years between the publication of the first and second volumes of his history of sexuality, but he refutes the idea that this represents a turn—or, worse, a return—to the idea of subjectivity that his earlier work had interrogated so brilliantly.
9 Gilles Deleuze and Félix Guattari, *What is Philosophy?*, trans. Hugh Tomlinson and Graham Burchell (New York: Columbia University Press, 1994).
10 Edward W. Said, "Thoughts on the Late Style," *London Review of Books*, vol. 26 (2004): 15.
11 Agamben, *Potentialities*, 238-9.
12 Deleuze, *Difference and Repetition*, 129.
13 For a thorough discussion of this relationship between Butler's work and that of Deleuze and Guattari, refer to my "Introduction" in Ian Buchanan and Marcel Swiboda, eds., *Deleuze and Music* (Edinburgh: Edinburgh University Press, 2004), 7-8.
14 Deleuze, *Difference and Repetition*, 129-131.
15 Ibid., 129.
16 Ibid.
17 Ibid., 131.
18 Ibid., 161.
19 Deleuze, *Pure Immanence*, 27.
20 Ibid., 26.
21 Ibid.
22 Ibid.
23 Lewis Carroll, *The Complete Illustrated Lewis Carroll* (New York: Gallery Books, 1991), 224. For Deleuze's discussion of the passage, see Gilles Deleuze, *The Logic of Sense*, trans. Mark Lester and Charles Stivale (New York: Columbia University Press, 1990), 29-31. See also Deleuze, *Difference and Repetition*, 155.
24 Deleuze, *Difference and Repetition*, xvii.
25 My argument in *Deleuzism* was precisely this: Deleuze's philosophy can be described as

dialectical, if this is what the dialectic is understood to mean. Ian Buchanan, *Deleuzism: A Metacommentary* (Durham: Duke University Press, 2000).

26 We "shouldn't enclose life in the single moment when individual life confronts universal death. *A* life is everywhere, in all the moments that a given living subject goes through and that are measured by given lived objects: an immanent life carrying with it the events or singularities that are merely actualized in subjects and objects." Deleuze, *Pure Immanence,* 29.

27 Cited in David Macey, *The Lives of Michel Foucault* (London: Hutchinson, 1993), 471. Details of the event itself are drawn from the same source. A different translation of the passage appears in Michel Foucault, *The History of Sexuality, vol. 2: The Use of Pleasure,* trans. Robert Hurley (New York: Vintage Books, 1990), 8-9.

28 Gilles Deleuze, *Francis Bacon: The Logic of Sensation*, trans. Daniel Smith (London: Continuum, 2003), 87.

29 Deleuze, *Pure Immanence,* 28-29.

30 Agamben, *Potentialities*, 230.

31 For an extended commentary on this scene, see Buchanan, *Deleuzism,* 127-140.

32 Gregg Lambert, "The Subject of Literature between Derrida and Deleuze: Law or Life?," *Angelaki* 5, no. 2 (2000): 85-6. If further evidence is required, one need only look at chapter three of *A Thousand Plateaus.* There Deleuze and Guattari use the persona of "Professor Challenger" borrowed and adapted from Conan Doyle to satirize themselves. What is significant about this chapter, for my purposes here, is they use this as an occasion to denigrate their disciples and epigones. See Deleuze and Guattari, *A Thousand Plateaus,* trans. Brian Massumi (Minneapolis: University of Minnesota Press, 1987), 39-74.

33 Deleuze makes countless references to the great traitors of literature and film, praising them for their willingness to challenge all assumptions. See, for instance, his comments on Shakespeare's *Richard III* and Herzog's *Aguirre* in Deleuze and Guattari, *A Thousand Plateaus*, 126.

34 Charles Dickens, *Our Mutual Friend* (London: Penguin, 1997), 440.

35 Deleuze, *Difference and Repetition*, 5.

36 Dickens, *Our Mutual Friend,* 440.

37 Deleuze, *The Logic of Sense*, 41.

38 Deleuze, *Proust and Signs: The Complete Text*, 95.

39 Deleuze, *Difference and Repetition*, 161.

40 Deleuze, *The Logic of Sense*, 48.

41 Ibid., 49.

42 Ibid.

43 Clinton's Treasury Secretary and later President of Harvard University Larry Summers's infamous statement—"The laws of economics … are like the laws of engineering. There's only one set of laws and they work everywhere" —is the apotheosis of this abuse of thought. Lawrence Summers, interview by Kirsten Garrett, *Background Briefing*, Australian National Radio, November 1991. Cited in Susan George and Fabrizio Sabelli, *Faith and Credit: the World Bank's Secular Empire* (San Francisco: Westview Press, 1994), 106.

44 Deleuze, *The Logic of Sense*, 49.

45 Fredric Jameson, "Politics of Utopia," *New Left Review* 2, no. 25 (2004): 47.

46 Deleuze, *The Logic of Sense*, 72.

The Politics of Prosthesis: Paul Against Neo-Pauline Universalism

Grant Farred

> *The end is … the question, and a question distinct from all those that are presented as problems.*
> —*Emmanuel Levinas,* God, Death, and Time.[1]

The entire issue here turns on a name. A name that, philosophically speaking, aspires to return to "universal" prominence. The name is Paul, as in the apostle, the most famous "convert" in the early history of Christianity. That Paul should long have occupied theological scholars and philosophers is, given the apostle's explicitly political tendencies, his epistolary gifts (what other New Testament figure writes so lyrically and provocatively of the political of his day?), and his propensity for dogma and institution building, hardly surprising. As the "founder" of Christianity, Paul was, after all, the "intimate of theologians Augustine and Luther, Calvin, Wesley and Karl Barth."[2] Freud, Heidegger, and Nietzsche all engaged Paul in their work.

However, since the discovery of the Gnostic Gospels[3] (in 1945, found buried in the desert sands of the town of Nag Hammadi, Upper Egypt, producing the Nag Hammadi library) and its publication (1972-77), the dominance of Paul and Peter's Church has been challenged. The Gnostic Gospels suggest that Paul and Peter's Church won out over other, competing Christianities, especially that incarnation advocated and led by Mary Magdalene. The Gospel of Mary Magdalene is the principle of the "lost" gospels recovered through the Nag Hammadi discovery. For the Gnostics, Magdalene was Christ's true heir because she was his intimate, perhaps even his wife, and they favored her version of the Church. The Magdalene Church was more democratic and egalitarian, less hierarchical, and nothing like the patriarchal Church that the male apostles eventually produced. In the democratic phrasing of Magdalene's

Gospel, "The Savior said, All nature, all formations, all creatures exist in and with one another, and they will be resolved again into their own roots."[4]

Subjected to an invigorated Gnostic and feminist criticism, it is appropriate that the name of the apostle Paul should in our moment articulate, above all else, the "questions" of universality and particularity. The dialectic between universality and particularity deriving from Paul in the time of the now, *ho nyn kairos*, can be thought as a Levinasian "question" because these issues are politically constitutive. These questions are philosophically distinct; they inform rather than being dependent on the "problems" that arise in relation to them. The philosophical re-turn to Paul is instructive because, in the contemporary struggle over his Judeo-Christian legacy, it reveals what is Pauline—or, what is desirable about a certain Pauline philosophy—in the politics of the *kairos*.

It would be wrong to name Paul's return to philosophical prominence a "resurrection," however much the event of the Resurrection is, in different ways, the key Pauline moment for Badiou and Žižek. For this reason, the turn to Paul by contemporary philosophers makes clear that it is not enough to ask "Why Paul?" Rather, the question must be extended into specificity: "Why Paul now?" To what use is Paul being put at this particular moment? From where do the Pauline philosophers speak? What is at stake in this delineation of Paul? This neo-Pauline politics that is enunciated through the left philosophical discourses of Giorgio Agamben, *The Time that Remains* (2005), Alain Badiou, *Saint Paul: The Foundations of Universalism* (2003), and Slavoj Žižek, *The Puppet and the Dwarf: The Perverse Core of Christianity* (2003).[5] Published within two years of each other by, arguably, the leading Western and Central (in Žižek's case) European philosophers of our day, in which they are so inter-textual as to regularly reference each other's work on Paul, these texts do more than compel a reading together. Their coincidence poses itself as a Shakespearean inquiry: what is intellectually afoot? What ghostly stirrings in the politics of the now have contributed to produce this simultaneous turn to Paul? Why is ours, again, the time of Paul's reemergence? What is the political secret that Paul alone knows?

In truth, however, for all its philosophical cross-referencing, neo-Paulinism is not a politically monolithic project. (Žižek is especially prone in this regard, as he is extremely enamored of Badiou's work on the apostle.) Loosely conceived, Badiou, for whom Paul is the Maoist "anti-philosopher" and Žižek, for whom Paul is a "Leninist," can be said to represent one version of the neo-Paulinism. On the other hand, Agamben's Paul, who marks an instance of the "revolutionary messianic," constitutes a signal political disagreement with his fellow-Europeans. Finally, however, Žižek's Paul is too elliptical a figure, too much a "vanishing mediator,"[6] not the philosophical focus in the same way that the apostle is in Agamben and Badiou's work. For this reason, my argument is restricted to the latter two thinkers, although there is a significant amount of shared conceptual ground among these philosophers. Agamben's is a disagreement that, even as it never becomes antagonistic, at its core represents a serious challenge to Badiou's rendering of Paul.

In an attempt to frame the "question" of Paul's contemporary philosophical ubiquity in a different but not unrelated way, this essay introduces a "third" Paul, the literary Paul–"Paul Rayment," to be exact–of J.M. Coetzee's novel *Slow Man*. Coetzee's Paul is a diasporic European, born in France, raised by a Dutch stepfather for whom he has no affection, and is an avid cyclist. Paul is recovering from the amputation of a leg, the result of an accident with a car while riding his bike in Adelaide, the South Australian city where Rayment and Coetzee now live. Resignedly bitter about the loss of his leg, "[f]irst the violation, then consent to the violation," Paul is such a diasporic being that he calls Adelaide, with his customary understated *ressentiment*, not a "home" but a "domicile, a residence."[7] The literary Paul and the apostle Paul share, however, more than simply a name, though that is by no means an unimportant bond. Coetzee's character calls "St. Paul his namesake, his saint-name. … When he arrives at the gate, St. Paul (for other new souls it may be Peter but for him it will be Paul) will be waiting."[8] In this moment of St. Paul's umpteenth emergence into philosophical prominence, *Slow Man* provides a counterweight. Paul Rayment re-orients, as this essay demonstrates, the relationship of the universal to the particular. Paul's amputation introduces the prosthetic as a politics that reconfigures how the universal might be conceived in its relation to the particular. While the *Slow Man* particular frequently disarticulates the neo-Pauline universal, there are also moments in which the prosthetic functions as a complicated conjuncture of the two, the "extended, artificial" meeting place of the universal and the particular. Through the prosthetic, a specific kind of relatedness between the particular and the universal is revealed.

At the very conjuncture that Paul, formerly Saul of Tarsus, is bequeathed yet another philosophical life, Paul Rayment insists upon living in the time of dying. "A man not wholly a man. … [L]ooking back in regret on time not well used,"[9] the literary Paul is, in Agamben's terms, struggling against the "time that remains" in a remaindered body. Bound by a common name that has assumed, in the course of intellectual history, an uncommon signality and preoccupied with the intense vagaries of temporality, Coetzee's "literary" Paul—the apostle is, of course, himself profoundly literary, a prolific "man of letters"—enables an interrogation of the philosophical Paul through the diaspora. Born in Tarsus, converted on the road to Damascus, resident in Arabia for three years, Paul engaged with Peter and the apostles during his time in Jerusalem. He was active on behalf of the Church in Rome, then, in Badiou's terms, became a "militant voyager" for Christianity in "Cicilia, Syria, Turkey, Macedonia, Greece."[10]

It is precisely Paul's missionary tendencies, the "fundamentalist" Christian convert who relentlessly makes his way around the Judeo-Christian world, indiscriminately calling others to this newly founded faith, that produce in Badiou's representation the "*ex-centered* dimension of Paul's actions."[11] Paul is a "fundamentalist" in the sense both that he is at the fundament of the Church and, as important, that he is "flexibly dogmatic" in his belief, prepared to welcome both Gentiles and Jews into the Church, the "circumcised and the uncircumcised," but never wavering on the singularity of Christendom. As an apostle Paul does his political work because he can function in his world, in the world he is making as the missionary *sui generis*, without a primary locus: without a "home." (The apostle Paul represents the missionary, the bearer and speaker of a new truth, before there were any missionaries, the mobile missionary against whom all future missionaries would be measured.) Tarsus or the road to Damascus, in Badiou's psychic calculations, is little different, the fundamental experience of conversion apart, for Paul than Cicilia or Macedonia; Rome is the same as Jerusalem.

Badiou is unable to conceive of Paul's missionary work as (pre-)figuring a diaspora or to acknowledge that the apostle is in part a fundamental figure in Christian theology and the early political life of the Church precisely because of his perpetual dislocation; it is the apostle's un-rootedness, his lack of "real" connections to any one place, that makes him such an effective spokesperson for Jesus Christ. It is because of his diasporic proclivities that "Saint Paul" stands in such sharp contrast to Paul Rayment. Coetzee's Paul openly admits to the problematic of diasporic existence. As Paul remarks to Elizabeth Costello, the heroine of an earlier Coetzee novel (*Elizabeth Costello*) and herself something of a diasporic figure, now returned to unsettle the "slowed man,"

> I had three doses of the immigrant experience, not just one, so it imprinted itself quite deeply. First when I was uprooted as a child and brought to Australia; then when I declared my independence and returned to France; then when I gave up France and came back to Australia. *Is this where I belong?* I asked with each move. *Is this my true home?*[12]

The deracinations that constitute the diaspora preclude an easy, "permanent" answer to the inquiry about "home" and "belonging," so Paul is "condemned" to live, not only as an amputee in the time of dying, but with the "remains" of several other times.

The remainder of the time left to live is not constituted only out of the time left over (to live), but also the time that is passed but is not yet passed. This is because the time accrues, multiplies, and complicates itself with each migration—each movement between North and South, each voyage between France and Australia. The "time that remains" represents a complex arithmetic, a series of temporal additions and subtractions that result in a time which is, "paradoxically" (because it is not really a paradox), at once being reduced by the very act of living and yet extends beyond the life of its own chronological time. The act of living in time produces, as it were, a time independent of the *chronos*. In the pithy philosophical terms of *Slow Man*, "*Those into whose lives you are born do not pass away.*"[13] There is, despite the finitude of life and the inexplicable, unalterable certainty of death as the "end" of (a) time, a transcendent permanence to time: the "remainder" succeeds into the "remainder." The individual life achieves an uncanny, unexpected atemporality simply by virtue of its "birth" into other lives, lives now "remaindered" ad infinitum into the "time of the born." Paradoxically, however, there is also a haunting finitude to the remainder. While those other lives "do not pass away," the individual life is vulnerable to erasure, to the process of "passing away" even as it survives, we might say, prosthetically—contained within the "artifice" of other lives and literary memory. A life relocated, as both the apostle Paul's and Paul Rayment's are, from one (diasporic) articulation to another.

In his turn, Badiou can only explain the absence of a diasporic discourse through its negation. For Badiou, Paul is not a (diasporic) proselytizer but a figure of that epistemology that invalidates the history of movement between places, that history of human migration that can claim a distinct name. Paul, as indicated in the subtitle of Badiou's work, is the "founder of universalism." As such, "all true universality is devoid of a center,"[14] ensuring that there is no need to account for diasporic movement, no need to recognize the particular difficulties of transition, of asking "is this my true home?" Such a Levinasian question, which opens immediately on to issues of gender and domesticity, has no interest for the subject of universality. It is precisely this neo-Pauline discourse of universality that Coetzee, as unlikely author of the diaspora, interrupts. Coetzee is a South African-born novelist who, despite his many "native" novels (*Dusklands, The Life and Times of Michael K, In the Heart of the Country*, and, of course, most controversially, *Disgrace*) is widely regarded as more universalist than diasporic in his literary concerns. He is the "international" (South) African writer, author of, most notably in this regard, *Waiting for the Barbarians*, *Foe*, and *The Master of Petersburg*. It is ironic, then, that it should be the (white, "expatriate") South African novelist who iterates the diasporic Paul as the disruption of the neo-Pauline *kairos*.

Saliently, Coetzee reorients the discourse about the diaspora in two crucial ways: racially and geographically. In *Slow Man* the diaspora becomes a "*bildungsroman*" of relocations, from the North to the South (childhood), from the South to the North (adolescence/young adulthood), from the North (back) to the South (adulthood); there is also contained within this trajectory a colonialist mapping of European movement— "settlement" in the Antipodean South—without the overtones of imperial conquest. Immobile, or, only partially mobile, Paul can be said to represent the post-imperial European not so much exhausted by movement as chronically unable to make a place in a world defined by diasporic populations—a world in which Australia is peopled by immigrant Anglos, Croats, Greeks, Irish, and French, among others. By virtue of his whiteness and his class, Paul disarticulates the prevailing representation of the diasporic subject: black or brown, Third World, impoverished, and assigned only the most menial of tasks. Typical of the complexity of Coetzee's fiction, the diaspora is critically "defamiliarized" and reconceived in *Slow Man*. Having himself recently relocated from Cape Town, South Africa to Adelaide, Coetzee has produced in Paul Rayment an articulation against Badiouian universality, a process that the "Slow Man" transforms into inquiry about neo-Paulinism: Why universalism? Why this strident European philosophical advocacy for universalism now?

Neo-Pauline Universalism: An Old Secret

> *[T]he event of a second mystery does not destroy the first. On the contrary it keeps it inside it unconsciously, after having effected a topical displacement*

> *and a hierarchical subordination: one's secret is at the same time enclosed and dominated by the other.*
> —*Jacques Derrida,* The Gift of Death[15]

For Badiou, Paul functions as the urgent inscription of, if not a "new" universalism, then a new need for universalism, a historical demand borne of what Badiou perceives to be a "crisis of truth." Writing as a leftist philosopher against the backdrop of neo-liberalism's putative triumph over (almost) all forms of socialism, Badiou asks: "What, in effect, does our contemporary situation consist of? The progressive reduction of the question of truth (and, hence, of thought) … ends up in a cultural and historical relativism that today constitutes at once a topic of public opinion, a 'political' motivation."[16] Badiou's real argument, as can be glimpsed here, is against "cultural relativism," the main political product of identity politics, that offspring of the New Left so abhorrent to Badiou. Identity politics is, in Badiou's estimation, responsible for the disarticulation and subsequent "demise" of the "old" Left's universalist project—that is, the Maoist, Leninist (European) left. It is a state of political affairs to which Badiou is firmly opposed: "All access to the universal, which neither tolerates assignations to the particular, nor maintains any direct relation with the status—whether it be that of dominator or victim—of the *sites* from which its proposition emerges, collapses when confronted with this intersection between culturalist ideology and the 'victimist' [*victimaire*] conception of man."[17] It is the rise of the "particular," the triumph of a "culturalist ideology" and a "victimist" politics that Badiou resists through the apostle.[18]

Paul stands for Badiou as that figure of the (Christian) political for whom "*universalist singularity*" is the only mode of militant being.[19] When Badiou extrapolates from this claim, "Universalizable singularity necessarily breaks with identitarian singularity," he is arguing not only that the "universal" is distinct from the "identitarian," but he is campaigning against the "disruptive" political effects of the particular.[20] Badiou is "intolerant" of the "particular," always refusing any recourse to a minoritarian discourse that privileges one experiential mode because it amounts to little more, in his estimation, than the narcissism of small differences: what he names "puny liberal differences."[21] This is an economical rhetorical maneuver because not only is Badiou dismissing the political import of difference (it is only "puny" and therefore historically inconsequential), but he is also aligning the "identitarian" movement with liberalism, explicitly reserving for universalist struggle alone the claim to the radical or the revolutionary. The identitarian is always, in Badiou's calculation, less than—in other words, "puny." His critique of the particular provokes, because of the history of political struggles around identity from the 1960s, and sharpened immeasurably from the late-1970s through the 1990s, a series of questions about the reasons for Badiou's antipathy. What political place, what history of struggle, we might inquire, would Badiou assign "suffering" derived from racism, "oppression" rooted in ethnic hatred, or "routine degradation" founded upon sexual orientation? Why is it so necessary, like Badiou, to be critical of it because it is only particular to a single constituency?

Its particularity, its understanding of itself as different, as incommensurable with others/other instances of resistance, its liberal inconsequentiality inherently disqualify the identitarian from constituting the grounds for a universalist struggle. The universalist is for Badiou the only political—not cultural or feminist, the patriarchy clearly declared in the designation "man"—resistance worthy of the name "struggle," although he might insist upon its proper designation, "revolution," so as to distinguish it from the particularity of feminist or cultural struggles. Particularity stands in contradistinction, for Badiou, to what Paul's birth as a political subject represents: the inauguration of universalist discourse, the "advent of a subject," the post-Resurrection Christian—convert or born—created as subject through the articulation of the "Christ event."[22] We might, of course, easily substitute the indefinite article "a" for its proper replacement, "the," so as to signify the "advent of *the* subject," which is clearly how Badiou intends to mark Paul's coming into political being. Badiou's is a minimalist political imaginary, pared of everything except the fact of Christ dying on the cross and being resurrected: "The rest, all the rest, is of no real importance."[23] It is a dismissive logic, Badiou's, impatient—implicitly—with the kind of political energies, commitments, and deliberations that make up and sustain a resistance borne out of particularity.

It is also a logic of subject formation that fails to take account of the feminist critique produced by scholars of the Magdalene.[24] For his part, Badiou disingenuously tries to divorce Paul from religion. According to Badiou, "Basically, I have never really connected Paul with religion."[25] By several historical accounts a "fallen woman," it is to the Magdalene—not the (male) apostles—that the event of the Resurrection is announced:

> Jesus saith unto her, Mary. She turned herself and saith unto him, Rabboni; which is to say, Master.
>
> Jesus saith unto her, Touch me not; for I am not yet ascended to my Father; but go to my brethren, and say unto them, I ascend unto my Father, and your Father; and *to* my God, and your God.[26]

It is this revelation, this act of enunciation, from Jesus to Mary, that makes the Magdalene the "apostle to the apostles,"[27] the emissary of the Resurrection—the (bearer of the) Word of Life. Without the words, "go unto my brethren, and say unto them, I ascend to my Father," of the particular subject, woman, the apostle Paul can have no political project, no Church to found because he would have no knowledge of the Christ event. The Magdalene's articulation functions here as Christ's representation to the world, in his (constitutive) absence—she acts in and on behalf of his miraculous reemergence into a transcendent presence. Jesus is spoken in his absence by the (female) part that Paul's Church will diminish in its (triumphalist) account of the Christ event. Paradoxical, then, that the Pauline universal would be impossible without the "intervention," "translation," and "transmission" by the particular. It is the Word of Woman that makes possible Pauline Man, that political subject that so preoccupies Badiou. (It is, of course, exactly this debate about the particular—

Woman—that has, in part, fueled the current controversy about Dan Brown's hugely popular novel, *The Da Vinci Code* in which Jesus and Mary Magdalene are married. Which in itself, of course, provokes a series of "Pauline" questions: Why? Why now? How does this articulation of the Magdalene as Christ's prosthesis complicate the understanding of the Pauline debates, of the popularity of the Gnostic recuperation, or of its occlusion and repression?)[28]

For Agamben, the struggle mobilized by identity is constituted out of the "rest, all the rest," that which he names the "remainder." The "remnant," that which exists outside of Badiou's revolutionary "core," represents that site of (Badiouian) articulation from and for which the "particular" has no purchase. Because it is "ex-centered," displaced from the hub of universalist politics, the particular has to be particularly aware of itself as "the rest," because that is the time from which it articulates. The "rest," the leftovers of universalist dominance, is the time that is not included within the ambit of the universal, the time that is not presumed to possess a historical temporality, that exists only as a fragment, a scant narratological "remainder" of political "victimization," or the repression of a people's "culture."

Through the discourse of the "remainder," Agamben critiques Badiou's fundamentalism by reorienting—or, de-orienting, we might say—Saint Paul as universalist. More to the point, Agamben claims that Paul's universalism is itself only possible if it is conceived as a fragmented politics: "It makes no sense to speak of universalism with regard to Paul, at least when the universal is thought of as a principle of cuts and divisions, and the individual as the ultimate limit of each division. In this sense, there is neither beginning nor end in Paul, only Apelles' cuts, the division of division, and then a remnant."[29] In other words, "the rest, and all the rest," matter; there is no Letter from Paul without the Word of Mary Magdalene, no Pauline Scripture without the specter of the Gnostic Gospels, no patriarchal writing sans its "buried" feminist counterpoint; there is no universality without the (resisting) subsumption of particularity. There is no understanding Paul's complicated "universalist" status without accounting for the "remnant" that derives from the "principle of cuts and divisions."

There can be no Paul, no Church, without the specter of Mary, and the "formation" of the Magdalene Church (founded upon "All nature, all creatures" that "exist in and with one another") that was lost to history because of Pauline repression (the fear of women because of sex; the fear of women as sex) and dogma (the notion of "One Holy Catholic and Apostolic Church"). There can be, if we are to think the philosophical and the literary together, no Paul of Rome and Turkey who is not also, simultaneously, divided, "cut" into the political fiber of Paul of France and Australia, that Paul who claims the apostle as a name(-sake) that is more than simply a name because the Biblical Paul is written into him, that literary text in which the Magdalene returns as "Marijana," the diasporic Croatian nurse who tends to the amputated Paul. ("Marijana" is, of course, the Slavic equivalent of "Marianne," a derivative of "Mary.") In contrast to the marked absence of the Magdalene in Badiou's work, in *Slow Man*, a new relationship, a complex one, made up of physical and emotional dependency (Paul's), financial dependency (Marijana's), desire (almost all of it emanating from Paul), and a shared diasporic past, is produced between "Paul" and "Mary Magdalene."

If Coetzee's Paul were stripped of his "raiment," his now ill-fitting garments, revealed would be the philosophical imprint of Agamben's Paul—publicly visible in the ugliness of the "cut" limb. Saint Paul cannot be said to "begin or end" in either universality or particularity because the force of "division" is so rhizomatic that it cuts across, that it "traces" itself all over, the ontological body of both the One and the Many. Contained in every Pauline "remnant," therefore, is the narrative of universality that can only survive in and through its relation to particularity, a series of "cuts" that makes in-conceivable, a priori divided, any project with universalist ambitions. "It is," as Agamben suggests, "neither the all nor a part of the all, but the impossibility for the part and the all to coincide with themselves or with each other."[30] Moreover, in the repeated call for the universal, there is, in Derrida's terms, the secretly instantiated question: What of the particular? A question that sharpens into: Why militate so strongly against the particular?

The "secret" of Badiou's universalist project is, following Derrida's notion of the one secret being "enclosed and dominated by the other," the "other secret": the political use of Paul in the struggle against the particular; the secret of the female Gnostic Gospels eliminated from Biblical memory by Paul's heirs. Through the rearticulation of Paul, Badiou, as well as Žižek, reveals the "real" secret of the universalist project: the *raison d'être* for the denunciation of the particular. The particular must be written against in the cause of reinscribing the white, male, European philosopher as not only the source of all epistemology, but as *the* theorist of a radical left politics. The neo-Pauline European philosopher stands against the division produced by "puny" identitarian politics. The history of the particular represents a struggle and a set of accomplishments now everywhere under threat because of the self-same neo-liberalism that Badiou believes it subscribes to and has been co-opted by. It is this form of a dis-articulated left politics that Badiou indicts for having decentered the white male philosopher. The "truth content" of Badiou's thinking in this regard is, to say the least, dubious, but it accounts for the re-emergence of Saint Paul. It is ironic that Paul, who deems himself as the "least of the apostles, that am not meet to be called an apostle," whose "mission" derives from that historic encounter with the particular, should stand in with such catholicity, with such political force, for the project of white, Judeo-Christian, philosophical masculinity.[31] Or, is it simply that Paul's is, as we might expect from so relentless a proselytizer, a man so steadfast in his faith that he can easily be called a zealot, a false modesty? That Paul, who disingenuously declares himself not fit to be an apostle, "not meet to be called an apostle," really understands himself to be, as the Founder of the Christian Church, the leading—or the greatest—of the Christian Elect? After all, as scholars have argued, Paul did not hold his peers, especially Peter, James, and John, in high regard.[32]

There is, then, something probative about Badiou's inquiry: "No discourse can lay claim to truth if it does not contain an explicit answer to a very particular question: Who speaks?"[33] This is, however, precisely the question that Badiou, in his appropriation of Paul, does not confront: "Who speaks" Paul? Moreover, in order to follow

Badiou's interrogative lead and make it accountable to the politics of our moment, there is another urgent question to be asked: Who is Paul speaking? It is not simply that the enunciative act demands a response, but that the enunciative act must be aware of its own condition of speaking: the discursive "truth" must be compelled into its proper relationship with its own locus of articulation. The claim upon Paul, much like the claim upon truth, is made from a particular place, in a particular time, with a particular political end in mind. The speaker—the putative "Who"—must be considered in relation to her or his motivation. Much like the "Who" must be identified, so too the "Why" must be explicated.

The "particular" designates all those ex-centric to the universal, all those constituencies ignored, taken for granted, incorporated without ever having the particularities, as it were, of their condition assigned primacy—any place at the Badiouian "center." These are the struggles that women, raced communities, gays and lesbians, environmentalists, and the disabled, among others, took up because left universalism did not so much fail them—though it can certainly be said to have done that—as it did ignore them by assigning them to the status of the Badiouian "rest" which they so resented, resisted, and then crafted into a politics of their own. The struggles mobilized by identity constituted a critique of universalism. Saint Paul is now being pressed into service to counter that trend at, ironically, the very moment that this identity-based struggle itself now teeters firmly on the back foot. The universalist, neo-Pauline left is, whether it acknowledges it or not, joining forces with the triumphalist neo-liberal center and reactionary right. The neo-Paulinists are doing so at precisely, for many constituencies across the globe, that moment in history—our contemporary one—that is a most vulnerable juncture for race, ethnic and gender politics, as well as, it should be added, a politics of religion.

What Badiou wants to reinstall is the old "hierarchy of subordination," the rearticulation of a hegemonic Pauline Church in the moment of its confrontation with Mary Magdalene's reemergence. Badiou's neo-Paulinism is based on the discredited—by the proponents of and activists for the particular—notion of white, male, European philosophical and political preeminence. However, it is, as Derrida reminds us, precisely because secrets are so folded into each other that the advocating of one invariably leads to an unraveling that reveals the other. The secret of "hierarchical subordination," which is of course nothing but an open "secret" (in the sense that it derives its power from the fact that it is known and so does not need to be spoken), cannot be made public without allowing for the articulation of that which lies "enclosed." That which is "dominated" cannot, within the political, be "divided" from that which is dominant. Universalism cannot reveal itself without provoking into political life that which it names the particular. It is, whether or not he names it as such or leaves it vaguely denominated as "historical and cultural relativism," the politics of particularity: issues of race, sexual orientation, gender, and environmentalism, that Badiou advocates "sacrificing" in the cause of a Maoist leftism, a leftism now lent a philosophical and theological gloss by the marshalling of Saint Paul, the militant early Christian who stood, in Badiou's view, for the One. If Paul is Badiou's argument against division, then division is precisely the specter that returns as the very measure against which universality must be articulated. Difference, "division's" more appropriate name in its identity-politics formulation, can never be banished, and because of it, universalism is condemned to the Sisyphean struggle that so occupies Badiou.

"That lumpish thing": Amputation Into a Particular Politics

> *The remnant is the figure, or the substantiality assumed by a people in a decisive moment, and as such is the only real political subject.*
> —*Giorgio Agamben,* The Time that Remains[34]

The particular of Coetzee's amputated, diasporic Paul disarticulates Badiou's Saint Paul by demonstrating how the part is more powerful than the whole, the Many more powerful than the One. Part Western European, part Australian, and, secretly, part (South) African, not-so-secretly diasporic, Paul's inability to make of himself a "whole" out of the parts—either by subsuming some, repressing others, or repressing still others—makes manifest how difficult to obtain the One is. There is always more than one part in political play, always more than one particularity at work in and on the political subject. There is, for this reason, a close relationship between the (absolute) part and the (absolute) whole. Even as it is necessary to keep operative the tension between the part and the whole, it is also important to think this oppositionality as, following the topography of Paul's body, a prosthesis.

Part of the act of living without a part, the severed limb, is coming to terms with the new artifice of the body. Through the difficulty of relating to his "crippled self," Paul—who rejects the use of a prosthetic limb and a recumbent, a bicycle made especially for the disabled—struggles to find a new name for himself.[35] A name, that is, which fits, a name appropriate to his "diminished" condition. None of the names he rifles through, "circumscribed life," "this unlovely new body of his," "a half-man, like an after-image," fit.[36] The secret of the rejected prosthesis is that it makes the prosthetic a ghostly presence—it becomes the site of repressed memory, becoming, in the process, a prosthetic limb, a "prosthetic" repository of physical and psychic memory. The amputated limb demands its own explanation: about why it is condemned to an "artificial" lack, about why it cannot be granted the prosthetic part that would make it prosthetically whole. The discourse of the prosthetic, which mediates (and displaces, it could be argued), the part-whole dialectic, emerges in an uncanny articulation in Paul Rayment's inability to command language, to own a language, to live in language comfortably. To make, that is, the speaking of (a) language autochthonous to his body.

For Paul the experience of dislocation even when located within the Whole, the sense of being particular even when there is the universality of language to do the work of relating, of making possible a permanent speaking as a member of the Whole, manifests itself both linguistically and physically. When Paul declares, with a memorably philosophical emphasis, "I am not the *we* of anyone," he is doing more than dissociating himself from any substantive relation to the nation. (There is for Paul

Rayment, of course, more than one nation in question. It could be France or Australia. His stepfather's Holland is surely not an option.) He is also elucidating the particularity of alienation within a shared—but not felt—language: "It is not I who speak the language, it is the language spoken through me. It does not come from my core, *mon coeur*."[37] Paul is in a prosthetic, complicatedly agential relationship to language: he is being spoken rather than "speaking" the language; he knows the formal rules of the language but he is never able to speak it with authority, with the sense that it is "his," that it is more than a prosthetic extension of him. The act of speaking is, for Paul, almost always a practice that he attaches to himself, a facility he contracts from the outside in order to function in the world. Language is not, unlike as it is with the linguistically deft "apostle," innate to Paul, something that flows naturally from (within) him, something that belongs naturally to him. Speaking is the prosthetic social part that allows Paul the pretense of a social wholeness, but it is also a part that is wholly unto itself, wholly outside him, non-constitutive of him.

It is the prosthetic experience of linguistic deracination, that rapid movement from childhood French to the teenage encounter with Dutch to living in English as an adult ("English came too late to me. It did not come with mother's milk"[38]) that denies the possibility of a universal, linguistically or psychically whole, "core." For Paul there is no center that will allow language, his language (whatever that might be, English, French) and the many languages (Australian English, the Croatian vowels of his nurse, the Greek widely spoken in Elizabeth Costello's Melbourne) he hears around him, to cohere, to hold subjects in a formal, dependable relation to each other. While Paul considers himself without a language, Derrida locates in this exasperation, this condition of linguistic impossibility, the kernel of a particularistic disarticulation: "Is one responsible for what one says in an unintelligible language, in the language of the other? … mustn't responsibility always be expressed in a language that is foreign to what the community can already hear or understand only too well?"[39] Here Derrida is making the case for the interrogative value of the particular: the "foreign" is that which interrupts the dominant, which enables another language—or, another articulation of the dominant language—to be heard. Spoken from the location of the particular, the minority constituency, we might say, the "foreign" irrupts into the discourse, making possible another kind of critical intervention, another kind of imagining of the political—the particular is what makes the universal foreign, philosophically strange to itself.

In the process of engaging the language of irruption, the particular restores the enfolded secrets of the universal to itself. This takes place through the process of defamiliarization, the violent linguistic confrontation with "what the community" cannot hear; the particular instigates the encounter with that aspect of its life that the community no longer "understands only too well." It is Paul's doubt, his uncertainty about his place in language, his prosthetic relationship to the act of speaking, that makes, according to Derrida, an entirely different series of questions necessary: "As often happens, the call of or for the question, and the request that often echoes through it, takes us further than the response."[40] Paul can, even as he lives in the time of dying, live in a language he cannot inhabit, a language he cannot speak with affective or psychic fluency. Paul has to draw into question the particularities of his linguistic and discursive discomfiture. He has to move beyond himself, to that place where, like all diasporic locales, other languages echo, where other questions are opened onto because of the particular inadequacies of his "response."

For Paul, the prosthetic assists, because it reveals the artifice with which the diasporic subject deploys language, in the process of taking the possibilities for (linguistic) interrogation beyond itself. The diasporic subject takes Derrida's "question" "further than the responses" because it recognizes the value of the prosthetic: of taking the interrogative beyond that point where the "natural" body ends and into the "foreign" terrain of artifice, that "attached" location of thought where a different set of "natural" skills can be learned. And, moreover, skills practiced to the point where they enjoy a certain "natural," yet still unnatural (because the prosthetic is only "partly" the body's "own" limb), artificial facility. Through the prosthetic, the body can act as itself in excess of itself.

In physical terms, the traumatic, disconcerting presence of the "part limb," what Paul calls a "lumpish thing," demonstrates how the part, the particular part, the particular history of the part, can overwhelm the whole, reduce it to a "curtailed, humiliating, and humiliated state."[41] This is the power of the part: it enables Coetzee's Paul to dislocate the universalist project to those places—displaced, repressed places—where his name conjures up another meaning, another project: to think against the neo-Pauline philosophical of our moment, to create literary room for the diasporic Magdalene. The Pauline Church of universality must once again, much like after Luther and Calvin's Reformation movement, be disarticulated into the philosophical Many, into a series of philosophical parts in political conflict with each other, at odds with each other, resistant to the possibility of cooptation into the One that recognizes no political value in its part, in its apartness, in its prosthetic attachment, that represses Mary Magdalene's Gnostic apostolic qualities into St. Paul's singular Word: that silences Magdalene's knowledge. Emphatically phrased, because *gnosis* translates as "knowledge" from Greek, Paul's Word represses knowledge of the Magdalene. Contained in the Magdalene Church and the Gnostic Gospels is the most haunting secret of neo-Paulinism: its resistance to a resurgent, particularist, democratic *gnosis*; the historic knowledge of the particular as an old, vaunted critique of the Pauline suppression of opposition to its "universalist" dominance.

It is in the unexpected articulation of *Slow Man* that it constructs a Paul who separates Saint Paul into political usefulness through Rayment's falling into fragments, his breaking off of and from himself. As Paul remarks in one of his more acerbic moments, punning on Marx, "Thesis, antithesis, then prosthesis."[42] However, it is because Paul Rayment complicates the notion of a "prosthetic" wholeness that he is able to make aesthetic—"literary," if you will—the politics of particularity. It is the part, the broken part, that, like all particulars, suffers from a broken, scarred history, a history of the particular that has had many brushes with political, economic, and cultural death, that Paul's ambivalence about the prosthetic—even as he rejects the artificial limb, so he from time to time considers the appendage—makes disturbingly public. It is, for Paul, an ugly thing, this amputated limb, something he can barely look at himself, but he will not hide, give himself an artificial mobility, a public wholeness. Instead, he resigns himself to the "detestation of the lumpish thing he will henceforth have to lug around with him."[43]

"Detestation" or no, Paul revels, almost, in his newfound partness, this reduction of his body, this marking of his body as remarkable because of its reductions, that leaves him marked as Other, different, whenever he encounters the world, either in his own home or on the street—where Elizabeth Costello is apt to drag him from time to time. It is through this Paul, the unheroic, agnostic, diasporic, unsightly, ordinary, and unsaintly, that Coetzee installs the part as the site of a grounded, if reluctant, disaffected politics of particularity—the politics, we might say, that revolves around the unspeakable, that "lumpish thing." The politics of the particular is, Coetzee might be said to suggest, rarely a thing of beauty. Historically, however, it is always necessary, however aesthetically unpleasing and however much it is unwelcomed by the neo-Paulinists. The particular is always both immanent, politically manifest, and imminent, a single articulation away from making itself visible—from announcing itself as the rejection of the prosthetic wholeness of the universal.

The true epistemic violence of the particular is its capacity to reveal itself, in public, in its full de-formation. It speaks its difference viscerally; it makes public that point at which it breaks off from the universal. It will not, it cannot, by virtue of its unprosthetic self-representation, incorporate itself into—accommodate itself to—a universality that will not understand how its "deformities" came about, that will account for its dislocations. Phrased within the historical narrativization of the novel, "Limbs have memories."[44] The body, amputated or not, is the repository of a history from which it cannot be severed and that is so deeply encoded within it that even the mechanical reduction of an arm or a leg cannot eradicate that memory. The "memories of the limb" represent that place called the politics of the particular: it is that place and time where the body of the particular, the body that has to live by and with the complications of its identity, displaces the narrative of political resistance, survival, and occasional respite, from one site to another. It is in his difficulty with "inhabiting" language, in his struggle with the prosthetic, in his refusal to name himself a "victim," that Paul Rayment most emphatically refutes Badiou's notion of the identitarian as the politics of the "*victimaire*." Paul's act of living in the time of dying is about the struggle for identity: the grasping for a name that fits the diminished body, the body that struggles to live its own particularity, without, as much as it resents that body, relinquishing the body. In Paul Rayment, the name of the white European male must grapple with how it might live a name, with how "Paul" is in itself an inadequate marker of the diasporic body that is surrounded by other diasporic bodies. The female bodies that occupy his domestic space, the nurse-love object Marijana, newly relocated from Dubrovnic on Croatia's Dalmatian Coast, and Elizabeth, whose Irishness Paul has great difficulty with, each speak their own diasporic history—the former recent and unfamiliar, the latter old but disconcerting because of Elizabeth's refusal to respect his privacy, both Catholic women who, in one form or another, have been diasporized by sectarian violence.

The memory of the political is, by force of historical struggle, consolidated: from its rhizomatic scattering throughout the limb to its concentrated location within the "lump," the only place on the body where the politics of the particular are most radically visible. The "lumpish thing" functions, in Agamben's terms, as the "remnant of the figure"; it is the "only real political subject" precisely because it conducts politics in its full ugliness: always cognizant of the mutations, the truncations, the gnarled quality of politics. It does not require an aesthetically whole—"wholesome," we might suggest—project in order for it to assume an effective "substantiality." It is its contraction, into consolidation through the inscription of defeat, loss, violence, and amputation (the sacrifice entailed in political struggle) onto its body, that makes the particular not only out-standing—salient—in its politics, but always potentially capable of "decisive" action. The body scarred by politics is the body that is, wisely, scared of political combat but also the repository—Coetzee's "limbs of memory"—of a political fortitude: the body poised, in all its imperfections, with all its history of political failure on full public display, for encounter. The particular has to remember itself, understand how it came to be, like the Gnostic Magdalene, remnant rather than dominant, because its body is so mauled by that process, so suppressed as to bury itself—as the only form of historical survival, of prolonging its existence—in the sands of North Africa. The particular is a body that, unlike Paul Rayment's single unfortunate encounter with a car, has had many painful accidents, many long erasures from history.

For this reason, the "lumpish thing" insists on standing out, on being politically salient, on constituting itself as the political outside. In the terms of *Slow Man*, Paul Rayment will not allow for the reinscription of the particular into the universal. Through Paul the abject, amputated body comes to represent the virtue of separation rather than suture. This might be the specter of "victimization" that Badiou fears most: the "substantial remainder," that subject of the political for whom the particular is the only way to be, that subject who cannot prostheticize itself into universality—the prosthetic subject who cannot be proselytized, despite Paul's immense capacities as radical organizer of the militant. In contrast to the apostle Paul's immensely powerful physical presence, there is Paul Rayment's "lumpish thing." The amputated leg constitutes the abject thing that most effectively, and affectively, upholds the principle of the prosthetic, historically gendered parts. ▪

I want to thank Jane Juffer and David Johnson for their readings of this essay. Jane and David were thoughtful and incisive in their responses, generous with their time, always witty in their remarks.

....

1 Emmanuel Levinas, *God, Death, and Time*, trans. Bettina Bergo (Stanford, Calif.: Stanford University Press, 2000), 14.

2 Howard Grant Timms, *Saint Paul: the Foundation of Universalism*, http://www.uwo.ca/theory/skandalon/skandalon/pdf_files/sk_rev_1_4h.htm.

3 The Gnostic Gospels consist of thirteen codices, texts previously thought to have been lost or destroyed during Early Christianity; the recovered gospels, in addition to Mary Magdalene's, include the Gospel of Thomas, Philip, and the Gospel of Truth. See Elaine

Pagels, *The Gnostic Gospels* (New York: Random House, 1979) for an authoritative critique of the Nag Hammadi discovery.

4 *Gos. Mary* 4.22, Pagels.

5 Žižek's *The Fragile Absolute: or, Why is the Christian Legacy Worth Fighting For?* is the companion piece to *The Puppet and the Dwarf*, elaborating many of the same thematics. See Giorgio Agamben, *The Time That Remains: A Commentary on the Letter to the Romans*, trans. Patricia Dailey (Stanford, CA: Stanford University Press, 2005); Alain Badiou, *Saint Paul: The Foundation of Universalism*, trans. Ray Brassier (Stanford, CA: Stanford University Press, 2003); Slavoj Žižek, *The Puppet and the Dwarf: The Perverse Core of Christianity* (Cambridge, MA: MIT Press, 2003); and Žižek, *The Fragile Absolute: or, Why is the Christian Legacy Worth Fighting For?* (London: Verso, 2000).

6 Žižek, *The Puppet and the Dwarf*, 10.

7 J.M.Coetzee, *Slow Man* (New York: Viking, 2005), 8, 197.

8 Ibid., 33.

9 Ibid.

10 Badiou, *Saint Paul,* original emphasis, 19.

11 Ibid., original emphasis. All terms in quotations throughout the text are mine, if not cited directly.

12 Coetzee, *Slow Man,* original emphasis, 192.

13 Ibid., original emphasis, 8.

14 Badiou, *Saint Paul,* 19.

15 Jacques Derrida, *The Gift of Death*, trans. David Wills (Chicago: University of Chicago Press, 1995), 9.

16 Badiou, *Saint Paul,* 6.

17 Ibid.

18 Badiou's antipathy toward cultural struggle, what we might name in institutional terms "Cultural Studies," is shared by Žižek. See, for example his critique of cultural struggle in *Welcome to the Desert of the Real: Five Essays on September 11 and Related Dates* (London: Verso, 2002).

19 Badiou, *Saint Paul,* original emphasis, 13.

20 Ibid.

21 Ibid.

22 Ibid., 49.

23 Ibid., 33.

24 See, in this regard, Marina Warner, *Alone of All Her Sex: The Myth and the Cult of the Virgin Mary* (New York: Knopf, 1976); Susan Haskins, *Mary Magdalene: Myth and Metaphor* (New York: Konecky & Konecky, 1993); and Katherine Ludwig Jansen, *The Making of the Magdalen: Preaching and Popular Devotion in the Later Middle Ages* (Princeton: Princeton University Press, 2001).

25 Badiou, *Saint Paul,* 1.

26 John 20: 16-17.

27 See, in this regard, Ann Graham Brock, *Mary Magdalene, The First Apostle: The Struggle for Authority* (Cambridge: Harvard Divinity School, 2003); Holly E. Hearon, *The Mary Magdalene Tradition: Witness and Counter-Witness in Early Christian Communities* (Collegeville, Minn.: Liturgical Press, 2004); and Jane Schaberg, *The Resurrection of Mary Magdalene: Legends, Apocrypha, and the Christian Testament* (London: Continuum International Publishing Group, 2002).

28 *The Da Vinci Code* has been on the *The New York Times* best-seller list for almost three years. Dan Brown, *The Da Vinci Code* (New York: Doubleday, 2003).
29 Agamben, *The Time that Remains,* 53.
30 Ibid., 55.
31 Corinthians 1, 15:9.
32 See Gerald Massey's essay, "Paul the Gnostic Opponent of Peter, Not an Apostle of Historic Christianity," www.africawithin.com/massey/gm1_paulpeter.htm.
33 Badiou, *Saint Paul,* 17.
34 Agamben, *The Time that Remains,* 57.
35 Coetzee, *Slow Man,* 26.
36 Ibid., 38, 33.
37 Ibid., original emphasis, 192, 198.
38 Ibid., 197.
39 Derrida, 74.
40 Ibid., 115.
41 Coetzee, *Slow Man,* 14.
42 Ibid., 62.
43 Ibid., 14.
44 Ibid., 60.

Figure 1. Francisco Goya, *Allegory of the City of Madrid*, 1810. Oil on canvas, 260 x 195 cm. Museo Municipal, Madrid.

The Disasters of War: On Inimical Life

Ian Baucom

Among the less celebrated of Francisco Goya's vast catalogue of drawings, etchings, and paintings is a canvas he was commissioned to produce by Bravo de Rivero, a municipal councilor in Madrid, in September of 1809. The councilor had been instructed by the mayor of Madrid to arrange for "a portrait of our present sovereign" and approached Goya to produce the work.[1] In theory, this should have presented no great difficulty. Goya had been a court painter for decades and had already produced numerous royal portraits. But, as events transpired, de Rivero's charge to Goya proved more than a little difficult to fulfill, if only because the question of who, precisely, might legitimately qualify as Spain's "present sovereign" was at the time the subject of one of the more brutally violent disputes of nineteenth-century European history. The official answer was Jose I, the erstwhile Joseph Bonaparte, older brother of Louis Bonaparte, whom the emperor had installed as Spanish monarch the year before after efficiently managing the sequenced abdications of Fernando VII and Carlos IV. Carlos immediately made peace with his surrender of power, but his son Fernando proved rather more intransigent in his ambitions, as did the greater bulk of the Spanish people who, inspired by reports that the French were attempting to kidnap Fernando's 13-year-old brother, Prince Francisco de Paula, took to the streets of Madrid on the second of May, 1808, and so began what is variously known as the Spanish War of Independence, the Peninsular War, and the world's first guerilla war—the brutal six-year conflict that was to become the subject of three of Goya's indisputably most famous works: the *Second of May* and *Third of May* (figures 2 and 3) and the series of 80 aquatint engravings commonly known as *The Disasters of War* (figure 4).

As my title suggests, it is these latter works in which I am primarily interested, but I want to begin with the painting commissioned by de Rivero, the canvas which ultimately came to bear the title *Allegory of the City of Madrid* (figure 1),

Figure 2. Francisco Goya, *The 2nd of May, 1808: The Charge of the Marmelukes*, 1814. Oil on canvas, 266 x 345 cm. Museo del Prado, Madrid.

because its curious history manages to contain in miniature the primary questions I want to raise. I will develop those questions in more detail in what follows; for the moment let me sketch their main contours simply by saying that the charge Goya took up in accepting de Rivero's commission is one that remains with us, and not just analogically but quite historically so. It is the charge of understanding what sovereignty might consist of in the ongoing moment of its modern transition and reinvention, of determining how it might be grasped, imagined, depicted.

Goya's answers to those questions were as simple and complex as those thrown out by the upheavals and reactions that had forced Spain and much of the continent into the situation of crisis in which it found itself in the first decades of the nineteenth century. I will not attempt to rehearse the history of the French Revolution or of its transition, under Napoleon, into an empire (and global Enlightenment war-machine), but it is perhaps fair to say that the fundamental question at the heart of both the Revolution and Napoleon's wars of conquest was not altogether different than that which Councilor de Rivero implicitly asked Goya to answer: who is sovereign? Or, more precisely, who is "present sovereign"? That qualification, admitting as it did the contingency of whatever answer one might choose to give, may be said to contain within itself the radical uncertainty of the times. The question was not simply one of

Figure 3. Francisco Goya, *The 3rd of May, 1808: The Execution of the Defenders of Madrid*, 1814. Oil on canvas, 266 x 345 cm. Museo del Prado, Madrid.

asking who, or what, might hold or pretend to sovereign authority but, as a consequence and a condition of posing and responding to that question, of acknowledging that sovereignty could not be said to possess some fixed principle of coherence. It is not only the person of the sovereign or the representational logic of sovereignty which such a question throws into doubt but the chance (and therefore the fact) of sovereignty's alterability, its only, ever, historically determinate verifiability, its case-specific historicizability. To pose the question of who, or what, might be sovereign in France in 1789 or Spain in 1809 was not simply to ask who might be king but to submit sovereignty to the general epistemological condition of the age, an age that had learned to think, precisely, in terms of the age, an age that, as James Chandler has demonstrated, had discovered in the thorough-going historicism of all categories of social life and thought its own epistemological principle of coherence.[2]

Subject to a relentless historicist interrogation, the identity and nature of the "present sovereign" emerged from the various crucibles of late-eighteenth and early-nineteenth century European thought as something unlike what it had been on the near side of the Enlightenment event-horizon, and the entirety of its renovation so thoroughly solicited the attention not only of the overtly political sciences but also

Figure 4. Francisco Goya, "And it can't be helped" ("Y no hai remedio"), Plate 15 of *The Disasters of War*, circa 1810-1815, published 1863. Etching, 14.5 x 16.5 cm. The copperplate is in the Calcografía Nacional, Madrid.

of the literary and plastic arts that it can be understood as one of the great tasks of both the political and the aesthetic revolutions that attended the transition from the pre- to post-Enlightenment (the transition which, in an aesthetic vein, we tend to shorthand as the passage from neo-classicism through romanticism and into realism) to resolve that question. Certainly that can be taken to be the argument, though it is never quite stated as such, of what remains one of the great studies of the post-Revolutionary emergence of realist aesthetics: Georg Lukács's *Studies in European Realism*. Lukács mentions neither Goya nor any other painter in his book. His subject is the evolution of the realist novel, and his two great heroes are Balzac and Tolstoy, but what he observes of Balzac and Tolstoy is in many respects true of Goya also, and, indeed, it is in the deeply Lukácsian realism of his art that I understand Goya to have found the terms of his response to the riddle of sovereignty posed by his age and encapsulated in Councilor de Rivero's commission.

If the Romanticism to which Balzac, Tolstoy, and Goya's work emerged as an antithetical response had vested sovereignty in the type of authentic personality and affective inwardness (or, as Lukács has it, had rendered sovereign the "type" of "man" "sublimate[d] into [a] purely mental-psychological process"), then, on his account, realism also constructs itself from human types but turns those types outward from an inner world of feeling to set before its protagonists minds and challenge its readers and itself to map the "totality of objects" which collectively compose the entirety of an historically particular social world.[3] "In the works of a great realist," as he puts it, "everything is linked up with everything else. Every phenomenon shows the polyphony of many components, the intertwinement of the individual and the social, of the physical and the psychical, of private interest and public affairs."[4] Rather than abandoning itself, its readers or its characters to that polyphonous, intertwined, and potentially infinite "total" world, however, the realist novel, Lukács further argues, orients its maps of totality by discerning a social center of gravity around which all of its linked objects and all its representative human types orbit, a defining force that disposes and directs the movements of the "totality of objects" through a given social order's gravitational field. Lukács calls this "the moving center" ("the great realists," he insists, "always regard society from the viewpoint of a living and moving centre and this centre is present, visibly or invisibly in every phenomenon"[5]), and, as this definition suggests, it is in depicting or grasping the nature of this moving center that realism offers its response to the riddle of sovereignty that the age had put before its political, social, and artistic thinkers alike. The "moving center" is realism's principle of sovereignty, the animating, directing, governing force it understands to hold sway over a social totality.

How then does the realist tradition, book-ended on one side by Balzac and on the other by Tolstoy, define, for Lukács, the moving center everywhere present within and immanently sovereign over the totality of objects? In two key ways. Balzac's "instance" of this moving center, Lukács argues, is "capital, which he—correctly at that time—saw incarnated in financial capital. … From Gobseck to Nunsingen, Balzac creates a long procession of the immediate representatives of this demoniacal force. … Balzac's world is permanently saturated. … Whether the immediate theme is love or marriage, friendship or politics, passion or self-sacrifice, … [this force] is ever present as an invisible protagonist and … [its] invisible presence visibly colours every movement, every action of all Balzac's characters."[6] Tolstoy, on the other hand, is for Lukács "the poet of the peasant revolt that lasted from 1861 to 1905. In his life work the exploited peasant is this visible-invisible ever-present protagonist. … [Everything] hinges consciously or unconsciously on problems which are more or less immediately linked with this central problem."[7]

Closer scholars of Balzac's and Tolstoy's work might dispute the discrete persuasiveness of these analyses. I want, however, only to comment on the broader characteristics of that form of sovereignty they reveal. Whatever particular shape it might take, Lukács's moving center is an immanent rather than a transcendent principle of sovereignty. It is something contemporaneously resident within and materially productive of a self-renovating social order, a force disposed not to the conservation of society but to the constitutional dis- and re-establishment of social life. Whether incarnate through all the speculative transactions of finance capital or in the surging anger of a populace in revolt, the moving center is a force of creative destruction and destructive re-creation, a vastly distributed network of urgencies, desires, and, above all, violence. I will return to this bundle of figures. But first I want to return to Goya and to the response he fashioned to Councilor de Rivero's commission. In its first incarnation, that response was disappointingly simple. Asked to create a portrait of Spain's "present sovereign," Goya produced not an image of one of those immanent, distributed, socially dis-and re-organizing "moving centers" that Lukács discerned in Balzac and Tolstoy but a portrait of the king. Which meant, in 1809, Jose I, Napoleon's brother. The resulting composition, as Robert Hughes observes, was a largely unoriginal Rococo piece.[8] The bulk of the painting is occupied by a crowd of tribute-offering figures: a trumpet-sounding Fame, Victory bearing a laurel wreath, and a female personification of the city of Madrid pointing to a gilt-framed oval within whose circumference Goya set his image of the imperially imposed sovereign.

Or so he did on completing the canvas in 1810. Two years later, however, threatened by the combined forces of the guerilla insurgents and their British allies, Jose abandoned Madrid and his claim to sovereignty over the city. So Goya painted him out. The question was what to put in his place. Fernando VII had not yet returned to the city, and Spain was without a king. What the country now possessed, however, was a constitution—newly drafted by an assortment of Enlightenment-inspired intellectuals, among whom Goya, on the whole, counted himself, and ratified by the short-lived Cortes of Cadiz in 1812. So in the place of the retreated and erased Jose, Goya painted the word "Constitución," the document which claimed to hold present sovereignty over Spain. Within the year, however, Jose returned to Madrid, and Goya painted out "Constitución," replacing it once more with the monarch's portrait. Then, in 1813, Jose was forced to retreat from the city again, so his image was for a second time removed and Goya had one of his assistants repaint "Constitución" within the framed oval, where it remained until 1826 when, in honor of the now re-established Fernando VII, who on resuming the throne had promptly abolished the constitution of Cadiz, an image of the restored Bourbon monarch was put in its place, this time by Goya's successor as court painter, Vicente Lopez. While that alteration marked the end of Goya's work on the canvas, it did not resolve the ultimate appearance of the serially metamorphosing image of sovereignty mirrored in the painting's oval frame. The canvas was reworked on two further occasions. First in 1843 when the government of the city of Madrid ordered the portrait of Fernando removed from the canvas and "Libro de la Constitución" ("Book of the Constitution") put in its place and finally, again, in 1872 when the constitution, as emblem of national sovereignty, was erased for the final time and in dual homage to the popular uprising that began the end of French rule in Spain and to Goya's now-iconic representation of that revolt, the words "Dos de Mayo" (the "Second of May") were placed in its stead.

So then: the monarch, the constitution, and the revolutionary people—three images serially appearing in and disappearing from the gilt-edged mirror locked within Goya's otherwise forgettable rococo painting; three competing and alternating images of who, or what, could claim to hold sovereignty over Spain during the turbulent decades of the nineteenth century; three images in which we might see the signature imprint of those historical forces that even the most unimaginative of genre pieces cannot entirely banish from itself and in which we might also see a fore-image of that more radical violation of baroque protocols Goya was to accomplish in the work he began to produce at exactly the moment that he quit retouching the *Allegory of Madrid*, handed that task over to an assistant, and commenced fashioning that more radically, and awfully, realist depiction of what he had come to understand as the true moving center of Spanish life: the suite of engravings commonly entitled *The Disasters of War*, the work that I understand to be Goya's ultimate, if indirect, response to Councilor de Rivero's commission.

And that indeed, is the opening point I want to make. Forgettable as it is, the *Allegory of Madrid* belongs among the canon of Goya's significant work not only because its curiously shifting surface mirrors the shifting political history of the country over the early decades of the nineteenth century, but because it anticipates and frames the *Second* and *Third of May* and the *Disasters of War*, because those works—as the final appearance of the words "Dos de Mayo" within the *Allegory's* gilded oval suggest—may be understood as collectively composing Goya's ultimate portrait painting of the "present sovereign" currently exercising dominion over Spain and much of the continent. To the sequence king, constitution, and people which the *Allegory of Madrid* serially offered as its response to the riddle of sovereignty, we must thus add one more figure, indeed, for Goya, one conclusive figure: war—the demoniacal force that he discerned to be exercising its sovereignty over contemporaneous social life, the "protagonist" visibly or invisibly present in every phenomenon, the living and moving center that is to Goya's late work what finance capital and the insurgent peasantry are, for Lukács, to Balzac and Tolstoy: that immanent, violent, simultaneously creative and destructive force orienting and directing the swirling movement of the totality of objects circulating within a historically particular social field.

....

The king, the people, the constitution, and war. The first three of these terms occupy an easily recognizable position within standard accounts of the history of modern sovereignty, particularly the classically liberal accounts, whose validity it has been the purpose of a recent, broad and multiply articulated counter-Enlightenment discourse on sovereignty to dispute. If Michel Foucault's 1976 College de France lectures, subsequently published as *Society Must be Defended*, stand as the point of departure for much of that discourse, it is in part because of his thoroughgoing refusal to accept the legitimacy of a political history of Enlightenment and post-Enlightenment modernity, whose central narrative plots the displacement of the first of these figures of sovereignty (the king) by the third (the constitution) in consequence of the altered loyalty of the second: the people, who, by the terms of the liberal-juridical account, depose the sovereignty of the monarch by reinventing themselves as the authors of the law.[9] Foucault's argument, of course, is that rather than finding their sovereign will expressed by the law (and enshrined in the constitution), the people emerge from this putative exchange of sovereign authorities as, in effect, deprived of sovereignty altogether and find themselves, instead, resolutely disciplined and administered by the normalizing mechanisms of the state apparatus that ever-more-massively accretes itself around and effectively displaces the law and its institutions. For it is, Foucault insists, neither the law, nor an anterior model of kingly sovereignty now copied onto the law in juridical guise, which the state exists to preserve. As the king cedes to the state, sovereignty itself, far from finding itself now constitutionally dressed, passes like a ghost from history, and, with its passing, the old power of the sovereign (the power to let live or make die) is transformed into the new biopolitical power of the state, the power of governmentality, the power to make live or let die, the power exercised not by the king's apparent successor, the judge, but by his true replacement: the bureaucrat, the demographer, the urban planner, the health officer, the statistician. In the terms I have been using, Foucault too discerns a moving center of modern political life, an ever-present, visible and invisible protagonist, but that protagonist is the radically extra-juridical, post-sovereign, biopolitical power of the state to make live or let die, not the constitution.

And on this score, Giorgio Agamben—whose work has come to define a primary second strand in the contemporary discourse on sovereignty—provides an entirely different account of sovereignty's modern trajectory. For Agamben, in brief, sovereignty does indeed survive the advent of the modern, and it survives, moreover, in explicitly constitutional form. Indeed, from Latin antiquity through the present (as he argues in both *Homo Sacer: Sovereignty and Bare Life* and *State of Exception*), the history of sovereignty, is, for Agamben, a history of the sovereign capture of a sequence of constitutional orders through the serial activation of a principle, or reason, of state commonly organizational to every constitution: the state of emergency.[10] Far from seeing the sovereignty of the king either replaced by the constitution or vanishing behind its ideological garb, the history of sovereignty is, for him, a history of the king (or, more precisely, the emperor, the dictator, and the executive) eternally latent within the constitution, a history of the power conferred on one constitutionally authorized to suspend the constitution, a history, therefore, in which the constitutional order neither displaces an older order of sovereignty nor masks its disappearance but is and always has been the very secret of sovereignty. The history of sovereignty is thus, for him, coterminous with the extension and triumph of an unfolding, and ever-more-expansive, sequence of constitutional orders endlessly haunted *by*, and most meaningfully sovereign *in*, the moment of their suspension. That reading, needless to say, produces a rather gap-filled chronology of political history: after the Roman empire, there is in his work essentially nothing worth noticing until, with the twin events of the signing of the treaty of Westphalia and the inauguration of modern political theory announced by the 1651 publication of Hobbes *Leviathan*, a broadly contemporary (and long-durational) constitutional tradition marks its public appearance. The implications of this chronology deserve closer attention. For the purposes of this essay, however, I want to underline just two things: the first is this fundamental difference between Foucault and Agamben's two revisionary critiques of the liberal trajectory king-people-constitution, but the second is the nevertheless vital point of correspondence between them. Whatever their differences, Agamben does agree with Foucault in one crucial respect—the final territory conquered by the constitutional order, its ultimate and most massive frontier, is one co-extensive with the boundary of life itself; it is the territory of what Agamben calls bare life, the exact terrain Foucault associates with the new governmental, biopolitical power of the state. Whether constitutionally grounded or governmentally administered, whether named as exceptionally and enduringly sovereign or as post-sovereign, the measure of modern power, Agamben concurs, is biopolitical: the power to make live or let die, not the old power to make die or let live. Regardless, then, of whether the true sequence of political history is the king, the people, and governmentality[11] or an endless variation on the theme of the king within the constitution, modernity, Agamben suggests, is most crucially apprehensible as the triumph of the biopolitical and the consequent emergence of what he variously calls homo sacer and bare life as the definitive subject and type of post-Enlightenment political society.

In attending to the political realities of the modern, it then becomes almost secondary to decide what had seemed to be the main point of difference between his and Foucault's work: virtually secondary, that is, to decide whether modern power is post-sovereign or hyper-sovereign, governmental or exceptional. The more fundamental matter is to affirm that power is biopolitical, that it nourishes itself on its simultaneous capture and production of bare life. Biopolitics, in a word, is the moving center Agamben borrows from Foucault to become the key concept of modern political life—the sovereign protagonist found everywhere present in, and everywhere saturating, post-Enlightenment political history: the demonaical, visible, and invisible force canny enough to express itself in constitutional, governmental, exceptional, or bellicose guise. The continuing power of the state to destroy and to kill, the sovereign power to produce death on a mass scale—the power, in short, to wage war—thus need not, on Agamben's terms, be understood as in any meaningful way interrupting or calling into question the marching triumph of the biopolitical. For, on this account, war is not opposed to biopolitics. It does not contain within itself an alternate logic of sovereignty or disclose itself as an alternate "moving center" of political and historical life—as that final image of the "present sovereign" intimated by Goya's *Allegory of Madrid* suggests. To add "war" to the sequence king, people, and constitution is thus to add nothing to what is already encompassed by biopolitics: the true fourth term of modern political life. War, so conceived, does not lie outside the domain of the biopolitical. It is simply the pursuit of biopolitics by other means.

And that is precisely the conception I wish to contest.

In doing so, I am by no means alone. Indeed, the starting point of Foucault's 1976 lectures was precisely that we need to reverse Carl von Clausewitz's famous understanding of war as the extension of politics and to understand things exactly the other way around: a reversal whose pertinence to the contemporary "war on terror" Judith Butler has recently and brilliantly discussed to illustrate those ways in which the "anachronistic" power of the state to detain and kill those it deems irredeemably enemy to itself "vitalizes" a biopolitical governmentality perhaps more properly understood as the extension of war by other means.[12] In defining the irreducible ground of the political as the friend/enemy distinction, Carl Schmitt's writings, which stand with Foucault's (and Benjamin's) work as the other primary source of Agamben's thought, also provide strong cues to what it might mean to read the practices of warfare, and war-discourse's production of "enemy" rather than "bare" life, as fundamental to the trajectory of modern political history. And, most resonantly for my purposes here, Achille Mbembe, while drawing on both Foucault and Agamben, has begun to query the theoretical adequacy of the concept of biopolitics to the forms of political violence that characterize our historical moment. As he puts it in the series of questions which open and frame his essay "Necropolitics":

> Is the notion of biopower sufficient to account for the contemporary ways in which the political, under the guise of war, of resistance, or of the fight against terror, makes the murder of the enemy its primary and absolute objective? War, after all, is as much a means of achieving sovereignty as a way of exercising the right to kill. Imagining politics as a form of war, we must ask: What place is given to life, death, and the human body (in particular the wounded or slain body)? How are they inscribed in the order of power?[13]

To which questions I would add the following: If war, or what Mbembe calls necropolitics, is not to be understood as the mere extension of biopolitics by other means, then what is its relation to the biopolitical? In what ways might it both currently, and serially over the long-durée of our modern political contemporaneity, articulate itself as an alternate "moving center" of social, political, and historical life? To what order of power or of law does it attach itself? And, finally (and most pressingly for the purposes of this essay), if, for an alternately or simultaneously governmental and exceptional biopolitics, the central figure of modern political subjectivity is that which is apprehensible to Agamben as "bare life," then what is necropolitics' countermanding figure or type?

To which final query, borrowing a term from the history of international law and its elaborate discourse on enmity, I would reply: "inimical life."[14]

But to see why that proposition might be true and what it might imply, we need to return to the moment with which I began, the moment in which Francisco Goya found himself, the moment exactly coincident with the one Agamben associates with the merging of biopolitics and the state of emergency: that turn-of-the-nineteenth-century moment in which, tiring of the game of painting in and out the competing figures of the king, the people, and the constitution, Goya took up the question of war and began his great, realist suite of engravings on the wounded and slain human body, and found in these images of the disasters of war, in an imperial state's and an armed insurgency's determination to torture, rape, dismember and kill those it regards not merely as enemy but as resolutely inimical to itself, his ultimate response to Councilor de Rivera's commission: the true and awful portrait of that demonaical force I understand, then as now, to be making its claim to modern sovereignty.

....

The genius of realism, on Lukács's reading, lies not only in its ability to at once map "the totality of objects" and orient this totality in relation to a "moving center" but to embody its social vision in a series of representative human "types": "the central category and criterion of realist literature …, a peculiar synthesis which organically binds together the general and the particular both in characters and situations. … [I]n it all the humanly and socially essential determinants are present on their highest level of development, in the ultimate unfolding of the possibilities latent in them, in extreme presentation of their extremes, rendering concrete the peaks and limits of men and epochs."[15] As both that final appeal to the unity of "men and epochs" and the yoking of "characters and situations" indicates, to speak of the type is to articulate a broadly materialist theory of human personhood, to assert a fundamental unity between the person and the moment, men and their epochs. But the epoch from which realism derives its historically peculiar characters, is not, Lukács further indicates, internally consistent with itself. It is, instead, a split period of time. "Every great historical period," he insists, "is a period of transition, a contradictory unity of crisis and renewal, of destruction and rebirth: a new social order and a new type of man always comes into being in the course of a unified though contradictory process. In such critical, transitional periods the task and responsibility of literature are exceptionally great. But only truly great realism can cope with such responsibilities, … fulfilling the tasks imposed by history."[16] That task and responsibility, as Lukács then clarifies, is to map (in the confused, contradictory moment of its advent) what is coming-to-be, to trace the sovereignty that even now, in the period of its part-arrival, a future disposition of the "totality of objects" has begun to exert over the present ordering of society. This does not mean that for Lukács either the "moving-center" of any "great historical period," or the human types in whom it finds itself expressed are utterly sundered from "what-has-been." Rather, what-is-to-be both threatens to destroy what-is and to re-animate or "renew" some vital element of what-has-been. A period of "destruction *and* rebirth," the moment of transition with which realism concerns itself and from which it derives its types of human personhood might thus be better understood as one marked by the coming dominance of those forces which have been long latent, marginal, or potential within history.

For Lukács, as we have seen, there are primarily two such forces to which the realist tradition attends and whose coming sovereignty it maps: the revolutionary potential long latent within the peasantry and the rise-to-dominance of a long-developing species of finance capital. Both these readings seem plausible. My sense, however, is that alongside these two forces of social destruction and social re-creation, and alongside the types of the financier and the insurgent peasant, there is another force and another type circling the fringes and sometimes erupting at the center not only of Balzac and Tolstoy's work but of a broader realist tradition that would include Goya among its prime artists, a force and a type which I understand each of these figures, in their separate ways, to have discerned as fundamental to their historical moment: the force of war and the type of the enemy, or, more precisely, the type of the unjust enemy, the type of what I am calling inimical life.

By way of an initial justification of that claim, let me merely gesture toward the first novel Balzac completed in his *Comédie Humaine*: *The Chouans* (or, as Balzac had earlier called it, *The Chouans or Brittany in 1799*). The general structure of the novel, plotting as it does the failed Breton insurrection against Republican rule, is simple enough. And its primary generic form is evident too: *The Chouans* is a historical romance, very much in Scottian form, replete with a doomed romantic protagonist (Montauran, the young royalist leader of the revolt), with whose devotion to a lost cause (and lost historical order) we are invited, briefly, to sympathize before, in Ian Duncan's terms, "moving on" to the mournful and properly liberal knowledge that that cause and that historical past cannot survive the advent of the modern.[17] Sprinkled in amongst this potpourri of romance conventions are, however, some harsher nettles, narrative thorns inassimilable to the generic bouquet, as prickly to the novel's generic harmony as the odd appearance of the words "Constitución" and "Dos de Mayo" are to Goya's otherwise rococo *Allegory of Madrid*.

These aberrant fragments attend Balzac's treatment not of his main characters but of the novel's subordinate cast, primarily the rebellious Chouans, whose insurgency against Republican and Bonapartist rule the novel cannot quite contain within romance conventions and who Balzac treats, instead, in starkly, if somewhat incoherently, realist fashion. The Chouans' form of warfare and the mode of war the republican armies practice against them are, in particular, irreducible to romance form. If in Montauran, Balzac can find his romance protagonist and Commandant Hulot, the commander of the Republican army, can find a stereotypically just enemy, one deserving, particularly in the moment of his defeat, of dignified treatment, then, in the Chouans, whose "insurrection had nothing noble about it" and had "turned war into highway robbery," neither the soldiers of the republic nor the narrative can find anything so deserving of dignity or conventional treatment.[18] Where the novel can thus realize its terms of closure on the insurrection by substituting the body of Montauran for those of the peasants he has led, ensuring him a proper burial with due military honor, the insurrectionists permit no such narrative or military decorum. They kill, and are killed, brutally, mercilessly, discriminately. And it is in the representation of their killing and their being killed that the novel violates its romance conventions, achieves its awful realist breakthrough, and signals the destructive re-appearance of an historical type (the unjust enemy) and an historical force (what Carl Schmitt calls "unbracketed" war) which, since the conclusion of the wars of religion and the signing of the treaty of Westphalia, it had been, Schmitt argues, the greater burden of European international law to banish from the stage of continental history and reserve for what he calls the "free zone" of unlimited war "beyond the [imperial] line."[19] At the conclusion of the narrative's first scene of battle, the victorious Republican soldiery, finding themselves in possession of a single Chouan prisoner, thus find no reason to consider him subject to those strictures regarding the treatment of captured foes that will apply to Montauran when he is caught in the novel's final chapter. Instead, Balzac has them act as he knows, and reports, they were instructed to act by those published proclamations through which Napoleon declared Britanny to be subject to a law of war otherwise reserved for colonial subjects "beyond the line" of the *jus publicum europaeum*, ordered his troops to "be merciless" toward the "brigands" and "bandits" who opposed them, and "strike [down] … whoever after this Declaration dare still resist the sovereignty of the nation."[20] As Balzac, in what strikes me as the centerpiece of the novel's first realist tableau, quite simply and quite unromantically writes, "Two soldiers … drew back several paces, took careful aim at the Chouan, whose fixed eyes were not lowered before the gun barrels leveled at him, fired point-blank, and he fell."[21]

This is neither the novel's last such scene, nor the last moment in which nineteenth-century European realism takes note of precisely such a scene of violence unfolding within the boundaries of the European state system, nor the last time one of Lukács's great realists will take notice of the destructive force which, in the name of "the sovereignty of the nation," was exerting over the "bandits" and "brigands" of continental history an unbracketed, discriminate killing power formally reserved, since the conclusion of the wars of religion, for the subjects of empire living across the seas and beyond the amity lines of European public law. Nor is it the last time European realism will discover, in its "extreme presentation"[22] of the merciless slaughter of the prisoner of war, *the* refashioned domestic type in whom this demonaical force was to find its imperial necropolitical sovereignty embodied and brought home. The subsequent pages of the realist tradition are littered with such scenes; littered with dour apprehensions that a new (or renewed or returned) practice of unbracketed, discriminate war had begun to re-assert and re-expand its claim as the true moving center and sovereign of both imperial and continental social life; littered with the type of the unjust enemy, in whose public "declaration," military capture, and merciless destruction this force of war found the revived and extended secret to its claims to sovereignty. By the final sections of *War and Peace*, in Tolstoy's dual and lengthy treatment of the reciprocal execution of civilian "incendiaries" by the French army occupying Moscow and the equally brutal "extermination" of "many thousands of [captured] enemy soldiers" by the peasant and Cossack "guerilla" "bands" harrying the French army on its retreat from Moscow, "this kind of warfare" has not only "taken definite shape" as an historical practice but has come to occupy the center ground of the narrative.[23] Like their French antagonists, the guerillas, Tolstoy writes, "reckoned everything possible now,"[24] and in the surrounding pages of the novel Tolstoy paints his grim portrait of this world in which every form of killing has been made possible by the two sides' mutual determination to regard one another as little more than bandits, brigands, unjust not just foes, less and worse than enemies resolutely inimical to one another; the world in which the condition of men has become one, in Hobbes's terms, of perpetual war with one another; the world in which man is a no more and no less than a wolf to man (*homo homini lupus*); the world in which the fundamental subject of public history threatens to become not biopolitics' emblematic "homo sacer" but that "homo inimicus" who is the representative type of a necropolitical order of sovereignty no longer proper only to the "conflict zone" on the far side of the imperial oceans and seas.

By which I do mean the type *of* an order of sovereignty. For, what explicitly distinguishes Balzac and Tolstoy's apprehension and representation of this type is their common understanding that the portraits they are painting are not of men in a putative state of nature prior to the institution of the sovereignty of the state (or subsequent to its collapse) but of men who have become wolfishly inimical to one another by the will and decision of a sovereign power whose most fundamental and most precious power of command, whose very *arcana imperii*, lies in its power and need to articulate itself in relation to those it deems its "unjust enemies"—a morbid knowledge of the force moving at the (re)emerging and expanding center of historical things dually demonstrated in Balzac's publication of the "brigand" declaration that Napoleon issued in the name of the nation's—though truly the empire's—"sovereignty" and in Tolstoy's indication that what remained of the czarist government after the siege of Moscow found the secret to its continuing survival when it "recognized" "this kind of warfare," which, in imitation of the French, the Russian forces in the field were beginning to wage.[25]

Both Balzac and Tolstoy may have recognized this, may indeed have glimpsed in the unbracketed warfare of the Napoleonic era an image of the true, doubly uncanny (temporally recurrent and geographically "unhomely"), simultaneously residual and emerging sovereign of European public life; may even have discovered in their twin representations of the executed prisoner a figure for the type of the unjust enemy in whom this necropolitical order of sovereignty finds its secret and purpose and reason of being. But neither Balzac nor Tolstoy proved willing to wholly surrender their art to the mapping of this demonaical force or to the elaboration of the type in whom this order of sovereignty found its reason-of-state embodied. That task, as I have been suggesting, remained to Goya, in whose *Disasters of War* nineteenth-century continental realism finds its fullest expression of the type of the unjust enemy and its fullest depiction of that necropolitical force of war, which, rather than the king, the people, or the constitution (or in its canny manipulation and subsumption within itself of all three of these), had begun marking itself out as the moving center of this contradictory, future-anticipating and past-recuperating, empire-and-nation-mixing period of history.

....

"Yo lo vi"—"I saw it," Goya famously declares in the bitter caption accompanying plate 44 of his *Disasters* (figure 5). "And this as well," the caption of the ensuing plate announces. But what did he see? Art historians are in general agreement that Goya would not, in fact, literally have seen many of the scenes the *Disasters* depict. Most of the war took place outside Madrid, where, other than for a few short journeys (most notably one to the city of Zaragoza in October of 1808, several months after it was first besieged by the French), Goya spent the war years. That trip *would* have afforded Goya a first-hand view, however brief, not only of the massive destruction the city had suffered but of the violence and desolation the war had brought to the countryside through which he traveled, as it would have allowed him to see the wretched bands of civilians fleeing from city to town to rural hiding place and to observe the savage momentos both the French and the Spanish guerillas left behind them: the gibbeted bodies, the dismembered torsos nailed to trees (figure 6), the reeking corpse piles. So Goya would have both seen and not seen in detail, in particular, what the individual plates, each with its sardonic caption, invite us to see. There are languages for this form of seeing what has and has not been seen: the language of traumatic witness for one, the language of fiction (or as Lennard Davis has

Figure 5. Francisco Goya, "I saw it" ("Yo lo vi"), Plate 44 of *The Disasters of War*, circa 1810-1815, published 1863. Etching, 16 x 23.5 cm. The copperplate is in the Calcografía Nacional, Madrid.

evocatively put it, of the factual fiction) for another.[26] And certainly *The Disasters of War* is both a work of witness and a factual work of fiction, as it is, I have been suggesting, a fiction of a particular sort: a realist fiction. But I will not belabor that point, nor will I linger in detail on any of the particular engravings. Instead let me simply ask what Goya allows us to see by having us see the *Disasters* in the form he elected: as a series, a sequence of engravings, not as a single history painting.

There is, first, a narrative of sorts. The *Disasters* are conventionally divided into three parts. Plates 2-47 depict the guerilla war itself. Plates 48-65 are famine engravings, showing the terrible hunger and manifold death in Madrid during the year 1811-1812 when the combined actions of the French and the insurgents cut off the city's food supply. The final 15 engravings, which depict the violent, obscurantist reaction that accompanied Fernando VII's return to power, his abolition of the constitution and re-instatement of the inquisition and absolutist rule, are less obviously realist and approach, indeed, the level of allegory, or, more accurately, the form of the capriccio (mastered by Goya more than a decade before). In sequence, then, the plates facilitate what a single history painting can suggest but cannot, alone, unfold: a narrative, and a tragic one at that, one which seems to run the course of political and aesthetic history backward: first the realist tableau, then the baroque allegory it is supposed to succeed; first the people's revolt, then the suffering of the people, then the abolition of the constitution, then the coming of the king. It is as if, bearing horrified witness

Figure 6. Francisco Goya, "This is worse" ("Esto es peor"), Plate 37 of *The Disasters of War*, circa 1810-1815, published 1863. Etching and lavis, 15 x 20.5 cm. The copperplate is in the Calcografía Nacional, Madrid.

to this discriminate and merciless war, Goya asks us to see political and artistic time running in reverse. *The Impossible Revolution*, Gwyn Williams called his excellent book on the *Disasters*, and that title superbly encapsulates the tragic pessimism at the heart of Goya's history-reversing narrative of the war. But the series' narrative of historical reversal and revolutionary frustration also plots an impossibility of another sort: the impossibility of sympathy, the impossibility of taking sides. A revolution, Kant had argued in his famous essay on historical progress written a single decade before Goya began his work on the *Disasters*, is not, primarily, a sequence of events played out in the street or the field. It is, instead, an event within the mental life of the historical observer, an eventful determination to "invest sympathy" in one side or the other, putatively the side of "freedom."[27] And if Goya had only painted his *Second of May* and *Third of May*, whose appeals to the sympathy of the historical observer are clear, and left his report on the War of Independence at that, then we could say that he had invested the revolt of the Spanish pueblo against French Imperial rule with revolutionary possibility. The series of images which compose the *Disasters*, however, annul that possibility. There is, in this full run of plates, no side with which to sympathize, no party innocent of the most horrific violence, no revolution whose coming,

Figure 7. Francisco Goya, "Great deeds! With the dead!" ("Grande hazaña! Con muertos!"), Plate 39 of *The Disasters of War*, circa 1810-1815, published 1863. Etching and lavis, 15.5 x 20.5 cm. The copperplate is in the Calcografía Nacional, Madrid.

however brutal, betokens the possibility of progress. There is only war—unbracketed, merciless, discriminate—and, at its heart, at the collective center of this historical disaster, a fundamental indistinction of identity, a loss of singular identifiability, a stripping away of individual personhood at least partly achieved in every plate and fully realized in the most starkly violent of all the etchings: those plates such as 39: "Great deeds! With the dead!" (figure 7), in which it is utterly impossible to identify the hacked, dismembered corpses and parts of corpses decorating the peninsula's crucifixion trees as anyone or anything at all or as anything other than an awfully realist representation of a single and repeating type of human life shorn of all its sacred or transcendent possibility. French or Spanish, soldier or civilian, the human figures occupying Goya's 80 plates are all, eventually, intimations of, and variations on, this single type: the type of what I am calling inimical life.

....

But what is this "inimical" life? Is it not just another way of naming what Agamben calls bare life? Do Goya's *Disasters* not just provide further testimony to the triumph of the biopolitical, to the grim movement of homo sacer to the center of modern political life? My answer, unsurprisingly, is no. But now I will need to be little more than schematic in explaining why. As a way of approaching this question let me simply note that at the original Hobbesian point of departure of Agamben's modern genealogy of constitutionality, exceptionality, and bare life stands the very figure I have been discussing, a figure apprehensible here under its legal appellation as the bandit or brigand, a figure Agamben situates within that Hobbesian state of nature in which man is a wolf to man (*homo hominis lupus*), that state which, Agamben argues, the sovereign power of the Commonwealth (in its "originary political act") does not so much overcome as exceptionally enclose within itself.[28] Original to the modern appearance of Agamben's homo sacer is thus the legal figure of the bandit, brigand, or outlaw and the Hobbesian specter of the man who is a wolf to other men. Rather than seeking some explanation of the relation of the brigand or outlaw to this wolfish man in the contemporaneous legal discourses (particularly those in the emerging field of international law) with which Hobbes's *Leviathan* was in conversation, Agamben, however, effects one of his characteristic philological maneuvers, shifting register to an Indo-European etymology of the *wargus* that will permit him to trace this lupine figure back through Germanic antiquity to a Roman origin in the figure of homo sacer. And he does so, I suspect, because the alternative would have been to track the bandit, brigand, and outlaw not through the ancient philological register but through the early modern legal discourses on the enemy and because, for all the Schmittianism of his argument, it is Agamben's claim for the novelty of *Homo Sacer* that in the figures of bare life and the sovereign ban he has seen more deeply than Schmitt into the irreducible nature of the political, discovered in the triad state-of-exception, bare life, and the ban, a "relation more original than the Schmittian opposition between friend and enemy."[29]

If *Homo Sacer* did not, however, hold the friend/enemy distinction under its own ban, it might, rather than leaping backward from Hobbes through Germanic legend to Rome, have forced itself to confront a text that Agamben's very detailed reading of Schmitt would have suggested to him stands as an essential counterpart to Hobbes's *Leviathan* in the 1650/1651 *annus mirabilis* of modern political theory, a work not of constitutional but of international law: Richard Zouch's *Exposition of Fecial Law and Procedure, or of Law between Nations, and Questions concerning the Same*, a text which gives the bandit, brigand, and outlaw one of their first full modern legal treatments as that form of life sovereign power exists to overcome and which, by the logic of Agamben's own arguments, sovereignty thus does not so much overcome as include within itself as its exceptional condition of possibility.[30] The pertinent portions of Zouch's text are drawn from section seven of the *Exposition*, "Of Status among Belligerents," where Zouch provides an account of the various types of enemy "whom it is lawful to offend ... some of whom are of a worse and others of a better condition."[31] "Of the worse condition," he then goes on to clarify, "are those to whom the laws of war do not apply, such as traitors; ... robbers ... those who go about in the manner of enemies without the authority of a state; … [and] brigands ... such as those who infested the provinces of Cisalpine Gaul, and were harried by Crassus, but ... had no leader of sufficient mark to be called *enemies* of the Roman people."[32]

Common to all three of these worse types of enemy (the traitor, the robber, and the brigand), as that last statement and Zouch's ensuing paragraph indicate, is a failure to in fact satisfy the proper conditions of enmity, a failure to amount to "lawful enemies ... those to whom are due all the rights of war," a failure consequent on the fact that these worse-than-enemies lack "a State, Senate, Treasury." For these less-and-worse than enemies not so much of any *particular* state but of the very concept, possibility, or institutions of *the state-form itself*, Zouch ultimately has a single name: *inimici*, those with whom there can be no possiblity of "friendship" "legal intercourse" or political community.[33] If the state both has a limit and accords itself permission to exceed the limits it has set itself, it is, Zouch's *Exposition* suggests, in relation to such inimical life that sovereignty both fails to be and guarantees its exceptional sway. It is in regard to this set of less- and-worse-than enemies that a Commonwealth thus marks both its failure to exist and its sovereign capacity to except itself from its own laws of violence and so causes itself to be where it wills and decides to be.

And the main point I am making is that, when such life comes under the banner and the ban of sovereignty, it does not appear as something bare but, in its very inimicality, renders itself legible as something marked by a recognizable set of features, marked by its leaderless disorganization, marked by its radical institutionlessness, marked by its disregard (as Zouch elsewhere indicates) for commerce, marked by its propensity, in his terms, to "break the treaty of the human race, destroy commerce, and sweep the seas with war."[34] Nor is Zouch the last theorist of international law to so identify the inimical outlaw life in relation to which the war-making state constitutes its unbracketed, merciless sovereignty. 130 years after the publication of his *Exposition*, to cite but one further textual example, Immanuel Kant was to regard this less- and-worse-than-an-enemy just so, while adding an explicitly Hobbesian accent to his appraisal of that inimicus, or, as he put it, "unjust enemy" against whom, he asserted, "the rights of a state ... are unlimited in quantity or degree."[35] This rather startling statement comes from the section on International Right in Kant's *Metaphysics of Morals*, provides the sole exception to his general understanding of the grounds and limits of the state's "right to make war" against its enemies, and is immediately followed by his attempt to define who this "unjust enemy" might be: "But what can the expression 'an unjust enemy' mean in relation to the concepts of international rights ... ? It must mean someone whose publicly expressed will, whether expressed in word or in deed, displays a maxim which would make peace among nations impossible and would lead to a perpetual state of nature if it were made into a general rule. Under this heading would come violations of public contracts, which can be assumed to affect the interests of all nations."[36] Who, then, is Kant's "unjust enemy"? One, like Zouch's inimicus, who is unwilling to enter into a contract with sovereignty or its institutional forms; one, in more explicitly Hobbesian terms, who is unwilling to abide by the public contract on which Hobbes's commonwealth is founded: the contractual exchange of the fear of death for the promise of security. Against such an enemy, Kant determines, the rights of the state are unlimited. In waging war against such an enemy, he decides, the state is free to declare that the system of international rights is suspended, there are no rights that attach to this worse-than-enemy.

Figure 8. Francisco Goya, "Sad presentiments of what is to come" ("Tristes presentimientos de lo que ha de acontecer"), Plate 1 of *The Disasters of War*, circa 1810-1815, published 1863. Etching, 17.5 x 22 cm. The copperplate is in the Calcografía Nacional, Madrid.

In the two centuries since the 1797 publication of Kant's *Metaphysics* (and Napoleon's contemporaneous identification of the irregular, stateless enemies of the empire—the Chouans, the Muscovite "incendiaries," the Spanish guerillas—as exactly such a species of inimical life), the "unjust enemy" has continued to haunt the war-making projects of empire and the international law of war. In *The Nomos of the Earth*, Schmitt suggests that this "frightful enemy against whom our law has no limits" is, indeed, not simply a minor actor in international law but one of its crucial figures and temptations: the figure, indeed, of international law's undoing, the figure who, once constituted or named as such, causes the law to suspend itself or undo itself.[37] And it seems difficult not to recognize yet one further reincarnation of this inimical foe in the guise of that less- and-worse-than-an "enemy" against whom the United States has declared itself at war and in whose repeatedly declared existence this most recent imperial state has discovered the secret and key to its claims to sovereignty, its very *arcana imperii*. As the Schlesinger report on the abuse of detainees in Abu Ghraib prison indicates, the violence inflicted on those prisoners is indissociably linked to the February 7, 2002, memo, signed by President Bush, declaring Al Qaeda and Taliban fighters "unlawful combatants" and "unprivileged belligerents" to whom the Geneva conventions on the treatments of prisoners of war do not apply.[38] Reconfigured as the unprivileged belligerent, the inimicus and the "unjust enemy" have once again commanded center stage in the political theater of international law, the international war-making projects that law is intended to regulate, and the imperial pursuit of a necropolitical order of sovereignty.

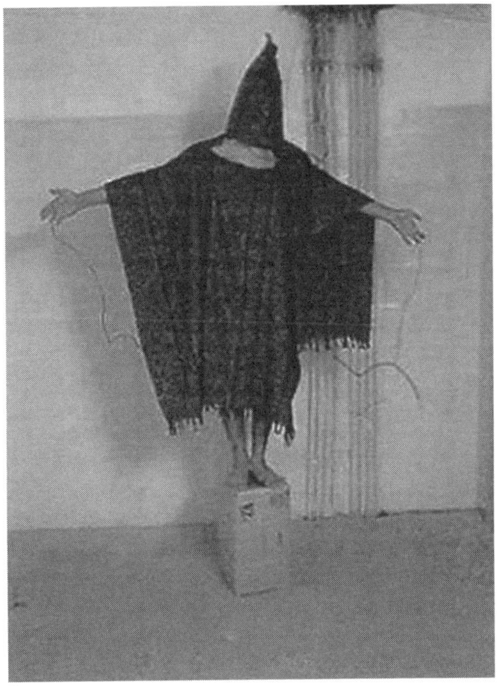

Figure 9. Photograph from Abu Ghraib Prison, released 2004.

....

With that melancholy thought in mind, let me close with just one last comment. I have said something about plates 2-80 in Goya's *Disasters of War* but not yet about the first engraving (figure 8). The plate depicts a kneeling man, his face wan and despairing, arms outstretched in crucifixion pose, a sort of double, as countless observers have noted, of the prisoner at the center of *The Third of May*. The accompanying caption is stark in its historical pessimism: "Sad presentiments of what is to come." The teleology of the plates which follow, as I have suggested, runs history in reverse, backtracks the liberal dream of the sovereignty of the people and the sovereignty of the constitution, sees the future in the nightmare of the return of the king and his re-assertion of a sovereign power to make die. If the period of historical time with which the *Disasters* concern themselves is thus one, in Lukács's terms, that, like every period of transition, expresses itself as "a contradictory unity of crisis and renewal, of destruction and rebirth,"[39] then the bleak, foreboding message of Goya's opening plate is that, in the disasters that imperial war visits upon the world (and in the "type of man" through whose conjoined production and destruction the necropolitical state finds the secret to its claim to sovereignty), time-present and time-future become time-past: what-is and what-is-to-be find themselves brutally replaying what-has-been. That does not mean that the disastrous period of historical time in which we find ourselves is what "had to happen" or that the discourses and imagery of the "unjust enemy" are what our present had to inherit from its long modern past—however closely the contemporary pornographic realism playing dubious successor to Balzac, Tolstoy, and Goya may find itself mapping one moment's image of the unjust enemy onto another's (figure 9). But it does perhaps imply that if we are to shake free from this nightmarish moment in which the sequence king, people, and constitution again seems to be running in reverse and in which a project of unbracketed, discriminate, imperial war has again asserted its claim as the moving center of the totality of things, it might be by recognizing, now, as then, that this is the "type" whose contours it is our "task" to trace and whose authority, meaning, and power it is our responsibility to contest.

Or let me put it this way: When in 2003, the two British artists Jake and Dinos Chapman bought an edition of the *Disasters* that had been published in 1937 by the Goya Foundation as an act of protest against the fascist bombardment of Guernica and other Spanish cities and then defaced the prints by drawing a clownish mask or cartoonlike animal head over the visage of every tormented figure in each of Goya's original plates, their iconoclastic labors predictably sparked a round of both outrage and approbation. Within a year of *Insult to Injury*'s initial exhibition, the Tate Gallery had published a set of study instructions for British high school students who found the work added to the list of those for which they were responsible on their art history A level exams. One of the instructions was the simple injunction: "Think about Iraq."[40] That is not exactly what I am asking. Rather, my suggestion is this: if we are inclined to ask what might hold present sovereignty over our moment, to trace its moving center, to track the force visibly and invisibly present in and saturating the current totality of things, we might do worse than to re-acquaint ourselves with the *Disasters of War* or, indeed, to offer ourselves this alternate, two-word injunction—"think Goya." ▪

....

1 Quoted in Robert Hughes, *Goya* (New York: Alfred A. Knopf, 2004), 304. See also Gwyn A. Williams, *Goya and the Impossible Revolution* (New York: Pantheon Books, 1976).

2 See James Chandler, *England in 1819: The Politics of Literary Culture and the Case of Romantic Historicism* (Chicago: University of Chicago Press, 1998).

3 George Lukács, *Studies in European Realism* (New York: Grosset and Dunlap, 1964), 7, 154.

4 Ibid., 145.

5 Ibid.

6 Ibid.

7 Ibid., 145-146.

8 Hughes, *Goya*, 305.

9 See Michel Foucault, *"Society Must be Defended": Lectures at the College de France, 1975-76*, trans. David Macey (New York: Picador, 2003), throughout but see especially pp 23-40.

10 See Giorgio Agamben, *Homo Sacer: Sovereignty and Bare Life*, trans. Danielle Heller-Roazen (Stanford: Stanford University Press, 1998) and Giorgio Agamben, *State of Exception*, trans. Kevin Attell (Chicago: Chicago University Press, 2005).

11 Foucault articulates this formula and most fully elaborates the emergence of the biopolitical in his lecture of March 17, 1976; see *Society Must be Defended*, 239-264.

12 See Carl von Clausewitz., *On War*, ed. and trans. Michael Howard and Peter Paret (Princ-

eton: Princeton University Press, 1976) and Judith Butler, *Precarious Life: The Powers of Mourning and Violence* (London and New York: Verso, 2004), 50-100.

13 Achille Mbembe, "Necropolitics," in *Public Culture* 15, no. 1 (2003): 12.

14 I take this term from Richard Zouch, the seventeenth-century theorist of international law. I discuss its meaning in Zouch's writing and a subsequent body of work on international law stretching from the mid-seventeenth century to the present in the following sections of this essay.

15 Lukács, *Studies in European Realism*, 6.

16 Ibid., 10.

17 Ian Duncan, *Modern Romance and Transformations of the Novel: The Gothic, Scott, Dickens* (Cambridge: Cambridge University Press, 1992), 86.

18 Honore de Balzac, *The Chouans*, trans. Marion Ayton Crawford (Harmondsworth: Penguin Books, 1972), 54.

19 Schmitt's argument, in brief, is that following the conclusion of the Wars of Religion and the signing of the Treaty of Westphalia, the continental European states managed to juridically limit (or bracket) the practice of war by shifting from a theory of just war to the concept of the "just enemy." While the theory of just war assumed an unjust enemy against whom any practice of violence was valid, the concept of the just enemy permitted states to wage a bracketed form of warfare against each other without needing to seek the total annihilation of one another. Since the enemy in this formula is "just" by virtue of being a sovereign state, war-making within the physical and legal territory of the European state-system remained bracketed, or, as Schmitt also puts it, non-discriminatory, i.e. not driven by a discriminate desire to annihilate an unjust foe. War practiced by European states outside the boundaries of the European state system, Schmitt further argues, was not however subject to such bracketing, nor were those imperial subjects against whom such war was waged recognized as either sovereign or, therefore, as "just enemies." "Beyond the line," of the*Jus Publicum Europaeum* and within an imperial zone formally marked off beyond the "amity lines" of the continental state system, Schmitt thus indicates, "was an 'overseas' zone in which, for want of any legal limits to war, only the law of the stronger survived ... the line set aside an area where force could be used freely and ruthlessly. ... Everything that occurred 'beyond the line' remained outside the legal, moral, and political values recognized on this side of the line," Carl Schmitt, *The Nomos of the Earth in the International Law of the* Jus Publicum Europaeum, trans. G.L. Umen (New York: Telos Press, 2003), 93-94. As Schmitt further argues (and as I discuss again later in this essay) this unbracketed imperial "conflict zone" (95) beyond the line has been associated by Hobbes and other writers from the mid-seventeenth century onward as analogous to the state of nature, the state of exception, and the state of siege. For a more recent and brilliant account of the interplay of imperialism, imperial war-making, and the emergence of modern orders of sovereignty, see Antony Anghie, *Imperialism, Sovereignty and the Making of International Law* (Cambridge and New York: Cambridge University Press, 2004).

20 Balzac, *The Chouans*, 98.

21 Ibid., 77.

22 Lukács, *Studies in European Realism, 6.*

23 Leo Tolstoy, *War and Peace*, trans. Rosemary Edmonds (London: Penguin Books, 1982), 1225, 1226.

24 Ibid., 1226.

25 Ibid., 1225, 1226.

26 See Lennard J. Davis, *Factual Fictions: The Origins of the English Novel* (Philadelphia: University of Pennsylvania Press, 1983).

27 See Immanuel Kant, "An Old Question Raised Again: Is the Human Race Constantly Progressing?" in *Kant: On History*, ed. Lewis White Beck (New York: Liberal Arts Press, 1963), 143-144.

28 Agamben's discussion of the bandit, brigand, and outlaw and the relation of this figure to Hobbes "man who is a wolf to man" is in *Homo Sacer, 104-111.*

29 Agamben, *Homo Sacer*, 110.

30 In his discussion of Zouch and other sixteenth- and seventeenth-century theorists of international law in *The Nomos of the Earth*, Schmitt strongly contends that both Hobbes's account of the state of nature and his discussion of the man who is a wolf to man are explicitly connected to the contemporaneous elaboration (within the emerging field of international law) of a zone of pure conflict and unbracketed war-making "beyond the line" of the *Jus Publicum Europaeum*: "For Hobbes the state of nature is a domain of werewolves, in which man is nothing but a wolf among other men, just as 'beyond the line' man confronts other men as a wild animal. The axiom *homo homini lupus* [man is a wolf to man] has a long history, which, with the land-occupation of a new world, suddenly became intense and virulent. ... In the 16th and 17th centuries, the *homo homini lupus* formula ... acquired a concrete meaning with amity lines, because now it was localized—it acquired its own space, recognized by Christian European governments, and, thereby, an unmistakable validity" (95-96). Among the legal theorists other than Zouch with whom Hobbes was in conversation, Schmitt singles out Francisco de Vitoria, whom Anghie also identifies as crucial to the intersecting histories of international law, imperial war-making, and European sovereigny discourse. Other prominent figures from the period include Balthazar Ayala, Alberico Gentili, and Hugo Grotius. For further discussion of the development of international law during this period, see William G. Grewe, *The Epochs of International Law*, trans, Michael Byers (Berlin and New York: Walterde Gruyter, 2000) and Richard Tuck, *The Rights of War and Peace: Political Thought and the International Order from Grotius to Kant* (Oxford: Oxford University Press, 1999).

31 Richard Zouch, *Exposition of Fecial Law and Procedure, or of Law between Nations, and Questions concerning the Same*, trans. J.L. Brierly (Carnegie Institute, 1902), 37.

32 Ibid., 37.

33 Ibid, 37.

34 Ibid., 38.

35 Immanuel Kant, "The Metaphysics of Morals," in *Kant: Political Writings*, trans. H.B. Nisbet (Cambridge: Cambridge University Press, 1970), 170.

36 Ibid.

37 Schmitt, *The Nomos of the Earth*, 169.

38 *Report of the Independent Panel to Review Department of Defense Detention Operations*, (http://stinet.dtic.mil/cgibin/GetTRDoc?AD=ADA428743&Location=U2&doc=GetTRDoc.pdf). President Bush's letter of February 7, 2002, is included as Appendix C of the report.

39 Lukács, *Studies in Europe an Realism*, 10.

40 Miquette Roberts, *Turner Prize 2003: Notes for Key Stage 5 Students and their Teachers* (http://www.tate.org.uk/britain/turnerprize/2003/turner_prize_2003_teachers_pack.pdf).

Thanatopolitics: On the Use of Death for Mobilizing Political Life

Stuart J. Murray

> *If one is not a human being, what is one?*
> —*Achille Mbembe*[1]

> *Go get slaughtered and we promise you a long and pleasant life.*
> —*Michel Foucault*[2]

"If one is not a human being, what is one?" To the extent that one *is*, one is, obviously, a human being—one's apparent humanity intimate with one's existence, one's subjective life. Or perhaps this is less than obvious, if existence and life are themselves rendered unspeakable or unthinkable, if existence and life are stripped of their salient meaning. Thus, in addition to asking "what" a human being is, a further question is echoed in Achille Mbembe's question, in the repetition of the "one," of a one that is many. There is perhaps no better preliminary definition of politics than this—the nature of the relation between the one and the many. What is a human being? In addition to this "what"-question, which we might call a question of content, the form of Mbembe's question is also and foremost an address to us, his readers. Thus, his question is moreover implicitly a "who"-question, a question that interpellates us in a certain way and demands a response from each of us—a question that calls human being into question and asks us what it means to *be* human, since the identity of these terms cannot be presumed.

But as long as we ourselves are in question, so too is our access to the normative conditions within which any adequate response to the human question might be formulated. Mbembe's question—both "what" and "who"—remains unanswered and in part unanswerable because it calls the oneness of the one into question: "If *one* is not a human being, what is *one*?" Who or what is the singular referent here? Am *I* the one, is it unequivocally *me*? Or is it rather some abstract, unitary *human being* in general, some universal notion of *the human*? And so, when he asks me, his reader, this question, Mbembe's formulation purposely begs the question of my own humanity, mobilizing a disturbing ambivalence in the very question of my life, right there where I thought it was most obvious, right there when I took myself as his unequivocal addressee. Shall I answer or remain silent? And if I speak, how can I be certain I will speak in the name of human being? What, Mbembe seems to ask, are the norms of my speech, and the norms of my being human?

Michel Foucault's apostrophization of the sovereign voice invokes no less of a normative crisis: "Go get slaughtered and we promise you a long and pleasant life." Here, with an ironic tone, Foucault characterizes the sovereign state as a power that both commands and promises. It is ironic because the promise directly contravenes the command: logically, if I am killed, my life will be anything but "long and pleasant." Yet there is another sense in which the command/promise is *not* meant to stand as self-contradictory. The command/promise is spoken to a *you* who, like Mbembe's addressee, is not one, a *you* whose oneness is radically put into play, whose oneness is spoken in the name of the many. The nameless "we" who both commands and promises speaks to an equally nameless "you," a "you" who is only ambivalently included in the "we," if at all. Clearly, the life that you are commanded to sacrifice, the existence you are commanded to revoke, is not the same as the life that you are promised. So how is it that my singular life—the only one I have to give—can be mapped onto a collective political life, the life of a nation or of a people whose oneness is meant to be unquestionable?

The strategic ambivalence of Mbembe's and Foucault's words calls to mind the well-known theory of the king's two bodies.[3] The king, the sovereign, is not one, and despite his death, his unending life is a sort of rhetorical and collective achievement purchased at the price of the many. The life of sovereign power is a life that is lived in the shadow of death—many deaths, nameless and innumerable, disavowed and forgotten. As Foucault remarks, "in terms of his relationship with the sovereign, the subject is, by rights, neither dead nor alive."[4] This paper will be about death, many deaths—ambivalent ones—not in the vain effort to name or enumerate them but to try to begin to understand how death informs our political life today. Admittedly, "death informing life" will seem counter-intuitive or even insane to us because, as Foucault has claimed, in the last two centuries we no longer properly *speak* of death. Discourses on death are as forgotten and disavowed as the nameless and innumerable deaths themselves. In the last two centuries, Foucault argues, political and sovereign discourses have focused instead on *life*. Life has eclipsed death. In the name of life, the "mass grave" has become popularized, making death(s) nameless and innumerable, obscure and obscured. In this vein, the sovereign command to "go get slaughtered" has nothing to do with (one's) certain death; it is spoken in the name of life, from the exquisite purity and goodness of the life that is promised to come, either here on Earth or in some heavenly New Jerusalem.

Our age is, therefore, the age of life, the age of what Foucault calls "biopolitics"—a politics that is organized by and for the control and regulation of life. Biopolitics is politics informed by a discourse on life that is *about* life as much as it appears, strategically, to *belong to* life itself, a natural extension of life's sacred—and thus unquestionable—value. Foucault summarizes the power of biopolitics as follows: "the endeavor, begun in the eighteenth century, to rationalize the problems presented to governmental practice by the phenomena characteristic of a group of living human beings constituted as a population: health, sanitation, birthrate, longevity, race."[5] Biopolitics is, then, the rational, sovereign regulation and control of the population. This remains the dominant political paradigm in Western democracies today, while it is increasingly inflected by neoliberal ideology. Life itself is regulated, maximized, and harnessed through governmental policy, free-market global capitalism, ever-increasing juridicization, medicalization, etc.—the moral mission of a "secular sacred." Such a view of life is promoted, discursively, as a universal good. It operates as a virtual cosmology for us, its subjects. And such a discourse makes it very comfortable, if not necessary, to disavow death as something almost immoral and alien, to forget that the price of life is often death itself. In the name of life, death is forbidden. What would it mean, then, to speak in the name of death? Is such speech possible?

Introduction: The Suicide Bomber

In this paper, I offer a modest discussion on the suicide bomber, whose own death, as well as those of his or her victims, necessitates a renewed discourse on death for our time. In recent years, a spate of books has appeared on suicide bombing, often focusing on the conflict in Israel-Palestine in particular. While these books frequently historicize the conflict(s), several of them are also very concerned to understand and to explain the causes or the "logic" of the suicide bomber. For instance, Robert Pape promises to deliver just such a "logic" in his book, *Dying to Win: The Strategic Logic of Suicide Terrorism*. And many of the books turn to an "insider" account: Barbara Victor's *Army of Roses* treats Palestinian women who are suicide bombers, for example, while Nadia Taysir Dabbagh's *Suicide in Palestine* lends a narrative voice to suicide bombers, as do Wendy Pearlman's *Occupied Voices*, Christopher Reuter's *My Life Is a Weapon*, and Anne Marie Oliver and Paul F. Steinberg's *The Road to Martyrs' Square*, to name but a few.[6]

Together, they deeply challenge the Western mass media's oversimplification of events and their conditions, offering a more complex—and arguably more just—picture of the social, political, and historical dimensions of the conflict(s). In an effort to debunk a mediatized and Orientalizing[7] discourse of the "typical" suicide bomber lustfully in pursuit of heavenly virgins, we find in these texts a whole range of themes, from a discussion of regional and global history and politics to relevant aspects of material, religious, and familial obligations. Here I cite from an empirical study by Scott Atran, whose conclusions are not atypical in this scholarship:

> suicide terrorists span a population's normal distribution in terms of education, socioeconomic status and personality type (e.g., introvert vs. extrovert). … Overall, suicide terrorists exhibit no socially dysfunctional attri-

> butes (fatherless, friendless, jobless) or suicidal symptoms (e.g., affective disorders, substance abuse, repeated suicide attempts). … They don't express "hopelessness" or a sense of "nothing to lose" for lack of life alternatives that would be consistent with "economic rationality" (i.e., if there is only one option, and no reasonable alternatives, you take it)—although despair is often the interpretation given by and to Western media in statements targeted for United States and European audiences.[8]

This image of the suicide bomber is probably not what first comes to mind for us. Indeed, the terrorist's very ordinariness might be shocking. But it is this ordinariness that the Western media must elide, or else it will be faced with questions it cannot easily answer. The media's fictions are more comforting.

Contrary to popular Western news media, then, discussions of suicide missions in "the Arab media emphasize expressions of hopefulness and 'everything to lose.'"[9] Pape concurs: his remarkable study includes detailed empirical facts about "every suicide bombing and attack around the globe from 1980 through 2003—315 attacks in all."[10] Based on his in-depth demographic study which probes the ostensible causes of suicide bombing, he concludes: "modern suicide terrorism occurs mainly in campaigns of suicide attacks carried out by organized groups for specific political goals and extending over a considerable period of time."[11] In other words, we are mistaken to emphasize the "psychopathology" or "religious fanaticism" of the suicide bomber him- or herself. Pape explicitly downplays the religious dimensions of the attacks, stressing that religion "is rarely the root cause."[12] Instead, he writes, "suicide terrorism is virtually always a response to foreign occupation."[13] This conclusion would not be contradicted by the many attacks in Iraq since 2003 and also now in Afghanistan; indeed, we might see these attacks as a resistance to the U.S. occupation of those countries.

This is not to deny that religion can play a complex role in recruitment, training, and so on, but it is to say that religion is rarely *the* "root cause," it is rarely *the* motivating factor. In fact, according to Pape's study, the majority of the world's suicide attacks were carried out by the Tamil Tigers, a group that is expressly *anti*religious. Jacques Derrida, in a discussion of the terrorist attacks on September 11, 2001, also succinctly expresses this view: "Every terrorist in the world claims to be responding in self-defense to a prior terrorism on the part of the state, one that simply went by other names and covered itself with all sorts of more or less credible justifications."[14] The nature of such competing claims makes it impossible to arbitrate between them and therefore impossible to determine the root "causes" or "reasons" behind suicide terrorism once and for all.

The argument of this essay *moves toward* a different kind of discourse. Insofar as this is possible, it is perhaps even hopeful in the face of such manifest hopelessness. I address neither the "causes" nor the "reasons" motivating the suicide bomber—I prefer to follow Mbembe and Foucault and call human being into question rather than impose some colonizing vision of causality or reason. I take inspiration from Mbembe, who sets the following challenge for postcolonial studies: "we need to go beyond the binary categories used in standard interpretations of domination, such as resistance vs. passivity, autonomy vs. subjection, state vs. civil society, hegemony vs. counter-hegemony, totalization vs. detotalization."[15] I therefore turn to a discussion on death, whether we choose to call it suicide or sacrifice. In Mbembe's words, we are forced "to discuss the status of *death-as-such* or, more precisely, of death's life or *the life of death*."[16] Through such a discussion, we might find that death—death-in-life—drives a wedge between conventional binaries and opens us perforce onto something new, inaugurating a new discourse, new hope for our living together. Thus, how might the death of the suicide bomber him- or herself begin to change the face of political life today? What is the rhetorical force of such death, with its myriad social, cultural, and political effects?

I argue that thanatopolitics—the politics of death—is both a response *and* a resistance to biopolitical power and to the Western conception of rational sovereignty with which biopolitics is allied. But it is more than this. While the resistance of the suicide bomber is sparked within the circuits of power, this resistance also approaches the absolute: he or she destroys the very condition of possibility for biopolitical regulation and control. Because the suicide bomber usually dies in the blast, for instance, he or she cannot be brought within the mechanism of justice. While suicide bombing is destructive, while it is clearly a force of negation, I argue that we must also understand this act as *productive*—it produces something, it has independent rhetorical effects which are not easily comprehended within a biopolitical logic. These effects impinge on everyday life and extend beyond war zones; their symbolic valence is unable to be contained or explained by our current moral norms or codes. How do we understand such death, the homicide–suicide, when it is explicitly carried out as a political act, an ultimate—and productive—act of refusal? What is "produced"? And how might this prompt us to reconsider our own faith in those liberal-humanist notions of the subject that have founded ethics and politics for so long? To begin to answer these questions, I address the effects of suicide bombing, and I read them as rhetorical, as effects which produce a particular response, a response that cannot be grasped through biopolitical reason alone. The hope is both to avoid the impasse imposed by the sovereign subject of liberal humanism, bequeathed to us from modern Enlightenment philosophy, and (at the other end of the spectrum) a postmodern nihilism that seemingly destroys the ethic of responsibility that is traditionally aligned with sovereign agency. Rather than terminating in a well-worn discourse that would blindly condemn these acts by reaffirming the sacred value of (biopolitical) life, I argue that a discourse on death will both challenge the hegemony of biopolitical reason while opening onto a renewed way of conceiving what is sacred in political life today.

The argument that follows has four main parts. First, I begin with a discussion on Foucault's concept of biopolitics: in particular, why a discourse on death will be a tremendous challenge for us today. In brief, our biopolitical terms are inadequate, and so, within this frame, the death of the suicide bomber will remain illegible and highly problematic. Second, I turn to Kant, who is one of the first philosophers in Western culture to discuss suicide. I look at how Kant views life and death vis-à-vis sacred human dignity or worth [*Würde*]. Kant touches on one reason why the "suicidal" aspect of the suicide bomber is so horrifying, and yet the activities of the suicide bomber forcibly blur the Kantian distinction between "suicide" and "sacrifice." In Kant, I argue, we find the roots of modern biopolitics as it has been taken up by the state—but, again, this is an ultimately fragile biopolitical logic that the suicide bomber threatens to disrupt absolutely. Third, in his work on the imagination and the sublime, once more it is Kant who helps us to think beyond the logical structures of biopolitics and to theorize the kind of disruption the suicide bomber's death represents. This means reading Kant against the Kantians, perhaps, and it offers a rhetorical model for ways we might begin to think outside of or beyond the horizons of our liberal tradition. And fourth, finally, my argument considers the explicitly rhetorical dimensions of death as they relate to wider aspects of bodily integrity and community. Here my reading turns to death in the spaces of everyday life, as excruciating as this may be, with the abiding hope that together we might begin to imagine new possibilities for shared political life.

Foucault: Biopolitics and the Silencing of Death Today

> *We're asked to live out our calling as Americans. We're asked to honor our own standards, announced on the day of our founding in the Declaration of Independence. We're asked by our convictions and tradition and compassion to build a culture of life.*
>
> —*George W. Bush*[17]

Death is unspeakable. It is silenced by the austere and pious rhetoric of nationalism, "honor," "compassion," and the "culture of life" itself. As he is signing the Partial Birth Abortion Ban Act of 2003, President George W. Bush repeatedly claims that "We're asked. . . ." However, we must ourselves ask: Who is this "we"? Who asks—or calls us? And in whose name? How are we interpellated by the sovereign doctrine of life itself? At the heart of such a discourse on life, death becomes the most intangible and invisible of problems—that which may never be asked. Even our best scientists, doctors, and jurists cannot say with certainty what death is as a concept or an event, and yet death casts a very long shadow over the history of our twentieth-century experience. In a Nietzschean vein, we might say that death hangs like a question mark, invisibly punctuating the lives of the living. And today, the conditions under which we might answer, by which we might properly *speak* of death, have become increasingly attenuated. Death never happens to *me*, never to *my* self. Death arrives as a veiled intruder, disguised as long-range military or police operations, televised terrorist acts, a virtual event, or as a "surgical strike." When it happens closer to home, death is understood, again, not on its own terms; instead, it occurs under sanitary conditions, as the mere cessation of life, the failure or limit of medical and political technologies whose principal task is to keep the living alive.

Foucault has famously charted the historical shift in discourse from what was once a discourse on death to our modern ideology of life. Classically, in pre-modernity, the discourse on death was conceived under Roman law as the *patria potestas*—the power of the family father who enjoyed "the right to 'dispose' of the life of his children and his slaves."[18] This power is summed up in the following formula: "to take life or let live." Here it was the sovereign's prerogative to revoke the life of his subjects or to allow them to live—an economy of death, as it were. Thus, in the classical theory of sovereignty, the balance of power "is always tipped in favor of death,"[19] with death as the rubric through which life was understood, almost by default. Life was that invisible-but-pervasive element that was always already there but announced only through its privation—by death, by the rule of the sword, the *gladius dei*.

In modernity, however, there is a reversal of sorts, and the balance of power is tipped in favor of life. "Life" or *bios* is now the rubric through which death must be understood. Life is no longer presumed as given but becomes discursively constituted in relation to political power—a biopolitics that is the purview of the modern sovereign state. Today, Foucault argues, the sovereign state exercises its control most explicitly by means of life, through the lives of the living. This takes the distinct form of regulating life and maximizing or prolonging it. The modern state intervenes with a self-proclaimed moral authority to affect the population's birth and death rates, aging, disease, hygiene, public health, and welfare; we are governed by ideological marriage laws, "pro-life" policies, "faith-based initiatives," and so on. The mechanism is technological as much as it is a self-righteous and onerous public morality. Thus, while classical sovereignty is summed up by the formula "to take life or let live," modern biopolitical state sovereignty has its own formula, namely, the almost godlike power "to make live and let die."[20] The shift from the classical to the modern must be stressed: from taking life to *making live* and from letting live to *letting die*.

Moreover, in modernity, *making live* and *letting die* become logical correlates; they go hand in hand, in proportion to one another. Life, we learn, must be produced and constantly tended. Life must be avowed; death disavowed. Life must be made; death is neither made nor unmade, it just happens, as it were. Thus it is only in modernity, Foucault writes, that we begin to properly *speak* about life—we *are compelled* to speak about it, while we fall silent on the subject of death. In Foucault's words, "death now becomes … the moment when the individual escapes all power, falls back on himself and retreats, so to speak, into his own privacy. Power no longer recognizes death. Power literally ignores death."[21] In the United States, for example, the death of the convicted criminal on death row is politically constituted as invisible, while the "life" of life, "innocent" life, achieves an anxious and repeated hypervisibility through State legislation (e.g., The Partial Birth Abortion Ban Act of 2003 and The Unborn Victims of Violence Act of 2004), religious fundamentalist teaching, the mainstream mass media, and the like. Within this scheme, some lives achieve political value while others are effaced and depoliticized. In a remarkable instance, Terri Schiavo's life was politicized through the promiscuity of State legislation, fundamentalism, and mass media saturation. Recall the histrionics of George W. Bush, the almost holy head of state, rushing to "save" the life of Terri Schiavo—"it is wise to always err on the side of life,"[22] he said—while as Governor of Texas he was famous for signing execution orders and for refusing to grant even a single pardon to anyone on death row. Such hypocrisies are themselves defended in the name of life. According to this logic, one can be ardently pro-life and yet just as faithfully committed to capital punishment: here the prisoner's death is rationalized first and foremost as that which will prevent the harm of life and save the lives of the living. It is as if the prisoner had already revoked his or her right to life, and, as such, in killing them we do no more than *let* them die—and for the greater good, at that. The prisoner falls back on himself, as Foucault would say, and his public and political death is cast as private and apolitical, a necessity best ignored. His life is life so patently unworthy of life that death is never death as such: he is *homo sacer*.[23]

Thus, "life" is swept up in a discourse, produced in and through discourse, through a discursive power-knowledge, vested by the sovereign state. In this view, living individuals cannot be said to "exist" de facto, as paradoxical as this sounds, but they must be *made* to live, subjects whose lives are perpetually manufactured and whose livingness and salvation are indexed by regulation, control, normativization, and state administration. Through burgeoning governmental and medical technologies, the individual's life now counts first as a biological member of the state's population, one biopolitical entity among a mass of others, or, as Foucault sums up, "man-as-species."[24] Effectively, the "individual" is displaced and becomes "regularized" by "a technology in which bodies are replaced by general biological processes."[25] And here, finally, the Other is "allowed" to die in order to promote the sacred health and well-being of the population—"us against them," those whose death is merely an unfortunate side-effect, quickly forgotten, disavowed: "the death of the bad race, of the inferior race (or the degenerate, or the abnormal) is something that will make life in general healthier: healthier and purer."[26] In Foucault's apostrophization, we hear the ominous echo of eugenics programs, starting with Francis Galton in Britain at the close of the nineteenth century and adopted in the early twentieth century by the Nazis, but also in much of Europe, America, and Canada. We can begin to understand how, under this modern biopolitical logic, "life" itself can become the ultimate apologia for *Rassenhygiene*, compulsory sterilization programs, "mercy killing" or state murder, and even genocide. And yet we proclaim very loudly that we have not actually "killed" anyone, that *their* death has not occurred by *my* hand, and that according to *my* idea of responsibility, based on my sovereign reason and autonomy, their death has just happened, a side-effect, perhaps, and so I as a single individual am not responsible.

But we must interrogate this logic and unearth the conditions of our own sovereign rationality, of our hegemony. We must ask ourselves difficult questions concerning terrorism and responsibility, like the following, posed by Derrida:

> [D]oes terrorism have to work only through death? Can't one terrorize without killing? And does killing necessarily mean putting to death? Isn't it also "letting die"? Can't "letting die," "not wanting to know that one is letting others die"—hundreds of millions of human beings, from hunger, AIDS, lack of medical treatment, and so on—also be part of a "more or less" conscious and deliberate terrorist strategy?[27]

Here, Derrida disrupts our biopolitical view that it is only the "terrorists" who take others' lives, directly or indirectly. Derrida disrupts the self-satisfied position of Western sovereignty, inviting us to rethink what we normally classify as terrorism, and, at the same time, he calls on us each to imagine the forms of responsibility we have within current geopolitics. We are asked to evaluate the force of our intentions and whether we can be—or ought to be—held responsible for what we do not—or cannot—willfully intend. We can hardly entertain the idea that our merely "letting someone die" is tantamount to terrorism, though Derrida's point is that we are ethically obliged to think in these terms—or to find the terms within which such a discourse could take place.

Here we arrive at a passionate critique of modern liberal humanism, including the brand of rational sovereignty with which it is coupled. In Mbembe's words, it is "the critique of Eurocentrism—a sort of singular subject that, while trying to pass for the universal *tout court*, always ends up legitimizing the violence of its irrationality in the very name of reason."[28] But such a critique does not entitle us to embrace wholeheartedly a free-floating sort of postmodern relativism as the cure. I do not believe that we ought to promote an empty and ultimately impracticable celebration of difference in which we can never say what is right and what is obviously wrong (even if this is a gross caricature of postmodernism positions). In the simplest terms, I would suggest that our current discourse is doomed, that we must try to work together to invent new ones, to find new modes of comprehension and communication, new ways of seeing. The challenge is to navigate a course *between* postmodern relativism and modern liberalism. On the one hand, relativism holds that ethical, social, and legal values will change across place and time and that we ought not to impose our own idiosyncratic values on others. On the other hand, liberalism maintains that *there are indeed universal human values* and that we can *know* them and must *act* upon them.[29] So here we are on the horns of a dilemma: it seems the choice is between a messy moral/cultural relativism that means we can never decide anything, or a liberalism, the very universals of which will always pose the threat of totalitarian violence. Although I have grossly oversimplified these positions, one of these two political models is all that seems tenable to many people today.

If we feel forced to choose between the rational sovereignty of modern liberalism, on the one hand, and postmodern moral/cultural relativism, on the other, this is because we lack political imagination, our thinking is monochromatic. How can we begin to imagine *new* forms of political subjectivity, *new* forms of political agency—maybe even a postsovereign subject? I would like to complicate things a little and set our imagination to work by asking whether the death of the suicide terrorist is really a suicide or whether it should rather be conceived as a sacrifice or some other emergent form of life. I turn now to the ambivalent death of the suicide terrorist because he or she captivates our imagination, but also because it is here that we might begin to imagine things otherwise.

Kant on Suicide

> *In honesty, if life is like this, and work is like this, death is more honourable.*
> *—Saeed, 21-year-old Palestinian male*[30]

Kant's depiction of life and personhood is important for us because it is a forerunner of the modern biopolitical discourse on life as this has shifted from the "religious" or "spiritual sacred" to a "secular sacred." In this view, biopolitics is a secularized state theology. Kant stands at the crossroads of theology and increasingly secular Enlightenment philosophies, precisely at that historical moment when spirituality and philosophy were going their separate ways.

Kant captures for us what is perhaps the additional or doubly incomprehensible horror in the act of suicide bombing—namely, the suicide itself. There is something about the suicidal aspect of these acts, I would suggest, that adds an inassimilable and morally grave dimension to the act itself—a "natural horror," as Kant calls it. Kant appeals to natural law, and, in this, his argument is at least implicitly religious. But his argument is just as applicable today if we understand that the divine prohibition on suicide has been secularized as a homologous prohibition on the part of the biopolitical state apparatus. In his *Lectures on Ethics*, Kant begins, significantly, by privileging the philosophical over the theological. He states: "Suicide is not an abomination because God has forbidden it; it is forbidden by God because it is abominable," which is to say, because it is "inherently heinous," because man "may not use his freedom against himself."[31] Turning his freedom against himself is, according to Kant, self-contradictory: "To use life for its own destruction, to use life for producing lifelessness, is self-contradictory."[32] Why? Because for Kant, freedom is the prior and enabling condition of life and, on principle, freedom cannot—must not—be abrogated.

Thus, for Kant, there is a higher principle than life. And this principle demands sometimes that I be willing to sacrifice my life. This principle is personhood, which is invested with dignity and a sacred value: "Humanity in our own person is an object of the highest esteem and is inviolable in us; rather than dishonour it, or allow it to be dishonoured, man ought to sacrifice his life."[33] Nevertheless, Kant wishes to maintain a sharp distinction between suicide and sacrifice, the one dishonorable, the other, supremely honorable. It remains impermissible, he writes, to commit suicide (defined as premeditated intent to kill oneself) in the course of self-sacrifice, however contradictory this sounds. When my death occurs as a sacrifice, it cannot stem "directly" from me, it cannot be by my own hand, but is understood, Kant claims, as the intervention of "fate." Thus, the soldier's death on the battlefield is "fateful." Insofar as it an invocation of Thanatos, this specter of death must not be conjured or willed by me. By these lights, we might fairly question whether the death of the suicide bomber meets the conditions of suicide in Kant's terms: is the suicide bomber's own death truly willed by him or her, or is this death a consequence of fate, part of a larger historical mechanism the particular effects of which are somehow beyond his or her control? Is this death, paradoxically perhaps, a preservation of his or her "humanity"?

A close reading of Kant suggests that this is in part possible. When it comes to our own life and the dignity or sacred value of our humanity, the rational will and autonomy of the individual agent is beholden to these higher principles. Therefore, although the death of the suicide terrorist might *literally* occur by his or her own hand, there remains a question of will and of responsibility, a question of whose hand this really is, and a question of honor and dignity. We may even speak of this hand figuratively, as an instrument of "fate." This suggestion might be outrageous to a Western subject who takes for granted the principles of autonomy and reason as the supposedly universal foundations of subjectivity. But, again, in his discussion of suicide terrorism, Derrida demonstrates that we must challenge this understanding of responsibility:

> there are historical and political "situations" whose terror operates, so to speak, as if by itself, as the simple result of some apparatus, because of the relations of force in place, without anyone, any conscious subject, any person, any "I," being really conscious of it or feeling itself responsible for it.[34]

Derrida challenges our taken-for-granted view of the subject as wholly rational, autonomous, free, and responsible; in this case, he or she is also the subject of "some apparatus" and of the "relations of force in place." There is nothing to suggest that any of us is ever wholly free from "some apparatus" or from the "relations of force in place." Nor is it clear that such freedom, were it possible, would be morally superior or more "advanced."

Kant writes: "If a man cannot preserve his life except by dishonouring his humanity, he ought rather to sacrifice it."[35] It is a complicated judgment, indeed, whether the preservation of the life of the would-be suicide bomber is somehow "dishonorable" to his or her humanity, but Kant is clear, "it is no suicide to risk one's life against one's enemies, and even to sacrifice it, in order to observe one's duties towards oneself."[36] Many who have tried to understand the living conditions of an occupied people or the horror and humiliation of watching family members raped and killed in front of them have argued just this. Scott Atran emphatically concludes, for instance, that "*suicide martyrs are not suicidal*."[37] He suggests instead that they die in order to preserve what they see as their humanity, their sense of a "common good." Thus, suicide bombers comprise "an emotionally bonded group of fictive kin who willfully commit to die spectacularly for one another and for what is perceived as the common good of alleviating the community's onerous political and social realities."[38]

It is of course impossible to catalogue a community's political and social realities; more complex still is the set of judgments and perceptions that motivate actions in the name of the common good. The point here is not to exonerate the terrorist's actions but to submit our own readiness to judge to an honest critique. We make a violent and narcissistic assumption when we take our own Western, individualistic approach to subjectivity as "natural" or "universal." Such a subjectivity—so foundational for the West since the Enlightenment—is not easily translated into some other cultures. For instance, according to one Palestinian author, the Arabic term that is commonly translated as "self," *naf*, can equally "be used in the sense of 'brother' or 'fellow Muslim.'"[39] She explains further: "the Islamic concept of the self is more collective and has more connection with the group or community than the Western individualistic, separated sense of self."[40] So when Westerners like President Bush declare that "freedom is on the march" and that it is our civilizing and moral mission to "spread freedom" throughout the world,[41] this is problematic on at least three counts: (1) it presumes that those in need of freedom are somehow less developed or primitive and that the Western notion of selfhood reflects a more advanced "historical progress"; (2) those who are the target of such freedom campaigns, if I might call them that, often correctly perceive "freedom" as thinly veiling what are in fact imperialist and neo-colonial objectives; and (3) this idea of "freedom" is itself based on the liberal humanist "self," which may have little or no currency in a particular culture. Moreover, if unreconstructed notions of selfhood and freedom are the basis for understanding life as we do, it is obvious that "life" will also fail as a universal, transcultural, or transcendent good.

We can see, then, that the suicide terrorist disrupts or begins to deconstruct our sovereign and biopolitical order of things. Indeed, I have highlighted the moral and epistemological ambivalence between suicide and sacrifice, between self and Other and community. In an instant, these deaths wrest control of life from the grip of our hegemonic biopolitical state. There is, then, an ambivalent specter of death that remains inassimilable and incomprehensible within sovereignty's hermetically self-referential discourse. Before working toward my conclusion, I would like to remain with Kant for a moment. In Kant, we find an unsuspecting ally when we turn to the *Critique of Judgment*, where Kant deals with an aesthetics of the sublime. I do not think we are wrong to see in the terrorist attack something sublime: the sublime can arrive as an incomprehensible beauty or an incomprehensible horror. The point is that here is something that *exceeds* the rational understanding. I also do not think we are mistaken in this moment to call for an aesthetics, which I take in its original sense as *aesthesis* or bodily "sensation." We must imagine ways to bring politics and aesthetics together critically. Political life cannot be based solely on economic rationality or ordered according to abstract concepts because it is about relations between people, relations that are sometimes beautiful, sometimes horrific, but relations that cannot fairly be understood or guided through the imposition of a logical calculus alone.

Kant on Imagining Otherwise

> *The imagination is free, so that, over and above that harmony with the concept, it may supply, in an unstudied way, a wealth of undeveloped material for the understanding which the latter disregarded in its concept.*
> —*Immanuel Kant*[42]

What is a death, when it is not one? How shall we begin to understand the added suicidal—or sacrificial—dimension of the suicide bomber? Is the body of this death "unstudied" or "a wealth of undeveloped material" in Kant's sense? And in what ways does the suicide bomber challenge our fixed concepts and capture our spirit, whether in sublime horror or in admiration? I am arguing that this added dimension is extradiscursive—or even nondiscursive, nonconceptual; it relies on a particular ethic or even an aesthetic.

For Kant, the imagination [*Einbildungskraft*] enjoys a kind of power or even an agency all its own. It *produces* something—in this case, images [*Bilde*]. Etymologically, the *Einbildungskraft* is a faculty or power [*-kraft*] that gathers the image [*Bild*] together into a kind of "oneness" [*Ein-*]; moreover, in German, *Bildung* means "education" or "formation," which connotes an active process. And curiously, the term *Einbildung* means "conceit," "fantasy," "illusion," or "fiction." In the *Critique of Pure Reason*, Kant writes:

> The products of the imagination are of an entirely different nature; no one can explain or give an intelligible concept of them; each is a kind of *monogram*, a mere set of particular qualities, determined by no assignable rule, and forming rather a blurred sketch drawn from diverse experiences than a determinate image.[43]

Thus, according to Kant, these images are of "an entirely different nature" than concepts, the products of reason and the understanding. The German word *Bild* loses something when rendered by the English translation, "image." On the one hand, a *Bild* is indeed a straightforward image or picture of something, a representation, and here we are justified to speak of it as a "product" of the power of the imagination. But on the other hand, a *Bild* is also much more: it is "the look" or "the face" that something presents to us from the world—the way something strikes our eye, the way it impresses us. For example, "The town *looks* friendly" or "The movie star maintains a certain *image*." Significantly, this "agency" does not wholly belong to the modern rational and autonomous subject. The imagination interfaces with the world, and the products of the imagination, Kant insists, *cannot* be understood conceptually—the imagination "schematiz[es] without a concept."[44] Instead, the *contents* of the imagination are "a blurred sketch drawn from diverse experiences," where the aspect of one thing suggests or conjures up a host of metaphorical relations to others. In the imagination, *content* relies on *form*; it is a way of seeing. Each image acts as a kind of "monogram." So the power or "agency" of the imagination is not simply *in* the subject or even in the subject's *mind*: it is not a *mental* power of representation, but almost a *worldly* power that takes place in between us and things.

The world in its pre-conceptual plenitude calls us to imagine new possibilities, different constellations, different relations—to see a new face, a new complexion, in those ultimately inassimilable faces that greet our own. The agency in question comes equally from the world, as it were—or perhaps even *in the first instance* it comes from the world, the way the world is presented to us, the ways in which the world mobilizes particular relations between its terms. This ethical work does not succeed when it fixes and remains steadfast to its definitions and conceptual structures, but is ethical insofar as it *keeps open* the space of imaginative difference, when it *puts into play* the space between self and self, and between self and Other. As Kant remarks in the *Critique of Judgment*, "the imagination is playing, as it were, while it contemplates the shape."[45] Such ethical work "at play" is a tremendously serious aesthetics; it should not laboriously close the gap by proposing "assignable rules" or conceptual legislation, but it operates through the implicit acknowledgment that this is impossible and that my reason reaches a *limit* here, that what I imagine is, as Kant says, a "monogram"—merely emblematic, partial, a truncated signature that bears the incomplete trace of my telling while motivating new interpretations and different signatures.

At the end of Kant's discussion on the imagination, he makes an oblique but unmistakable reference to a familiar biblical passage: "The letter killeth, but the spirit giveth life."[46] Appearing at the end, it comes as a kind of ultimate explanation—or "monogram"—for how the imagination works and its central importance in Kant's critical apparatus. The imagination, he writes, is what is "conjoined with a given concept" or "add[ed] to a concept"[47] but not as a mere supplement. Here Kant seems to admit that the concept *alone* is no more than a *dead letter*. The concept alone would promise death, unless the imagination breathes life into it. As far as aesthetic ideas go, the concept is clearly inadequate. No determinate concept can successfully represent aesthetic ideas. And here Kant does not hesitate to speak of the concept as a rational linguistic form which ultimately fails to be true to life: "no language can express it completely and allow us to grasp it."[48] Instead, he writes, we must "add to a concept the thoughts of much that is ineffable."[49] Thus, the imagination is the domain of the ineffable, of that which cannot be spoken in the here and now. This is what the imagination does, marrying an aesthetic affect and a rational concept—remarkably, through tropes, such as metaphors, "aesthetic attributes," and "kindred presentations."[50] In Kant's own words, the imagination works through a "feeling … which quickens [*beleben*: breathes "life" into] our cognitive powers and connects language, which otherwise would be mere letters, with spirit."[51] I find these passages remarkable for their sensitivity to the power of rhetoric as an essential and irreducible moment of human being.

Although we ourselves must breathe life into words in speaking them, the "we" here is not one; subjectivity is not sovereign. This "spirit" is not ours alone; it is not simply a "product" of the imagination, bestowed on an imaginary object through speech. It is a rhetorical spirit. Spirit comes from the world, and it captures us when we are in-the-world in a certain way. It is significant that Kant illustrates "spirit" at the beginning of this remarkable section through a discussion on fine art and human sexual desire. A poem, he writes, can be "quite nice and elegant and yet have no spirit."[52] Likewise, a story may be "precise and orderly," or an oration "both thorough and graceful," and yet neither may have "spirit." "Even about some women," Kant ventures, "we will say that she is pretty, communicative, and polite, but that she has no spirit."[53] In these cases, the worldliness of the thing itself fails to convey a spirit, fails to capture our spirit, fails to engage us aesthetically, in a world somewhere between objects and our conceptual representations of them.

Applying Kant's insight as a political commentary becomes essential if we are to understand those sublime political acts that "capture our spirit" but that fail to be fully explicable according to rational, conceptual discourse. The death of the suicide bomber him- or herself poses as just such an inassimilable remainder in the politics of armed combat, and it is Kant, here, who prompts us to argue for a metaphorical reading, a reading which marries aesthetics, politics, and ethics. If we fail to remain sensitive to these rhetorical and imaginative dimensions, we will fail to do justice to the way that the death—or sacrifice—of the suicide bomber impresses us most intimately. Indeed, there is an ethical imperative to mobilize a rhetoric of the imaginary so that images or impressions never contract into mere mechanical productions.

Conclusion: The Language of Everyday Life

> *Dropping cluster bombs from the air is somehow deemed, by Western leaders at least, to be morally superior. … Why dying with your victim should be seen as a greater sin than saving yourself is unclear.*
> —*Jacqueline Rose*[54]

In her short article, "Deadly Embrace," Jacqueline Rose offers a reading of the suicide bomber that pays close attention to the metaphorical dimensions of his or her act. This is *not* to argue that these deaths are "merely metaphorical": they are *not* unreal deaths, but if we are to begin to understand them in our age of biopolitics, we will need an engaged analysis of their *rhetorical effects*. And we do consider the suicidal aspect of these attacks to be disproportionately "sinful," as Rose suggests. But why? "Suicide bombing kills far fewer people than conventional warfare; the reactions it provokes must, therefore, reside somewhere other than in the number of the dead."[55] Hence, our strong moral reaction is provoked less by the number of the dead than by the *kind* of death it signifies.[56] First, there is the suicidal dimension of the death itself, which I have discussed above, and second, the attacks take place in the spaces of everyday life.

Rose claims the following: "You can die, but you can't commit suicide, on your own."[57] Her statement might first strike us as paradoxical. If we die on our own, would it not be truer still to say that we commit suicide on our own? After all, is this not the very definition of suicide? But this view assumes that the act of suicide ends at the moment of death, that the suicide does not live to haunt the places of everyday life. Unlike "natural" death, the suicide never really ends; it is an act of cruelty that has far-reaching social and historical valences. It is a wound that never closes. Whether or not it results in the literal death of others, our suicide is never entirely our own, never merely our own death. "All suicides kill other people," she writes, and we might add, the suicide continues to kill. It is not a trauma in the traditional sense; it is not an event that is strictly contained by the past, but its temporality is distinctly futural. It cannot, strictly speaking, be mourned. In his discussion on the suicide attacks of September 11, Derrida captures such a futurity, writing, "this weapon is so terrifying because it comes from the to-come, from the future, a future so radically to come that it resists even the grammar of the future anterior."[58] Thus, the suicide attack is an event that never *will have been*, and it is in this that it is so traumatizing, so inassimilable. "Traumatism is produced by the *future*, by the *to come*, by the threat of the worst *to come*, rather than by an aggression that is 'over and done with.'"[59]

For those who are haunted, this kind of death becomes a way of life. It represents what Rose calls an "unbearable intimacy" and a "passionate identification": "you take the enemy with you in a deadly embrace."[60] I would argue that our horror is, in part, deeply connected to bodily integrity and all that this vital integrity represents—from the dignity of the human person to the containment of political states and the imaginary inviolability of state sovereignty. Here it is not just the livingness of the body that is integral; death, too, has become a vital site around which personhood and politics constellate. This is not just the death of the body—the *nekros*—pure and simple, but much more. Honoring the dead extends across cultures, each in its own way. According to Jewish custom, for instance, the soul (*neshama*) is said to remain close to the body until burial. The body therefore figures distinctly in the preparation and burial of the deceased, and the strict principle of *kevod ha-met*—dignity and honor of the dead—is followed. It is important for the body to be buried within one day of death; the body is ritually washed, dressed in shrouds of white linen, and committed to the earth. "For dust thou art, and unto dust shalt thou return."[61] The integrity of the body is of great importance. The sanctity of the body is maintained after mortal life has ended, and, for some, this means adhering to strict principles of bodily integrity after death.

I would like to conclude by turning to some graphic and disturbing images. These depictions and the experience they convey might give us some insight into the language of everyday life for the suicide bomber and for his or her victims. These images are not meant to be gratuitously violent, like those we have grown too used to seeing on television, nor are they meant to be easily dismissible, as, for example, through an argument about the "banality of evil." I hope, for a moment, that they mark the interruption of all argument, in part through their incommensurable everydayness and the attack on integrity that these depictions convey. In this way, I hope they fire the imagination. We must dwell with these images, allowing the imagination to be met by the world. We must resist our sovereign will to impose too quickly a rational judgment on these scenes, to colonize them. In fact, as I suggested above, Kant's point is that we *cannot* fairly impose our reason and that, in order to do so, we would have to turn away from this unbearable reality rather than face its truth.

First, I offer an account by one member of Israel's volunteer police auxiliary called ZAKA, a Hebrew acronym that stands for "Identification of Victims of Disaster." Comprised of volunteers numbering at least 900, this ultra-orthodox group arrives on the scene of suicide attacks not just to save the lives of the living—biopolitically—but to identify and gather the pieces of the dead so that the entire corpse can be buried on the day of death, if possible. The matter-of-factness of this volunteer's account adds to its unbearable pathos:

> The powerful C4 explosives now being used as the primary blast component in a Hamaside bomber's attack are so powerful that the 5 mile per sec-

> ond blast front generated by the detonation wreaks its destruction in about 1/1000th of a second. ... Mostly, C4 just blows things apart. Into tiny fragments. It even destroys finger nails so thoroughly that sometimes it can take a few days just to figure out how many people were blown apart by the blast. Body fragments can be rendered into pieces half the size of a dime. The bones of the Hamaside bomber are rendered into shards that themselves inflict damage on others.[62]

Victims of suicide attacks are not merely "embraced," to use Rose's term, or cloaked in the exploded body of the bomber. They are penetrated by it. The attacker's body is literally weaponized. Shards of bone become human shrapnel. The body of the bomber and the bodies of his or her victims become inextricable; it is impossible to separate one from the other. This is for many the language or currency of everyday life: finger nails and dimes lose their everyday familiarity, destroying the world as we know it. They become grotesque. Ritual cleansing of the deceased becomes impossible on two counts: not only are these bodies in pieces, but it will be impossible to determine where one body ends and the other begins.

One cannot help here but to conjure horrific associations to the Nazi death camps, where the dead were routinely referred to as "*Figuren*"—forms without a face, as it were, nameless and innumerable, nobody and everybody at once. The attacker is forever a part of his or her target. Blood has mixed with blood. In this light, the act of the suicide bomber can be said to *exceed* murder because the death is both literal *and* figurative. Arguably, the crime is not just against the victims and their loved ones but against all those for whom their blood is a powerful metaphor and for whom their splintered bodies represent the broken integrity of a people.

The attack destroys not merely the dignity of the living but the dignity that we assign to death itself as something absolute and irreversible, as something that is shrouded in ritual and symbology. As Scott Atran has written, "The primary target is not those actually killed or injured in the attack, but those made to witness it."[63] The witness remains to try to make sense of the attack, ensuring its inassimilable futurity, not just in relation to his or her own life, which is implicitly threatened, but through the specter of death, death-in-life. But we need not assume that the witness is the one who remains alive. The dead can witness, too, and it is a thanatopolitics that comes from their "perspective." In the Islamic context, the power of the dead as witness is made explicit in the language itself: "The Arabic word for a martyr, *shaheed*, means 'witness,' as in 'a witness to the truth.'"[64] This is undoubtedly counter-intuitive. To begin to understand, we would have to fully comprehend the body as the intersection of innumerable synecdochal relations. In other words, the body stands in for but also participates in a textured and irreducible reality, part of an everyday language or way of life that feeds the imagination, with hope or with despair.

Synecdochal relations bind together ethnic groups in multiplex ways. Attacks do not just kill but also terrorize when it is these bonds that are shattered. To give yet another illustration, this time from Palestine, consider the life-and-death effects of what some critics call "infrastructural warfare." Here again we must dwell with images of quotidian violence, almost a litany of them:

> fortified structures, military posts, and roadblocks everywhere; buildings that bring back painful memories of humiliation, interrogations, and beatings; curfews that imprison hundreds of thousands in their cramped homes every night from dusk to daybreak; soldiers patrolling the unlit streets, frightened by their own shadows; children blinded by rubber bullets; parents shamed and beaten in front of their families; soldiers urinating on fences. … *[B]ulldozing*: demolishing houses and cities; uprooting olive trees; riddling water tanks with bullets; bombing and jamming electronic communications; digging up roads; destroying electricity transformers; tearing up airport runways; disabling television and radio transmitters; smashing computers; ransacking cultural and politico-bureaucratic symbols of the proto-Palestinian state; looting medical equipment.[65]

This kind of death exceeds biophysical death. It is not the mere cessation of life and not even merely an attack on the conditions of possibility for life itself, even though these attacks, from both sides, take place in "the spaces of everyday life."[66] The effect is a form of death, death in life—a death that "labor[s] under the sign of the future."[67] Our existential uncertainty in regards to death is here radicalized and made Real; the specter of death punctuates the language of everyday life through the perpetual threat of attack in the marketplace and in the home, where we ought to feel most alive, through unexploded landmines, and sometimes in the process of birth itself, as rape victims bear the enemy's children, children who are a living testimony to a form of death, to blood mixed with blood. This is a death which is not one: it proliferates and remains, as "the possibility of being there when the others (in this case the enemy) are no longer there."[68]

These images wash over us and, I hope, suspend—for an instant—our role as intellectuals, disrupting the possibility for epistemological mastery, alienating us from our comfortable traditions and familiar tasks, interrupting the banalization of evil.

Dwelling with these images invites an ethic of discomfort,[69] a hesitant comportment towards that which cannot be contained by sovereign rationality: it is a wound that will not close. The point is not to try to explain or even exonerate the suicide terrorist after-the-fact but instead to try to work towards a communication of what life and death might mean under these conditions, a communication that draws on the language of everyday life and which has as its vital source these images. And so, if we start with these sublime and inassimilable images and work towards the communicability of the incommunicable, as Derrida might say, we might dwell in the openness of human language as a way forward. As Mbembe writes:

> What is necessary is that we use the uncertainty as an epistemological asset in learning to read and to write and to act. … Radical politics consists … of patiently moving along the rift, throughout these sites that seem to have been deserted by the forces of life. For in these spaces apparently doomed

> to nothingness and to radical negation lie unsuspected possibilities, those, even, that authorize us to resuscitate language and hope itself.[70]

Against this fragile collective project, fundamentalisms of all stripes work tirelessly to close up our language, to foreclose on hope, in the name of the absolute. Indeed, the risk is always that the ambivalent and *poietic* openness of language will be exploited by sovereign power. In the place of this ambivalence and promise, where we might imagine a vital proliferation of discourses and distinctions, sovereign power works to displace and to silence the language of everyday life, obsolescing the political and replacing it with a majestic lie. So this is also a call for vigilance.

Admittedly, this vigilant communication is irreducible to some succinct idea or other; I am unsure what vigilance would look like here or what terms we might eventually share. We are wrestling here with disparate images and affects, far from the kingdom of reasonable ends and far from any heavenly New Jerusalem. In this sense, there is no prescription for communicative action because the future belongs to all of us, and has yet to be forged, together, from inauspicious moments like these. Our vocabulary, our comportment, and our vigilance must be anti-fundamentalist and must recognize universal values, perhaps, without imposing a project of universal morality. It means opening up language and communication in ways that do not presume epistemic certitude (this alone is a monumental task). It means that those who adhere to different moralities might imagine and eventually meet within a space of mutual understanding—without necessarily arriving at a consensus, without holding out for any preconceived project of "communicative reason," and without committing ourselves—and each other—to such austere absolutes. Mbembe invokes the African tradition of the "shadow song," the *chant d'ombre*: "a song that can only be captured and truly understood by the entirety of the senses, and not by hearing alone."[71] Inspired by this tradition, like Mbembe, we might imagine "a mode of writing that would lead the reader to listen to that shadow song with her or his own senses."[72] Our writing must learn to sing and to dance—and, if only such a gift were so easy, the reader's imagination would suffer less abuse!

With Foucault, we might call this a "spiritual" rather than an "epistemic" or properly philosophical relation. Foucault offers us some preliminary clues in his last work on ethics as the care of the self. Of central importance for Foucault is the kind of relation the self has with itself as it crafts a life for itself, as it struggles with the terms of a meaningful life and, implicitly, a meaningful death. In some sense, we might even think of this self–self relation as what Kant calls "the duty to oneself"—a duty that can demand self-sacrifice—rather than the absolute preservation of one's life over all else. In his lecture course from 1981–82, *The Hermeneutics of the Subject*, Foucault argues that there are two distinct ways to understand the self–self relation: (1) philosophically or conceptually, which is particular to the modern context, and (2) spiritually, as a relation of care, derived from the Ancients. In explaining these two modes of self-relation, Foucault returns to the self–self reflexivity of the Delphic injunction, which we moderns presume to be the wellspring of philosophical wisdom: "Know thyself" [*gnōthi seauton*]. Again, the kind of self–self relation that

Foucault has in mind here is not primarily epistemological; it is not first and foremost a modern relation of philosophical knowing, either cognitive or conceptual. Rather, it is a relation of being, a *spiritual* relation founded in care—"the care of the self" [*epimeleia heauton*].

This mode of care is irreducible to an epistemological statement, a code, or a succinct set of propositions or practices. An ethics of self-care cannot be prescriptive, cannot be codified. Instead, it is, as Foucault writes, "both exercise and meditation . . . , a number of actions exercised on the self by the self, actions by which one takes responsibility for oneself and by which one changes, purifies, transforms, and transfigures oneself."[73] We might think of this as the practice of "conversion" in the pursuit of truth: "in and of itself an act of knowledge could never give access to the truth unless it was prepared, accompanied, doubled, and completed by a certain transformation of the subject."[74] With this, Foucault has effectively turned the history of Western philosophy on its head, challenging the notion that the truth alone will set us free and that our access to this truth is mental rather than spiritual. With the Ancients, spirituality and philosophy go hand in hand; they have not yet been torn asunder, as they are, increasingly, by Enlightenment rationality. The self-relation is, then, an attitude toward both self and world, an embodied relation in the *Lebenswelt*, a social, political, and historical exercise [*askēsis*], an ethic and an aesthetic. The self–self relation is, therefore, an ethical relation for Foucault because the self must struggle to invent the terms by which it will relate to itself and to others—these terms are not ready-made, they are not simply prescribed as part of a moral code.

For my argument, the most important and provocative mode of self–self relation is the "meditation on death" [*meletē thanatou*]—a mode of self-transformation which appears toward the end of Foucault's lectures. Like the relation of care, this "meditative" relation must not be understood as mere psychological contemplation or *noēsis*. It is not a simple mental exercise by which we would seek to gain mastery over a concept. Rather, meditation works to transform the subject in his or her entirety, precipitating a spiritual "conversion to self." It is a kind of training, a spiritual putting-into-practice, and, above all, it is "to perform an exercise of appropriation"[75]—the appropriation of one's own death. It is never categorical, in the Kantian sense; it is never reducible to a normative practice. Significantly, meditation on death is "not a game the subject plays with his own thoughts," Foucault writes, "but a game that thought performs on the subject himself."[76] Death is, then, that "game" that is constitutive of the subject; it is that relation—an ultimately unmanageable risk—that will constitute the terms of the relation, of the relata, of the self reflecting on itself, a self which is not one. The "thought" here, the "thought" that plays with us, is a thought uncontained by our thinking, an unthinkable thought that is, if you will, the very condition for our thinking, that which sets the limits of the thinkable.

If this is true, we shall begin to see that the self is an activity of *expropriation*: becoming a self will involve ceding the self to a relation that marks the prior condition of its very selfhood. In Derrida's terms, faced with a suicide terrorism that is itself "unappropriable," the only way forward is through the "expropriation"[77] of the subject from itself—a form of death, surely. The event of death is not merely a limit to my understanding and to the idiom that informs it; the event is not simply privative but is productive, actively separating me from my self-certainty and my particular and comfortable way of being-in-the-world. In such an intimate relation with death, death becomes the condition of life. The subject's own undoing is, at once, the intimate possibility of its existence and the meaning of its life as ethical life. Thus, meditating on the death of the suicide bomber, in its multiplex affective, rhetorical, and symbolic valences, might occasion a new departure in ethico-political discourse.

We must press forward into such a discourse, toward new mythographies, perhaps, or toward a postnational and postsovereign understanding of human relations. It is, perhaps, a time to mourn together, to keep a vigil, and to invent new symbols that will come to occupy the spaces of indescribable loss, the spaces of everyday life, to make this loss and this life somehow livable. And lastly, it is, perhaps, a time to contemplate our own death, the death of our sovereign subjectivity, the willful expropriation of who we think we are, the death of our own moral and intellectual narcissism, and the willful suspension of our will to contain the world as a piece of rational knowledge. Paradoxically, *this* death—you might even call it a suicide—may prove to be the ultimate condition of our continued life together. ▪

The author gratefully acknowledges the support of the Social Sciences and Humanities Research Council of Canada, which has made this work possible. Earlier versions of this paper were presented at the 2005 American Political Science Association Annual Meeting in a panel titled "Theorizing the Political Sacred" and also as the keynote address, "Statements of Exception: Insurgency and the Politics of Dying," at the 2006 York University International and Security Studies Conference, "Exceptional Measures for Exceptional Times: The State of Security Post-9/11," in Toronto, Canada.

....

1 Achille Mbembe, *On the Postcolony* (Berkeley and Los Angeles: University of California Press, 2001), 174.

2 Michel Foucault, "The Political Technology of Individuals," in *Power: The Essential Works of Michel Foucault, 1954–1984*, vol. 3, ed. James D. Faubion (New York: The New Press, 1994), 405.

3 Cf. Ernst Kantoriwicz, *The King's Two Bodies: A Study in Medieval Political Theology* (Princeton: Princeton University Press, 1985).

4 Michel Foucault, *"Society Must Be Defended": Lectures at the Collège de France, 1975–1976*, trans. David Macey (New York: Picador, 2003), 240.

5 Michel Foucault, *The Essential Foucault*, ed. Paul Rabinow and Nikolas Rose (New York: The New Press, 2003), 202.

6 The interested reader may consult Scott Atran, *In Gods We Trust: The Evolutionary Landscape of Religion* (New York: Oxford University Press, 2002) and "Genesis of Suicide Terrorism," *Science* 299 (2003): 1534–39; Nadia Taysir Dabbagh, *Suicide in Palestine: Narratives of Despair* (Northampton, MA: Olive Branch Press, 2005); Philip B. Heymann, *Terrorism, Freedom, and Security: Winning Without War* (Cambridge, MA: MIT Press, 2003); Chalmers Johnson, *The Sorrows of Empire: Militarism, Secrecy, and the End of the Republic* (New York: Henry Holt and Company, 2004); Mark Juergensmeyer, *Terror in the Mind of God: The Global Rise of Religious Violence*, 3rd ed. (Berkeley: University of California Press,

2003); Walter Laqueur, ed., *Voices of Terror: Manifestos, Writings and Manuals of Al Qaeda, Hamas, and Other Terrorists From Around the World and Throughout the Ages* (New York: Reed Press, 2004); Anne Marie Oliver and Paul F. Steinberg, *The Road to Martyrs' Square: A Journey into the World of the Suicide Bomber* (New York: Oxford University Press, 2005); Robert A. Pape, *Dying to Win: The Strategic Logic of Suicide Terrorism* (New York: Random House, 2005); Wendy Pearlman, *Occupied Voices: Stories of Everyday Life From the Second Intifada* (New York: Thunder's Mouth Press/Nation Books, 2003); Christopher Reuter, *My Life Is a Weapon* (Princeton and Oxford: Princeton University Press, 2004); Barbara Victor, *Army of Roses: Inside the World of Palestinian Women Suicide Bombers* (Rodale Press, 2003).

For a more theoretically inflected discussion, please see Talal Asad, *Formations of the Secular: Christianity, Islam, Modernity* (Stanford: Stanford University Press, 2003); Iain Boal, T. J. Clark, Joseph Matthew, and Michael Watts (Retort Group), *Afflicted Powers: Capital and Spectacle in the New Age of War* (New York: Verso, 2005); Judith Butler, *Precarious Life: The Powers of Mourning and Violence* (New York: Verso, 2004); Jacques Derrida, "Autoimmunity: Real and Symbolic Suicides—A Dialogue with Jacques Derrida," in *Philosophy in a Time of Terror: Dialogues with Jürgen Habermas and Jacques Derrida*, ed. Giovanna Borradori (Chicago and London: University of Chicago Press, 2003), 85–136 and *Rogues: Two Essays on Reason*, trans. Pascale-Anne Brault and Michael Naas (Stanford: Stanford University Press, 2005); Terry Eagleton, *Holy Terror* (Oxford: Oxford University Press, 2005); Diane Enns, "Bare Life and the Occupied Body," *Theory & Event* 7, no. 3 (2004); Foucault, *"Society Must Be Defended"*; Achille Mbembe, "Necropolitics," trans. Libby Meintjes, *Public Culture* 15, no. 1 (2003): 11–40; Jacqueline Rose, "Deadly Embrace," *London Review of Books* 26, no. 21, November 4, 2004, http://www.lrb.co.uk/v26/n21/print/rose01_.html, and *The Question of Zion* (Princeton and Oxford: Princeton University Press, 2005). This list is, of course, by no means complete.

7 Edward Said, *Orientalism* (New York: Vintage, 1979).

8 Atran, *In Gods We Trust*, 134–35.

9 Ibid., 135.

10 Pape, *Dying to Win*, 3.

11 Ibid., 20.

12 Ibid., 4.

13 Ibid., 22. In the Iraqi context, under American occupation, I would suggest that any religious/nonreligious distinction has become more difficult to discern. Naturally, the mainstream U.S. media prefer to depoliticize these events, assuring us that recent suicide attacks have been carried out by Islamic fundamentalists.

14 Derrida, "Autoimmunity," 103.

15 Mbembe, *On the Postcolony*, 103.

16 Achille Mbembe, "*On the Postcolony*: A Brief Response to Critics," *Qui Parle* 15, no. 2 (2005), 18.

17 George W. Bush, "President Bush Signs Partial Birth Abortion Ban Act of 2003," *The White House, Office of the Press Secretary*, November 5, 2003, http://www.whitehouse.gov/news/releases/2003/11/20031105-1.html.

18 Michel Foucault, *The History of Sexuality, Volume 1: An Introduction*, trans. Robert Hurley (New York: Random House, 1978), 135.

19 Foucault, *"Society Must Be Defended,"* 240.

20 Ibid., 240ff.

21 Ibid., 248.

22 George W. Bush, "President Participates in Social Security Conversation in America," *The White House, Office of the Press Secretary*, March 21, 2005, http://www.whitehouse.gov/news/releases/2005/03/20050321-7.html.

23 Cf. Giorgio Agamben, *Homo Sacer: Sovereign Power and Bare Life*, trans. Daniel Heller-Roazen (Stanford: Stanford University Press, 1998).

24 Ibid., 246–47.

25 Ibid., 249.

26 Ibid., 255.

27 Derrida, "Autoimmunity," 108.

28 Mbembe, "Brief Response," 3.

29 More specifically, this points to a troubling paradox deep within liberalism itself. On the one hand, we each wish to be counted as equals, each with equivalent rights (and responsibilities, although this is perhaps too seldom remarked), while, on the other hand, we demand to be recognized in our uniqueness or difference because we understand that we will lose our dignity, as Kant would say, if our "equality" implies that each one of us is exchangeable for another. How, then, do we balance equality with irreplaceability, two presumably competing desires? If we stick to a rights-based view, there is a dilemma because the underlying substance of those rights is at once the basis of our sameness *and* difference; that is, there is a dilemma if we persist in conceiving of rights as *properties* or *predicates* of the "substantial" human *person* or *subject*. Sadly, much of modern analytic philosophy continues to hammer away in this tedious fashion, unable to break the spell of its own discourse.

With neoliberalism, the paradox of liberalism persists in a particularly insidious and globalizing fashion. Here, we are supposedly free and equal according to the terms of the "free" market; indeed, some neoliberals will argue that it is thanks to the independent fairness of the market's terms that each can find in them a means for the expression of his or her uniqueness. But in this way, the market becomes both means and end at the same time. And the cruel myth, of course, is that there is equal access for all, that the market's terms are independent and fair. Neoliberalism must utterly disavow the often-criminal infrastructural inequalities it relies upon and perpetuates. Moreover, it must also deny the charge that any expression of uniqueness within its terms may ultimately ring hollow. Some have argued that a fundamentalist and increasingly politicized Islam is a response to just these hypocrisies of neoliberalism (e.g., see Boal et al., *Afflicted Powers*).

30 Quoted in Dabbagh, *Suicide in Palestine*, 200.

31 Immanuel Kant, *Lectures on Ethics*, trans. Lewis White Beck (New York and London: Harper and Row, 1963), 119–20.

32 Ibid., 148.

33 Ibid., 156.

34 Derrida, "Autoimmunity," 108.

35 Kant, *Lectures on Ethics*, 156.

36 Ibid., 150.

37 Atran, *In Gods We Trust*, 134.

38 Atran, "Genesis of Suicide Terrorism," 1534. To give a sense of the numbers, in his book *In Gods We Trust*, Atran cites a survey of 900 Muslim adolescents during the first Palestinian Intifada (1987–1993) in Gaza: "For males, 81% reported throwing stones, 72% burned tires, and 29% tossed Molotov cocktails (vs. 51%, 9%, and 5%, for females, respectively); 73% of males reported being verbally abused, 66% were hit or kicked, 63% shot at, and 23% imprisoned (vs. 38%, 19%, 20%, 3% for females). Involvement in violence was not strongly

correlated with depression or antisocial behavior. In fact, adolescents most caught up the Intifada displayed a strong sense of individual pride and social cohesion. This was reflected in their activities: for males, 87% reported delivering supplies to activists, 83% visited families of martyrs, and 71% cared for the wounded (vs. 57%, 46%, and 37% for females)." Atran concludes: "The studies indicate that both psychosocial (unattached males in supportive religious and peer groups) and socioecological factors (small cells organized under charismatic leadership) shape the causal network of interconnected representations, emotions, and behaviors that are broadly characteristic of contemporary suicide bombing. Individual psychopathology seems not to be an important factor here" (135).

39 Dabbagh, *Suicide in Palestine*, 25.

40 Ibid., 26.

41 George W. Bush, "President Participates in Social Security Conversation in America." However, one need not look far for countless instances of "freedom" or "liberty" in Bush Administration rhetoric. For example, reading the Fifth State of the Union Address (February 2, 2005), we find 17 sentences containing the word "freedom" and 6 containing the word "liberty." Cf. "State of the Union Parsing Tool," *www.style.org*, http://www.style.org/stateoftheunion/parse/?q=freedom&q2=liberty.

42 Immanuel Kant, *Critique of Judgment*, trans. Werner S. Pluhar (Indianapolis: Hackett, 1987), 185; §49, Ak 317.

43 Immanuel Kant, *Immanuel Kant's Critique of Pure Reason*, trans. Norman Kemp Smith (London: Macmillan, 1933), 487; A570/B598.

44 Kant, *Critique of Judgment*, 151; §35, Ak 287.

45 Ibid., 77; §16, Ak 229.

46 2 Cor. 3:6.

47 Ibid., 185; §49, Ak 316.

48 Ibid., 182; §49, Ak 314.

49 Ibid., 185; §49, Ak 316.

50 Ibid., 184; §49, Ak 315.

51 Ibid., 185; §49, Ak 316.

52 Ibid., 181; §49, Ak 313.

53 Ibid.

54 Rose, "Deadly Embrace."

55 Ibid.

56 Recall Pape's study, which documents every suicide attack from 1980 through 2003 (see note 6 above). Pape documents a total of 315 attacks globally. The vast majority of these attacks would have targeted a civilian population. If we are just looking at the numbers, however, we might at the same time consider the number of civilians who have died as a direct result of the purportedly legitimate actions of states, including the U.S. To take just one small sample, according to *www.iraqbodycount.org*, to date "the minimum number of civilians reported killed by military intervention in Iraq" is 38,355. ("Iraq Body Count," *www.iraqbodycount.org*, June 14, 2006, http://www.iraqbodycount.org/.) This carefully documented figure say nothing of those who have died as a (more or less) indirect result of years of American-sponsored U.N. sanctions against Iraq from 1991 through 2003—sanctions that led to a lack of clean drinking water, malnutrition, disease, and a lack of medical supplies. In 1999, UNICEF reported: "under-5 mortality more than doubled from 56 deaths per 1,000 live births (1984–1989) to 131 deaths per 1,000 live births (1994–1999)." ("Iraq Survey Shows 'Humanitarian Emergency,'" *www.unicef.org*, August 12, 1999, http://www.unicef.org/newsline/99pr29.htm.) According to these figures, more than 500,000

Iraqi children would have perished in the 12 years of sanctions. Also see David Cortright, "A Hard Look at Iraqi Sanctions," *www.thenation.com, The Nation online*, November 15, 2001, http://www.thenation.com/doc/20011203/cortright. While these remarkable figures cannot exonerate the suicide bomber, we are forced to conclude that some deaths count politically more than others and that this is not a numbers game. We must look elsewhere for the particular significance of thanatopolitics.

57 Rose, "Deadly Embrace."

58 Derrida, "Autoimmunity," 97.

59 Ibid.

60 Rose, "Deadly Embrace."

61 Gen. 3:19.

62 William P. Welty, "The Healer of Souls," *ZAKA Rescue and Recovery website*, 2005, http://www.zakausa.org/zaka_press.cfm.

63 Atran, "Genesis of Suicide Terrorism," 1534.

64 Dabbagh, *Suicide in Palestine*, 30.

65 Mbembe, "Necropolitics," 39, 29.

66 Ibid., 36.

67 Ibid., 37.

68 Ibid.

69 Cf. Michel Foucault, "For an Ethic of Discomfort," in *Power*, 443–48.

70 Mbembe, "Brief Response," 43.

71 Ibid., 20.

72 Ibid.

73 Michel Foucault, *The Hermeneutics of the Subject: Lectures at the Collège de France, 1981–1982*, ed. Frédéric Gros and Arnold Ira Davidson, trans. Graham Burchell (New York: Palgrave Macmillan, 2005), 11.

74 Ibid., 16.

75 Ibid., 357.

76 Ibid., 357–58.

77 Derrida, "Autoimmunity," 90.

Contributors

Eric Alliez is Senior Research Fellow at Middlesex University (London). His publications include *L'Œil-Cerveau: Histoires de la peinture moderne* (with Jean-Clet Martin, Vrin, forthcoming), *La Pensée-Matisse: Portrait de l'artist en hyperfauve* (with Jean-Claude Bonne, Le Passage, 2005), *The Signature of the World, or, What is Deleuze and Guattari's Philosophy?* (Continuum, 2004), and *Capital Times: Tales from the Conquest of Time* (University of Minnesota Press, 1996).

Merav Amir is a PhD candidate in the Cohn Institute for the History and Philosophy of Science and Ideas at the Tel Aviv University. Her fields of research are critical cultural studies, political theory, gender studies, and queer theory. Her MA thesis researched the social and cultural implications of developments in the new reproductive technologies. She is currently working on her dissertation, which analyzes modes of embodiment in the context of the Israeli-Palestinian conflict.

Ian Baucom is professor and chair of the English department at Duke University, where he works on twentieth century British literature and culture, postcolonial and cultural studies, and African and Black Atlantic literatures. He is the author of *Out of Place: Englishness, Empire, and the Locations of Identity* (Princeton University Press, 1999), *Specters of the Atlantic: Finance Capital, Slavery, and the Philosophy of History* (Duke University Press, 2005), and co-editor of *Shades of Black: Assembling Black Arts in 1980s Britain* (Duke University Press, 2005). He has edited special issues of the South Atlantic Quarterly on Atlantic Studies and Romanticism.

Jean-Claude Bonne is professor and past director of studies at l'Ecole des Hautes Etudes en Sciences Sociales in Paris, where he teaches the history and theory of medieval art. In addition to the recent publication of *La Pensée-Matisse: Portrait de l'artist en hyperfauve* (Le Passage, 2005) with Eric Alliez, his books include *L'art roman de face et de profil: Le tympan de Conques* (Le Sycomore, 1984) and *Le sacre royal à l'époque de* *saint Louis*, in collaboration with Jacques Le Goff, Eric Palazzo, and Marie-Noël Collette (Gallimard, 2001).

Ian Buchanan is Professor of Critical and Cultural Theory at Cardiff University. He is the author of *Fredric Jameson: Live Theory* (Continuum, 2006) and *Deleuzism* (Duke University Press, 2000).

Sarah Clift is a Teaching Fellow at the University of King's College in Halifax, Nova Scotia, Canada. She is completing her PhD dissertation, "Committing the Future to Memory," in the Department of Social and Political Thought at York University in Toronto, Canada. Research interests include philosophies of memory in the eighteenth and nineteenth centuries, contemporary theory and criticism, and the intersection of historiography, politics and memory. Her English-language translation of Jean-Luc Nancy's "Forbidden Representation" has recently appeared in *The Ground of the Image* (Fordham University Press, 2005), and she is currently working on a translation of Nancy's *Noli me tangere*, set to appear in late 2006.

Grant Farred teaches in the Literature Program at Duke University. His most recent book is *What's My Name?: Black Vernacular Intellectuals* (University of Minnesota Press, 2003). His forthcoming publications include *Phantom Calls: Race and Globalization of the NBA* (Prickly Paradigm Press, 2006) and *Long Distance Love: A Passion for Football* (Temple University Press, 2007).

Matteo Mandarini is Visiting Fellow to the Centre for Philosophy and Political Economy at the University of Leicester (UK). He is the translator of Antonio Negri's *Time for Revolution* (Continuum, 2004) and *The Political Descartes* (with Alberto Toscano, Verso, 2007). The focus of his research is on French post-structuralism and Italian workerism and post-workerism.

Stuart J. Murray is Assistant Professor in the Department of English at Ryerson University in Toronto, Canada. He received his PhD in Rhetoric from the University of California, Berkeley. Recently, he held a Social Sciences and Humanities Research Council of Canada (SSHRC) Postdoctoral Fellowship in the Department of Philosophy at the University of Toronto, where he maintains his affiliation as a Senior McLuhan Fellow at the McLuhan Program in Culture & Technology. His research interests include the philosophy of technology, philosophy and rhetoric, Foucault, biopolitics, and bioethics.

Rachel Smith is a PhD candidate in English at Rutgers University. She is currently working on a dissertation entitled "The Future Breach: The Politics of Time in Contemporary American Culture," which explores the political implications of destabilizing traditional concepts of futurity in contemporary cultural works.

POLYGRAPH
AN INTERNATIONAL JOURNAL OF CULTURE AND POLITICS

NUMBER 19 (2007)

CALL FOR PAPERS

AUGUSTINE, OUR CONTEMPORARY

Issue Editor: Russ Leo

The Polygraph Editorial Collective invites papers on any aspect of St. Augustine of Hippo's work—on Augustinian concepts; interventions in the history of Augustinian exegesis (or in the exegesis of Augustine's considerable body of work); non-modern, pre-modern, and modern determinations of his thought which inform our own contemporary preoccupations or occlusions; or the assessment of his importance to current theologico-political controversies. Augustine's import to intellectual history has yet to enter the emergent conversation on "political theology" or the phenomenology of religion in any substantial way—a particularly striking absence given the scope of writing by and on Augustine shaping numerous philosophical and theological archives as well as the recent interest in religion (and Paul in particular) across a number of disciplines. Important works on Augustine are integral to numerous contemporary debates on grace, law, the Word, the messiah/messianism, sovereignty, belief, and secularism.

Encounters with Augustine enable new or renewed meditations on love, translation and historicity; projects of autobiography and subjectivity in the afterlives of the Confessions; epistemologies of memory and origin, where Augustinian determinations of conversion or original sin complicate our readings of events and iteration; theories of temporality; or diagrams and negotiations of religion and the secular state after Hegel's *Phenomenology of Spirit* or Marx's *Capital*, in their confrontations with the City of God. Given the rich history of Augustinian reading, our task remains one of retrieval as well as reappropriation. What are the resources of love in and after Augustine? What are the demands of grace? Who are Augustine's interlocutors and what are their terms, from the Pelagians, the Donatists, and the Manicheans to Heidegger, Derrida, Arendt, Vattimo, Lyotard, Wittgenstein, and Agamben? What has been done with Augustine, in or against his name? What does it mark? What is the import of a theology of grace to philosophy? To ethics? To feminism? To race? To political economy? Moreover, what is the status of the City of God, given attendant religious controversies and our contemporary "secular" occasion?

Deadline for submissions: January 31, 2007

E-mail complete manuscripts to the issue editor at russell.leo@duke.edu. More information and guidelines for authors are available at http://www.duke.edu/web/polygraph.